THE ENGLISH NOVEL IN HISTORY 1840–1895

The English Novel in History 1840–1895 refocuses in cultural terms a particularly powerful achievement in Victorian narrative – its construction of history as a social common denominator. Using interdisciplinary material from literature, art, political philosophy, religion, music, economic theory and physical science, this text explores how nineteenth-century narrative shifts from one construction of time to another and, in the process, reformulates fundamental modern ideas of identity, nature and society.

This analysis of a cultural discourse positively requires multidisciplinary treatment in order to bring into focus the dimensions of the cultural discourse in question. The view from a single cultural site, or from a single academic discipline, obscures the breadth, the power, and the implications of such broadly functional cultural phenomena. Making comparisons across conventional intellectual boundaries, this book locates those markers, and those systems or markers, that inform knowledge and project in Victorian narrative.

Students, advanced undergraduates, postgraduates and specialists will find this text invaluable.

Elizabeth Deeds Ermarth is Saintsbury Professor of English Literature at the University of Edinburgh and Director of the Postgraduate School.

THE NOVEL IN HISTORY
Edited by Gillian Beer
Girton College, Cambridge

Informed by recent narrative theory, each volume in this series will provide an authoritative yet lively and energetic account of the English novel in context. Looking at the whole spectrum of fiction, at elite, popular and mass-market genres, the series will consider the ways in which fiction not only reflects, but also helps shape contemporary opinion. Incisive and interdisciplinary, the series as a whole will radically challenge the development model of English literature, and enable each period – from the eighteenth century to the present day – to be assessed on its own terms.

Other titles in the series include:

THE ENGLISH
NOVEL IN HISTORY
1840–1895

Elizabeth Deeds Ermarth

London and New York

For Roland Vargish Ermarth

First published 1997
by Routledge
2 Park Square, Milton Park, Abington, Oxon, OX14 4RN

Simultaneously published in the USA and Canada
by Routledge
270 Madison Ave, New York NY 10016

Transferred to Digital Printing 2007

Typeset in Baskerville by Routledge

British Library Cataloguing in Publication Data
A catalogue record for this book is available from the British Library

Library of Congress Cataloguing in Publication Data
Ermarth, Elizabeth Deeds, 1939–
The English novel in history 1840–1895 / Elizabeth Deeds
Ermarth. – (The novel in history)
Includes bibliographical references and index.
1. English fiction–19th century–History and criticism. 2. Social
classes in literature. 3. Literature and history–Great Britain–
History–19th century. 4. Literature and society–Great Britain–
History–19th century. 5. Social classes–Great Britain–History–
19th century. 6. Great Britain–Social conditions–19th century. 7.
Great Britain–History–Victorian, 1837–1901. 8. Pluralism (Social
sciences) in literature. 9. Power (Social sciences) in literature. 10.
Sex role in literature. I. Title. II. Series.
PR878.S6E76 1996 96–23044
823'.809358–dc20 CIP

ISBN 0–415–01499–9 (hbk)
ISBN 0–415–01500–6 (pbk)

Publisher's Note

The publisher has gone to great lengths to ensure the quality of this
reprint but points out that some imperfections in the original
may be apparent

CONTENTS

PREFACE

This volume refocuses in cultural terms a particularly powerful achievement of Victorian narrative: its construction of history as a social common denominator. 'In' history, all sorts of social problems – problems of corporate order and personal identity – appear in new light because they appear serially. 'In' history, all sorts of social problems become susceptible to recuperation, restoration, revision, repair.

The cultural and intellectual tools for this achievement had been available for several centuries, since the era of humanist Renaissance, but they were long occupied in other media and at other tasks. The tradition of humanist representation, whether in art or in politics, or even in mathematics, already had flourished for more than four hundred years when, in the early nineteenth century, realist, historical narratives explore the *social* implications of that tradition. Novels especially constitute experimental laboratories for defining and exploring a new construction of corporate order.

Such a project positively requires multidisciplinary treatment in order to bring into focus the dimensions of the cultural discourse in question. The mutation in narrative sequence during the middle of the nineteenth century belongs to a large, dynamic, immensely varied field of practices and deflections across the whole range of cultural production. Perhaps it is no longer necessary to affirm this, although in many ways people tend to forget it. Cultural assumptions are, by definition, forgettable. An especially determined and delightful demonstration of this fact appears in Luis Buñuel's film, *That Obscure Object of Desire* a film it is possible to watch from beginning to end without recognizing that the woman who obsesses the male protagonist is played by two entirely different actresses. How is this possible? It is possible, as the sly surrealist knew, because perception is three-quarters censorship; because when we 'perceive' something we rely to a larger extent than we allow upon certain markers, like class or gender role, that are culturally composed and that have nothing to do with the evidence in front of our noses.

PREFACE

To locate those markers, and systems of markers that inform knowledge and project, requires, at the very least, comparison across conventional intellectual boundaries. The view from a single cultural site, or from a single academic discipline, obscures the breadth, the power, and the implications of such broadly functional cultural phenomena. This volume thus compares material not customarily related, in order to locate a problematic; it does not attempt other, quite different work such as determining exact influences or discovering neglected writers.

Two words about method. First, the selective bibliography necessarily omits much of the valuable scholarship that has informed my thinking and writing about time, language, feminism and literature over many years; for obvious reasons, the trace of those sources must remain in the footnotes to my *Realism and Consensus* (1983), and in the bibliographies to my *George Eliot* (1985) and *Sequel to History* (1992). Second, the author cannot in good conscience invite the reader to skip around in the book at will. As the preceding paragraphs have made clear, the four chapters develop an argument about history and society. They alternate between general points and revisionary discussion of texts, so that a section on a particular writer, Thackeray for example, specifies a more general point that could significantly be missed by anyone deciding to skip straight to the Thackeray section.

Chapter One, 'Narrative and Nature', moves from the beginning to the end of the period between 1840 and 1895 in order to locate certain pressure points at which narrative developed new formations. This chapter necessarily assumes to some extent the definition of history as a particular kind of formality that is not explained fully until the second chapter. Chapter Two, 'The Idea of History', discusses a convention at the heart of Victorian narrative form, whether in novels, science or painting: a convention so much at the heart of cultural narrative still that we continue to take it for granted despite its extraordinary artificiality. Nothing could be more abstract than the realistic conventions that underwrite historical narrative, and nothing more central to the novel form after 1850. Chapter Three, 'Society as an Entity', deals with the particular construction of social order that the historical convention makes possible, one that competes with other, naturalized structures of obligation. Chapter Four, 'Dilemmas of Difference', treats problems like class and gender that faced an English culture newly intent upon the political and social forms of democracy. In all chapters the discussion moves between general points and particular attention to texts, sometimes in a revisionist spirit.

Elizabeth Ermarth
Edinburgh, 1996

ACKNOWLEDGEMENTS

I especially welcome this chance to thank the patient people who have supported me through the project. My General Editor, Gillian Beer, has been a paragon of patience with an author preoccupied, first with another book to finish, then with various transatlantic moves. My thanks to her for asking me to write this book in the first place, and for treating my explanations as explanations, not excuses. Thanks, too, to the generations of editors, editorial assistants and others at Routledge who have at intervals politely asked whether or not I was on course.

Various institutions have supported the writing of this volume, including the Universities of Edinburgh and Maryland. The Fulbright Foundation gave me a Senior Fellowship and a wonderful year in Cambridge; Churchill College shared its many resources, including the loan of the most beautiful printer I have ever seen; and St. Deiniol's Library in Clywd, Wales, provided an invaluable opportunity to complete some fundamental reorganising.

Several generations of students and colleagues have provided a continuing conversation about the issues raised here: they are by now too many to count, but are gratefully remembered. Thanks especially to Jo Ann Argersinger who has made much possible in her multiple roles as friend, Provost, colleague, sister and wit. Thanks to Margaret Noll for research support and for useful insights, especially about Mrs Poyser's butter. Thanks, finally, to Sandra Nichol upon whom I have relied during the past several months: on her tact and efficiency in helping to run a graduate school, and on her ability to translate air-borne messages into hard copy and lost files into bytes.

Tom Vargish, miraculously, remains witty and generous after all these years. Thanks, Tom, for surviving in relatively good humour the never-to-be-repeated experience of finishing two books simultaneously in one household; for carrying the pram and its inhabitant up the cliff in San Marino; for writing useful, venturesome, interdisciplinary books in elegant style; for incautiously

ACKNOWLEDGEMENTS

living at high altitudes; for showing what it means to be a legendary teacher; for equanimity in the face of sometimes incomprehensible Fate; and for giving up taupe.

Finally, this book is dedicated to Roland Vargish Ermarth who has always had to cope single-handed with parents forever writing and travelling, and who has honourably and courageously met the challenges of each new game: definitely the man of the match.

1

NARRATIVE AND NATURE

PROLOGUE: A PATTERN AND A PURPOSE

Detective stories represent in a most familiar manner a narrative code characteristic of the nineteenth century. Then, as now, detective narratives re-inscribe over and over again, in books or other media, a post-Enlightenment faith in rationality and, more to the point, in the naturalness of reason. A character in Graham Greene's novel, *The Honorary Consul*, explains the ritual value of such narratives of disclosure:

> There is a sort of comfort in reading a story where one knows what the end will be. The story of a dream world where justice is always done. There were no detective stories in the age of faith – an interesting point when you think of it. God used to be the only detective when people believed in Him. He was law. He was order. He was good. Like your Sherlock Holmes. It was He who pursued the wicked man for punishment and discovered all.
>
> (Greene, 1974: 238)

Unlike bitterly ironic versions in le Carré-style detective plots which depend on deconstructing this faith, the garden variety detective stories still reassure us; their soporific value lies in their assertion that it is natural for human measures to work. Mystery and contradiction are only apparent. No matter how egregious the crime, no matter how gratuitous the act, Sherlock Holmes can always discover the secrets that explain what seemed opaque, and can explain it to his doubting interlocutor, Dr Watson – a figure reminiscent of the hapless Socratic interlocutors in Plato's dialogues. Where Watson is likely to complain that something makes 'no sense', Holmes always understands that absolutely everything has meaning: that 'there's a pattern and a purpose in it'. Holmes's enduring popularity rests on his affirmation of this truth. The narrative

1

always reveals an 'elementary' causality; it always illuminates Watson's disbelief. What such narratives codify is faith in a rationality with almost infinite extension. The narrative code enshrined in these stories is one where ignorance and unbelief can be illuminated by unknown facts discovered and secrets revealed. It is a code evident in almost all Victorian novels, perhaps in all plotted novels of suspense, from the superlative achievements of Charles Dickens and George Eliot to the lesser ones of Charles Reade, Wilkie Collins and Conan Doyle.

The narrative code that features the unearthing of secrets plays on those ambiguities between social and natural order that so rivets the attention of nineteenth–century readers. If a civil law is broken, Holmes repairs the rift in social function by discovering the secret, establishing causality, and isolating the individual agent responsible. But what is the relation between civil law and that wider, but still-rational, arena that is governed by laws of other kinds, laws that have to do with everything from chemical reactions to human nature? Does social law depend upon the same rational system that produces natural law? The 'solution' of a crime, like the resolution of dissonance in harmonic music, reaffirms the existence of a single system of explanation and interpretation.

Here the detective story, and all the plots based on it, verges on very deep waters. Its faith in rationality is as deep, as abstract and as old as the Greek principle of non-contradiction. What is at stake in any particular case is nothing less than faith in 'natural' powers of intuition and reason. These powers, while obviously cultivated in the case of Sherlock Holmes, still seem somehow outside of and even prior to sociality: a kind of natural talent that, potentially, can be shared, even by a Dr Watson. This peculiar symbiosis between human rationality and total rationality has been described by Michel Foucault, as well as by Graham Greene's character, as a religious, not a logical move.

But such soporific narratives contain a potentially fatal ambiguity about the relation between nature and history. Does human rationality discover Reason, or put it there? Is it individual human reason that gives the world its meanings? Or is that rational order already there to be discovered and assimilated, a thing to which humans aspire? As consumers of narrative, do we seek particular causes, or Cause itself?

Such systemic ambiguities figure importantly in nineteenth-century narratives, although generally they become explicit only after 1850. Something happens to narrative in the middle of the nineteenth century, something favourable to the historical aesthetic in which the detective code makes sense, and unfavourable to the kind of providential explanation that operates so prominently in novels before mid-century.

What is most important in this chapter is a shift in the very construction of nature and in the differing narrative codes at stake in that shift. Before mid-century, 'nature' generally appears in novels as something hospitable to human aspiration. Fifty years later, nature generally appears in narrative, to the extent it appears at all, as something inhospitable to human meaning. In short, Victorian novels move from one to the other of the two constructions of nature that Thomas Carlyle announces in *Sartor Resartus*: one a nature that is the 'living garment of God', and the other, a nature that is, morally speaking, a 'dead mechanism'. In early Victorian narrative these two visions provide fruitful ambiguity, providing ostensibly historical and social narrative sequences with rhetorical burdens. Around mid-century, as the historical aesthetic gains an almost sudden ascendancy over the providential, mid-century novelists experiment with an entirely social, secular construction of human possibility. Great moralists like Charlotte Brontë or William Thackeray seek justification in nature, while George Eliot or Anthony Trollope refer all questions of moral agency and social justice to entirely socialized human action. Towards the end of the century, these ambiguities between natural and social explanation resurface in Thomas Hardy to serve an essentially tragic vision of nature. The mid-century social novel thus marks a shift from the one construction of nature to the other, and a reformulation of narrative code.

NARRATIVE WITH CLOUDS OF GLORY

Before 1850, Nature with a capital 'N' appears in narrative as a divinely formed setting for human affairs. Nature remains essentially anthropocentric, even three centuries after Copernicus (1473–1543) refocused cosmology away from earthly affairs. Novelists of the nineteenth century inherit this morally intelligible, man-centred nature from Romanticism, from the Enlightenment, and from Renaissance humanism. Wordsworth's 'Ode on Intimations of Immortality', for example, quite overtly naturalizes individual identity:

> The Soul that rises with us, our life's Star,
> Hath had elsewhere its setting,
> And cometh from afar:
> Not in entire forgetfulness,
> And not in utter nakedness,
> But trailing clouds of glory do we come
> From God, who is our home.
>
> 'Intimations' Ode, lines 60–66

The 'soul' (not, we note, the 'self') belongs to a divinely organized scheme of nature. Society figures only negatively, as a 'prison house' that twists and reduces natural order. A Wordsworthian suspicion about social conditioning and historical explanation permeates much of the best fiction of the 1840s. The novels of Charlotte, Emily, and Anne Brontë particularly associate social usages with corruption and the good life with 'natural' inspiration; but they are by no means alone. An apparently social novelist like Thackeray offers the same distanced view of society as a corrupt and limited arena in a larger moral order. These novelists employ a narrative sequence that is primarily rhetorical, not historical; time produces nothing new; only the same, same old stories.

To begin with such assumptions about social possibility means that, as Graham Greene's character suggests, the possibilities of plot sequence are to some extent already settled. Plot involves departure from or arrival at truths that remain beyond question, truths that are 'natural'. Such plots are often episodic and based on the journey trope: the idea that life is a road with a moral destination, a pilgrim's progress of the kind Wordsworth's poetry invokes and that has powerful narrative antecedents in Bunyan's *Pilgrim's Progress* and Milton's *Paradise Lost*. In such narratives there are no open-ended possibilities, no alternative outcomes. The niceties of causal sequence have less importance than the re-inscription of familiar stories about the Christian pilgrim's progress in this world, or the fall from grace. They tend to be picaresque because they put no priority on the complex causalities and open-ended possibilities characteristic of historical, social novels.

Less accomplished writers than the Brontës or Thackeray may simply imitate the narrative sequence, without doing much to activate the assumptions from which such sequences derive. Many hundreds of nineteenth-century novels, sometimes optimistically called 'histories', put the voice and manners of the time into this functionally conservative narrative structure. Geraldine Jewsbury's *The History of An Adopted Child* (1853) rambles sentimentally through the experiences of a young girl brought up by harsh grandparents, whose absentee mother turns up and retrieves her, only to die leaving the girl to live with a friend and, eventually, to marry into a comfortable life. Defoe is behind such novels, not Walter Scott. The picaresque traditions of typological narrative inform them, not the social traditions of historical narrative (Ermarth, 1983: 3–92; Fish, 1973: 74).

Even a more accomplished novel like Robert Louis Stevenson's adventure book, *Kidnapped* (1886), has a similar grammar; it depends heavily on nature for its interest, although a demystified nature composed of brambles and other obstacles, and it has a similarly episodic sequence devoted to a series of adventures of an orphaned youth who is sold into high-seas slavery, escapes by shipwreck, and makes his way back to Edinburgh and his inheritance after weeks of wandering through miles of Scottish countryside and having to cope with everything from extreme thirst to outlawed Jacobins. The 'point' of such tales does not lie with the complex influences of social development, but instead with various social situations along a journey, however remote from a pilgrim's progress that journey might seem to be. Development over time is not an issue in such texts, or is only a marginally important issue. The social context is a frame, not a focus.

This complicity between nature and 'man' generally sets apart such novels from the more sceptical social narratives of the nineteenth century, political narratives as well as literary ones. The Wordsworthian language positively relishes this anthropocentric complicity. To describe 'the Soul' as our 'Life's Star', and to say that at birth we come from God 'trailing clouds of glory', certainly implicates nature in human growth. A star is like my soul, my divinely-given nature like a sunrise. The sunrise is not, to use a phrase of Conrad's, 'purely spectacular'; the sunrise is implicated in my progress, and in some way even guarantees the divinity of my nature. The star provides an objective correlative, perhaps even a warrant for the very existence of my soul.

Such projection of human characteristics into nature appears in scientific as well as literary narrative, and especially in the most contemporaneously influential scientific writing of the century, Darwin's books on *The Origin of Species* (1859) and the *Descent of Man* (1871). Though Darwin is discussed most fully in Chapter Two of this book (The Idea of History), it is worth noting here how his use of narrative language projects human qualities on to nature, and even preserves conventional and even conservative constructions in that language. *Descent of Man* especially relies on metaphors that naturalize certain human values. For example, males compete in the battle for survival, females do not, although often in some nations 'women are the constant cause of war', as they are implicitly in the rest of the animal kingdom (Darwin, 1979, I: 418; II: 312–15, 323). Accumulation is a value (the female ant that accumulates more is 'superior' to the scale insect that does not). 'Equality' in numbers between the sexes does not bear essentially on fertility, but considerable time is spent discussing 'equalizing the sexes' (ibid., I: 315ff.). Productiveness is a value (ibid., I: 318) and even a sign of higher intelligence and moral sense in some animals as opposed to others. Implicit comparisons between animal and human 'breeding' thread the text (e.g. ibid., I: 274; II: 403). By

5

considering gradation in a historical horizon, Darwin employs a method with radical potential; at the same time, however, he retains some of the language and values of a religious, and essentially ahistorical discourse, including and especially the implication that nature itself admits of value classification, if not hierarchy. In such ways conventional and unacknowledged values creep into the scientific description.

Later in the century, Kipling provides a literary version of such anthropomorphic projection in *Jungle Book* (1894) and *Second Jungle Book* (1895), where animal tales are human stories masked. Kipling effects a complete colonization of nature by human language, human interests, human competitions and jealousies. This feat has its charm for children, but it extinguishes nature as anything very mysterious, or even as anything other than human. His writing takes to extremes the analogic relation between the human and the natural. To discuss social agendas through projection on to animals not only tames the animals, it universalizes the projected human agendas, which is to say, it renders them in effect 'natural', essential, and thus secured beyond human influence or effort. Thus colonized, Kipling's nature universalizes the particular social and personal concerns he represents. Such an effort had obvious local interest to England as a colonial power confronting black-skinned natives half a world away.

But though Kipling presents only a particularly egregious example of anthropocentrism, neither he nor Darwin nor Wordsworth are alone in deploying the analogical technique that links nature in complicity with man. That use of metaphor has been a cultural value since the Renaissance, and belongs to humanism. The French novelist, Alain Robbe-Grillet (English versions of most of his writing are shamefully unavailable in Britain), argues in his seminal essays on the novel that 'belief in nature is the source of all humanism' (Robbe-Grillet, 1989: 57), and that this complicity between nature and humanity is the keynote of humanist tragedy. Humanism makes man the measure of all things, not just by an arm's length in painting (the *bracchae*-length measures of Quattrocento realist painting), but by the inscription of human agendas over the face of the entire universe. Darkness 'broods', the stars are 'beacons'; and when humans misbehave, all nature feels the wound (Milton's *Paradise Lost*, IX, lines 782–784, 1000–1001).

This analogical habit remains especially strong in novels of the first half of the nineteenth century. For example, in Charlotte Brontë's *Jane Eyre* the eve of Rochester and Jane's would-be sinful marriage also is Midsummer Night's eve; their rhapsodic hopes find expression in terms of 'the shining stars [which] enter into their shining life up in heaven yonder' (C. Brontë,

1966: 280; ch. 23); and the horse-chestnut under which they meet is struck by lightning during the night's storm, leaving 'half of it split away' (ibid.: 284–5). This is no mere accident of weather, and the split tree is more than a 'symbol' of the division between Jane and Rochester. This is nature's comment on their plans; it is a moral warning.

English novels of the 1840s, especially those by the Brontës, Thackeray and the early Dickens, generally depend upon a narrative code that is rooted in a religious tradition and still naturalizes both personal and social life. Its causal explanations, even where they may use historical conventions, remain fundamentally providential in their narrative codes. This 'providential aesthetic' (Vargish, 1985) provides narrative codes that depend to a considerable degree upon readers who make certain religious assumptions about how nature operates. I am indebted to Thomas Vargish's discussion of this important dimension of Victorian narrative, *The Providential Aesthetic in Victorian Fiction*, 1985. The providential discursive framework has immense flexibility, as its currency from Bunyan to Dickens shows; but its 'histories' always belong to a timeless, apocalyptic pattern where origins and ends are not in human hands. The Providential Aesthetic, then, belongs to that complex transition in mid-century between a naturalized and a secularized vision of nature.

Delightfully strange blends of the cosmic and the proto-historical appear in novels like *The Old Curiosity Shop* (1840–41), *Dombey and Son* (1846–48), *Wuthering Heights* (1847), *Jane Eyre* (1847), and *Vanity Fair* (1847–48). Depending as they do upon a tradition of religious assumptions about nature and personal life, they are novels that treat social constructs very sceptically. All minimize the ideal of development that John Stuart Mill enunciates so vigorously in his essay *On Liberty* (1859). At the same time, and within the constraints of providential narrative, they experiment with historical conventions in ways that focus the tensions between the natural and the social order.

NATURE KNOWS BEST: THE BRONTËS AND THACKERAY

Writers as apparently different as Emily Brontë and William Makepeace Thackeray nevertheless produce similar kinds of narratives. Charlotte, Anne and Emily Brontë all occupy readers with the tensions created by pursuing individual history in a natural context. While these tensions take on more laughing qualities in William Thackeray's writing, his treatment of individual experience resembles theirs much more than it resembles that of the historical novels of the later nineteenth century. His historical and urban settings, his verbal playfulness and intellectual wit, give his novels quite a different tonality from theirs, but not a different narrative code. This does not detract one iota from his brilliance or delightfulness, but as the section on him below makes evident, he writes, even in *Henry Esmond*, a different *kind* of narrative than the historical novels of Scott, Trollope or George Eliot. Chapter Two develops the important distinction between historical novels and novels that merely use historical material.

Each of the three Brontë sisters writes accomplished narratives in a style of her own. Anne's two novels, *Agnes Grey* (1847) and *The Tenant of Wildfell Hall* (1848), have a certain composure and intellectual strength that makes them seem still quite contemporary. Charlotte's four novels, *The Professor* (written first and published posthumously in 1857), *Jane Eyre* (1847), *Shirley* (1849) and *Villette* (1853), demonstrate an impressive range and a writing style that is practically unique in its successful combination of two quite different narrative codes. Emily's single novel, *Wuthering Heights* (1847), one of the best known and most original novels in world literature, has an eerie command about it that still defies explanation: it makes immensely original use of complicated and quite ancient narrative codes.

Despite their differences, however, all three novelists share certain assumptions and strategies. All their novels subscribe to a providential aesthetic, that is, to an economy where poetic justice prevails, where there is deep suspicion of social solutions, where 'nature' supports the individual will and is morally organized. The answers to important questions, consequently, lie at the margins of social order, not in the drawing room. Certain things are taken for granted that affect the narrative sequence: that individual will is 'naturally' effective; that social usages are trivial except as they reflect larger, metaphysical and 'natural' truths about individual life. These are not assumptions that make for the fine character delineation, or complex social causalities of a Trollope, a Meredith or a George Eliot. The nature novelist, assuming nature is divine, attends instead to the ways in which individual life adjusts in certain predisposed patterns within a moral cosmos. This lack of social observance or complex dialogue is not something to be explained biographically, as it often is in the Brontës' case as a consequence of their celebrated isolation, but instead something to be explained in terms of an entire discourse or a set of cultural values which differ crucially from the social and historical values more familiar after mid-century.

A case in point is Charlotte Brontë's (1816–55) heroine in *Jane Eyre* (1847), who still rivets readers as she did at her first publication. So real, yet so unrealistic. As a character she remains remarkably static as she goes from one stage of her journey to the next. In growing up to womanhood she repeats the same pattern of 'submission and rebellion' in one episode after another, from Gateshead to Moorhouse. This is because the book has a particular rhetorical burden: to teach her the lesson she needs to learn, which is how to avoid the cycle of submission and rebellion by avoiding idolatry. And that lesson can only *be* learned because she manages not to change her uncompromising moral and emotional intensity. She must keep her own counsel and act.

But in doing so, Jane has guidance from various 'voices' that come unbidden at crucial moments, as if from within herself and in solitude (usually at night): when she wants to change her situation a mentor-voice whispers 'advertise'; a Mother-voice counsels her to flee temptation; and the voice of Rochester calls her name at a crucial moment. Whatever name we give to these transcendent powers – conscience, God, nature – they clearly function to support Jane's own will to resist compromise and change. Such will power is not necessarily inconsistent with social life or even with good investments; it is by no means accidental in her providential universe that she can choose love over duty only after she has earned some money and a place of her own. But each little 'society' of equals, first with her cousins at Moorhouse and then with Rochester at Ferndean, remains a family group in a natural setting, and Charlotte Brontë insists upon the power of nature. Nature is enough to restore vision to a man like Rochester, blinded by too much experience of sociality; but also enough to help Jane focus her ambition in this world and not, through missionary sacrifice, in the next.

This novel, furthermore, presents a providential economy of virtue and reward that definitely exceeds the bounds of historical probability. If Jane had not gone back to her aunt's death-bed, she would never have learned of her uncle in Madeira; if she had not written to him from Thornfield announcing her marriage, he would never have been able to stop the wedding; and if she had not refused to be a mistress instead of a wife, the same providential uncle would not have left her his money. And so it goes. So many coincidences point both to the causalities of a consequential moral universe, and to the efficacy of Jane's will: providence and history, the vanishing points of two universes, meet in *Jane Eyre*.

When Jane finally does assert herself against St John Rivers's pressures towards duty – 'It was *my* time to assume ascendancy. *My* powers were in play and in force' – the assertion of selfhood has the ring of religious inspiration, and even of providential pattern, while the contextualities of social and historical fiction are more than a little irrelevant. Identity is established and maintained outside social boundaries, though sometimes tested in them. The strange, stagey episodes of Brontë's plot, and of her language, make it unsatisfying to read for realistic character and historical development.

Jane Eyre is a providential novel that demonstrates not just one but both the narrative motives characteristic of 'the providential aesthetic'. First, a 'providentialism of design' informs Jane's schematic pilgrimage, which is composed of a series of separate episodes that refine the moral outcome. This plot implies that divine causalities work in the world and work counter to historical and social causalities. Second, a 'providentialism of immanence' appears in the flashes of preternatural insight and communication that determine the plot (Vargish, 1985: 6–24). In Charlotte Brontë's novel, social order belongs to a providential agency that encourages the morally strong to seek domestic solutions and to avoid wider social contest. The smoking ruins of Thornfield stand as an emblem of the deep scepticism in this novel about social order as a context for personal moral development. Jane's conscience keeps her on the road and in the margin of a society that always threatens to change her for the worse. She moves in a typological universe and in a rhetorical sequence that strongly invokes Bunyan's in *Pilgrim's Progress*. From Gateshead, to Lowood, to Thornfield, the 'places' of the novel are rhetorical *topoi*, literally sites of argument. When Jane Eyre leaves Thornfield by the 'wicket' gate, a pilgrim's progress is clearly underway.

Charlotte Brontë carefully distinguishes this true, morally alive Nature from the mere lower-case nature of rocks and stones and trees. Lost on the moors, cut off from all friendship and human support, Jane's first, benign view of nature quickly turns pessimistic in a single short day of cold and hunger. Outside on the moors, Jane nearly starves. She turns fruitlessly to strangers, who conspicuously lack any generosity. To find her 'place', Jane must temper her uncompromising moral posture with a little friendship, in her case a sisterhood, and the convenience of inherited income; but she comes by these things naturally, as it were, through the kindness of those who coincidentally turn out to be long-lost relatives. When she survives moral testing, Jane's reward is a human consummation, albeit an exclusively domestic one. But specifically *social* identity is something that Jane Eyre conspicuously lacks.

Whereas in more fully historical novels by Dickens or George Eliot, change is a good in itself and to stand still is to atrophy, change in *Jane Eyre* is a necessary evil. To the extent that Jane worries about what she will become, she worries about decline and diminishment, not growth or development. Her story does not develop her identity so much as it submits her to trial and assigns her a place. The opening scene of the novel haunts the progress like an emblem: Jane claiming a space of her own in the window seat, protected by a curtain from the corrupt social world on one side and protected by the window glass from a harsh natural world on the other. This problem of what 'place' is hers continues to be the preoccupation of the novel. Jane gets older, her capacities enlarge, she inherits money, she goes through spectacular, not to say melodramatic, experiences; but she is as assertive at the outset as she is at the end. Her mind stays the same.

Given the anachronistic usage of words like 'self' and 'human' in discussing the Brontës, it should be remembered when reading a novel like *Jane Eyre* that these terms had scarcely any of their current functions before the early eighteenth century. In fact, modern usage developed broad currency surprisingly late, which is to say, well into the nineteenth century. The twentieth-century idea of selfhood, as Foucault said, should not be reconstituted where it did not find formulation (Foucault, 1985: 12). It takes a particular narrative construction of difference to produce the secularized, socially differentiated, historically and materially specified self. In its medieval and now-archaic uses, 'self' is a largely negative word used to signify selfishness or conflicted identity. When Shakespeare's Polonius counsels Laertes, 'to thine own self be true', he has been interpreted by modern readers to mean something positive, whereas it is quite probable that Shakespeare has given the word 'self' to Polonius in order to discredit it. When Carlyle in *Sartor Resartus* rejoices in 1833 over Teufelsdrock's liberating 'annihilation of self', he activates this older, Christian sense of the self as a blocking influence. Since the early eighteenth century, 'self' has had a different and a positive meaning in more than one sense: it connotes a positivity, which is to say, an entity that remains internally or essentially the 'same' despite outward or developmental changes; and this connotation has positive, not negative value.

Comparison of the two constructions of identity may help to keep their difference in mind. The identity of a naturalized soul is relatively static, simply because a rationally ordered 'natural' cosmos, in which every created thing has its 'natural' place, does not value essential change, however much it may value motion. Where perfection reigns, individual success can be measured by its resistance to influence, except in the rare instance where change of identity itself belongs to the divine order. A historical self, by contrast, is necessarily responsive to influence, for better or for worse; it is mobile; it changes; and it is by definition social. The fully historical, which is to say social, development of such individual selfhood remains surprisingly unimportant even as late as the late 1840s. After 1848, one is tempted to argue, and in tandem with historicizing sciences, theological Higher Criticism and European revolutionary activity, emergent social forms seem rather quickly to become more important and, with them, the historical development of individual identity.

In these novels of the 1840s, the entity once conceived in a variety of narratives (e.g. Bunyan's *Pilgrim's Progress* (1678), and Richardson's *Clarissa* (1748)) as a Christian 'soul' on a progress through this world, explores its worldly potential as a historical 'self' but without ever quite giving up the assumptions grounded in religion. Key among them is the assumption that individual identity has its definition and functions in a natural order of things. Society may or may not express that 'nature', but that issue remains secondary; all things human necessarily remain secondary in a divine cosmos. The identity that comes with such a formation may be a personal and flexible English identity, or the solidly atomic *cogito* of French philosophers, but it is a divinely given identity nonetheless, and one to be maintained by resistance, not improved by development. The plots of novels like *Robinson Crusoe* (1719)or *Pamela* (1740–41) accommodate these characters, part Christian soul and part historical self, loosely, in episodic and rhetorical sequences where causal development is not a primary issue because, as Graham Greene noted, the 'natural' or universal story already is known.

The word 'human' has a history similar to that of the word 'self'. Before about 1700 it is spelled with a final 'e', and 'humane' distinguishes mundane beings from supernatural ones. After 1700 the term 'humane' becomes restricted to descriptions of behaviour (e.g. courteous, sympathetic) and 'human' developed its distinctively modern and secular reference to attributes or qualities distinctive to mankind as a species, an entity in its own right. In other words, these etymological mutations imply a watershed separating a medieval idea of identity from the modern one that most Westerners now treat as second nature: the idea that human beings, like other objects, are not 'places' in a cosmic hierarchy, but entities possessing internal invariances that remain the same despite changes in position or external appearance (Ermarth, 1983: 3–63). The social implications of this idea are still being discovered in England.

This difference in linguistic function before and after the end of the seventeenth century suggests the kind of shift in usage that accompanies discursive reformation, in this case the reconstruction of the word 'self' to suit a world increasingly under the influence of secular and rationalizing influences. In the populous spiritual cosmos constructed by Christianity, however, a 'self' merely interferes with that divine 'converse of spirits' mentioned by Robinson Crusoe in 1719. A 'self' merely blocks the cosmic exchange of influence that maintains the divinely inspired order of nature.

In the nineteenth century, 'self' gradually takes on a new and positive definition from a context that changes because the definition of nature changes.

This context informs Charlotte Brontë's as it does all providential novels, and has crucial implications for interpreting her heroines, in particular Jane Eyre. Jane is not exactly a Christian soul any longer, but she is not yet exactly a socialized self, either. Her will has its scope at the margin of society; her history remains schematic; the identity that she calls alternatively 'my self' and 'my soul' performs heroic acts of resistance from beginning to end in a natural environment responsive to human will. Jane's 'self' resembles a Christian soul more than a historical person; this shows in her stirring assertion of equality to Rochester in the rose garden at Thornfield (another emblematic environment):

> Do you think, because I am poor, obscure, plain, and little, I am soulless and heartless? You think wrong! I have as much soul as you – and full as much heart! . . . I am not talking to you now through the medium of custom, conventionalities, or even of mortal flesh: it is my spirit that addresses your spirit, just as if we had both passed through the grave, and we stood at God's feet, equal as we are.
> (Charlotte Brontë, 1966: 281, ch. 23)

Such equality of souls requires no legislation; it belongs to a scheme of cosmic or natural justice not in human hands, except as self-control. In such a context the word 'self' has a distinctly religious flavour. When Jane confronts the temptation to stay as Rochester's mistress – 'who in the world cares for *you*? or who will be injured by what you do?' – her 'indomitable' reply is '*I* care for myself'. But this 'self' is very shortly described as a 'soul' ('I still possessed my soul').

Because the providential aesthetic is generally underestimated in reading such fiction, I have concentrated on only one of Charlotte Brontë's novels, but the general argument applies to all of them equally, and especially to her masterpiece, *Villette*. While Charlotte Brontë's heroines are never conceived as emergent historical entities of the kind we call 'selves', this is not because Charlotte Brontë could not conceive of such a thing but because she had other visions to pursue. The pleasures of her novels lie not in character development but in the dauntless, uncompromising revelation of the workings of conscience; in the revelation of a cosmos alive to moral courage; in the subtle pursuit of moral distinctions; and in some, but not all, cases in the satisfying fact that moral effort meets with a just reward (*Villette* is the apparent exception).

By comparison with Charlotte Brontë's novels, Emily Brontë's

13

(1818–48) single novel, *Wuthering Heights* (1847), hardly seems to emphasize anything like a Christian Providence, yet its reliance on 'nature' is absolute. Consequently it shares with *Jane Eyre* certain narrative dispositions: its faith in nature's power, its episodic plot composed of journals and letters, its suspicion of social solutions, and its emphasis on individual will. But as narrative, *Wuthering Heights* is much more sophisticated than *Jane Eyre*. Emily Brontë's originality as a writer of narrative lies, at least in part, in her direct focus on the problem of narration.

She effectively prevents historical time from forming by using a frame-tale that cuts up time into different units, or levels, particular to many different observers. There are at least a dozen narrators, all unreliable. *Wuthering Heights* has nothing to do with the reliable narrative hindsight that gives Charlotte Brontë's novels their feel of being at least rudimentary history; it has nothing to do, in short, with the narrative code that historical novels orchestrate fully after mid-century. In this novel the main narrative perspective belongs to the cold, cowardly Lockwood, who includes everyone else's narrative in his journal but who seems to comprehend little about the events he records. The housekeeper, Nelly Dean, who seems to him so 'very fair' an observer (Emily Brontë, 1965: 192), actually interferes with and blurs the social relations she supposedly manages; she attempts to 'smooth over' differences and difficulties, she betrays confidences, and neglects to carry out orders. In short, and quite unlike the narrator function that sustains the grammar of perspective in historical and social novels, her mediations are fatal to truth, to love, to clarity, to energy, to life itself. These two 'tellers', the housekeeper and the visitor, are everything that the main characters, Catherine and Heathcliff, are not. The hero and heroine may be destructive, especially when subjected to 'civilization', but the narrators, Lockwood and Nelly, are worse: he throughout a shrinking voyeur, she a destructive compromiser.

The sense of historical dislocation so impressive in this novel stems entirely from this carefully constructed unreliability of the narrative hindsight. A reality of passion and will and survival bursts open the fragile frame-tale of quotidian life represented by Lockwood and Nelly Dean. Linear causalities are scrambled; identities do not emerge so much as persist. The impossibility of historical relationship means that even the identities of characters do not remain separate and individualized. The name 'Catherine' refers confusingly to two different people, so does the name 'Linton' (it is both Edgar's last name, and the first name of Isabella's son); but these names are not used in ways that clarify these differences. Instead, these names act like switches, simultaneously sending attention in two different directions, and creating a chronic problem for readers stumbling on them who attempt to separate the one generation from the other. No matter how often one has read the novel, the narrative still generates this identity confusion. Although Emily's novel ends on a fragile note of reconciliation between nature and culture, as the creature of the drawing room and the creature of the moors bend their heads together over a book, the agendas of the novel all work in the direction of the moors. Those agendas also privilege an ethic of vengeance, not one of mobility and change. Motivated by Heathcliff's revenge, this story reproduces violent, non-historical patterns that render social justice impossible (Vargish, 1971). Even though the abused orphan becomes master of the house, he only repeats the child abuse that was visited on him. This violence ensures a perpetual break of continuity, a perpetual assertion of boundaries often expressed in terms of personal 'honour'.

In the end, the social order survives only by rejecting this inbreeding, by incorporating the stranger, and by secluding both native and stranger from a 'natural' world turned violent by its exclusions. This sophisticated novel does not by any means come down on the side of revenge over social justice, and shows with poignancy the terrors of abused children. But the novel does not exactly come out in favour of the conventional domestic environment either, taking an almost surrealist angle on the sublimations and deflections of 'good' middle-class people. It certainly casts doubt on those who mediate in other people's lives.

In any case, and whatever the thematic material in the novel seems to indicate, the entire *formality* of *Wuthering Heights* works against the mediations of history: against the double agenda of individualizing character and unifying the medium of events with a single historical perspective. In short, Emily Brontë's social messages, like Charlotte's, may *seem* remotely similar to those of later, historical, social novelists like late Dickens, Trollope and George Eliot. But if the message seems similar, the messenger is not. The whole novel fractures any common medium like historical time, thus rendering impossible any union, or re-union, in this world. Instead, it valorizes a timeless and 'natural' energy.

Anne Brontë's (1820–49) quiet, accomplished novels, *Agnes Grey* (1847) and *The Tenant of Wildfell Hall* (1848), have been less celebrated than those of her sisters, perhaps because they show divine nature working in more recognizable ways; but they have the same narrative codes: the episodic presentation, the assignment of causality to providence not history, the reliance on individual will in a natural setting. The novel moves from one drawing room to another, and one domestic scene to another, just as Bunyan's Christian moves through the 'places' of Vanity Fair. Helen Huntington, the heroine of her second novel, functions in the social hierarchy as Jane Eyre does – by withstanding it. While her morally bankrupt husband spends a lot of time in the city, she does not; and she ends morally and economically triumphant in a rural retreat not unlike Ferndean.

Despite its courageous treatment of issues that, more than a century later, we regard as 'social' issues – the secrecy surrounding domestic violence and drug dependency, the poisonousness of gossip, the destructiveness of English habits of educating children of both sexes, the symbiosis of abusive husbands and wives who are professional victims – these are not primarily social issues for Anne Brontë; or rather, for her, what we call 'social' issues are at bottom moral and religious ones. The abusive husband is paired in marriage with a professional victim, and Anne Brontë is direct and uncompromising as she analyses the mutuality of the human default. ' "I *don't* oppress her," says he; "but it's so confounded flat to be always cherishing and protecting; and then how can I tell that I *am* oppressing her when she 'melts away and makes no sign'? I sometimes think she has no feeling at all; and then I go on till she cries – and that satisfies me" '(Anne Brontë, 1979: 300). Though he is no paragon, the portrait of his wife, the doormat Millicent, bears him out. The assertion of human relatedness seems quite like what we find in George Eliot's novels, for instance when Brontë's heroine confronts the drinker with his responsibilities: ' "It is nonsense to talk about injuring no one but yourself; it is impossible to injure yourself – especially by such acts as we allude to [oppressing your wife, carousing] – without injuring hundreds, if not thousands, besides, in a greater or less degree, either by the evil you do or the good you leave undone" ' (ibid.: 300–1). But realistic as these episodes seem, they belong to a narrative that relies on already understood plots that have to do with salvation, not with the accomodations and compromises of realism and history.

The narrative sequence in *The Tenant of Wildfell Hall* marks 'places' or *topoi* just as certainly as if this were an oration of Cicero. The heroine, with her own abusive husband (ibid.: 346), has the confidence that the next life is recompense for this one and, unlike a Trollope novel, this narrative does not offer any irony on the point, or contextualize it in any way. The novel traces Helen's resistant refusal to collude in her addict husband's decline and death, in a plot 'development' that is mainly negative (ibid.: 432–7). Her weapons of resistance, moreover, are moral, not legal or social. Her *will* is like iron (ibid.: 405) and, in 'her uncompromising boldness' (ibid.: 85), she is forever teaching men, some of whom actually listen. Most tellingly, poetic justice rules in the end. The self-indulgent destroyer eventually destroys himself; the uncompromising wife, through enormous stress and difficulty, lives.

It would be more difficult to describe Thackeray's novels as 'providential' in any usual sense. Their moral centres are indicated mainly by their absence, and we do not yet have a theory of a 'providentialism of absence'. Yet they resemble providential novels more than they differ from them. Thackeray's greater social scope did not mask from Charlotte Brontë the kinship between them; it led her to dedicate the second edition of *Jane Eyre* to him as the 'great moralist' of the age. (In perhaps another tribute, her first written novel, *The Professor* (1846?, published 1857), has the same title as Thackeray's own first novel (1837)). Like hers, his narrative sequence is rhetorical, not historical; like her he maintains deep scepticism about social solutions and a reliance on a naturalized morality.

Though Thackeray spends more time in those drawing rooms that Jane Eyre so studiously avoids, his large 'set of people living without God in the world', with reverence for nothing but prosperity and an eye for nothing but success, belong to an episodic narrative process unfavourable to historical development. In *Vanity Fair: A Novel Without a Hero* (1847–48), nobody gets their just reward, and nobody has a really productive flash of intuition. The series of locally realist scenes belong not to history but to a puppet show presented, Hogarth-like, in a series of lifelike vignettes that repeat without mutual linkage a pattern of conflict and disappointment so constant as to seem like a kind of inverted version of Homeric *arete*.

Thackeray does not construct society as an entity; it is simply 'the world' and, as such, it is a moral bog. Such 'society' is an opiate for his characters, e.g. Becky Sharp, who 'loved society' and 'could no more do without it than an opium eater without his dram' (Thackeray, 1963: 623). In *Pendennis* (1848–50), Blanche reaches one moment of frankness that approximates the narrator's when she privately confesses to Pen her addiction to society: ' "I have been spoilt early. I cannot live out of the world, out of excitement. I could have done so, but it is too late. If I cannot have emotions, I must have the world" ' (Thackeray, 1871b: 415). The opposition between 'the world' on the one hand and 'emotions' on the other looks backward to the older opposition between mundane and 'humane' on the one hand and supramundane or spiritual on the other.

The local texture of Thackeray's novels often seems realistic and historical, and they rightly have been admired for the many quiet scenes where the narrator seems to fulfil the historian's function of maintaining a common, neutral medium which makes possible the mutually informative measurements, and thus the development of individual and social identities, that constitute historical narrative. Becky Sharp and Rawdon Crawley have a tacit understanding about 'taking' people at cards that implies a kind of private world we never see and a mutual consciousness

17

shared by them; the quiet friendship between Lady Jane and Rawdon seems to sustain a sequence of mutual understandings. Mutual respect and trust survives between Arthur Pendennis and his Laura in the interstices of worldly occupations. We rejoice in the rare moment of frankness between Pen and his erstwhile fiancee, Blanche. The innocence and need of small children, the experience of grief, the good-humoured endurance of those whose experiments fail: all inspire a generic 'human' sympathy. And in his essays and novels Thackeray conveys a sense of what life is like in the street, for the London greengrocer or tourists in Paris fleeing war, for art students in a French garret or a pedestrian at the Inns of Court.

Yet these scenes are contained in a framework that isolates them, rather than making them yield historical results. Where no emergent identities are being established, there is no need for sustained, continuous development or for the narrator–historian so essential to it. The journalistic forum, which gave both Thackeray and Dickens their start as narrative writers, seems particularly suited to these episodic novels, and an immediate offspring of the epistolary novel: so well suited, in fact, that we might conclude that serial publication may have been more a consequence than a cause of prevailing assumptions about what it means to tell a story.

In Thackeray's case these assumptions were inherited from eighteenth–century classicism, and opposed the historicizing romanticism of Walter Scott and subsequent novelists like Trollope and George Eliot who admired him. Thackeray laments the death of classicism in these terms:

Jacques Louis David is dead. He died about a year after his bodily demise in 1825. The romanticism killed him. Walter Scott, from his Castle of Abbotsford, sent out a troop of gallant young Scotch adventurers, merry outlaws, valiant knights and savage Highlanders, who, with trunk hosen and buff jerkins, fierce two-handed swords, and harness on their back, did challenge, combat, and overcome the heroes and demigods of Greece and Rome.

(Thackeray, 1872: 50)

Thackeray's allegiances with the eighteenth century are nowhere so evident as in his moralist's depreciation of historical consequentiality. The 'sentiment of reality' that Thackeray sought to give in this novel of the 1840s is itself a conspicuously ahistorical construction, in spite of its references to the Napoleonic wars and other local detail. *Vanity Fair*'s narrative maintains its vantage point at the margin of the relatively chaotic realm of social and historical events and keeps an eye on eternity, from which perspective all human plots look pretty much alike. It is not exactly the drama of Everyman, but it is the domestic affairs of Damon and Delia who are much closer to everyman and everywoman than to the developing characters in novels that emphasize historical causality.

While Thackeray partly materializes the realist medium of historical time in historical allusions and in local episodes, he contains such moments in sequences so arbitrary that they undercut the development of character and the formation of the neutral temporal medium that characterizes historical narrative (see Chapter Two). The vigorous, ironic voice of the moralist, with its cosmic view of origins and ends and its sad affection for human contrariness, watches over emergent patterns just as a historical narrator would do, but the patterns that emerge are so archetypal, so Bunyanesque in their cosmic universality, that they almost completely transcend their social particulars.

In fact, that is the point. The Napoleonic wars in *Vanity Fair* are a distant echo in the background of domestic wars between the sexes, between old and young, between rich and poor. There is scarcely any difference between power struggles, whether they are for Waterloo or child custody, even though the one struggle is 'great' and the other not. In *Pendennis* (1848–50), as in the extended collection of novels dealing with the same families on both sides of the Atlantic, *The History of Henry Esmond, Esq.* (1852), *The Newcombes: Memoirs of a Most Respectable Family, edited by Arthur Pendennis, Esq.* (1853–55) and *The Virginians: A Tale of the Last Century* (1857–59), we focus on the generic patterns found in individual lives. For example, when it comes to women, says the narrator of *Pendennis*, 'Men' are all one – 'Ajax, Lord Nelson, Adam'; and, ending the novel: 'every man' lives the same pattern of disappointment. This perception leads attention well beyond social boundaries and the concerns of individual development:

> If the best men do not draw the great prizes in life, we know it has been so settled by the Ordainer of the lottery. We own, and see daily, how the false and worthless live and prosper, while the good are called away, and the dear and young perish untimely, – we perceive in every man's life the maimed happiness, the frequent falling, the bootless endeavour, the struggle of Right and Wrong, in which the strong often succumb and the swift fail.

Character is not fate in these novels; Fate has a mind of its own. And so, the narrator concludes, we should be generous to the failings of Pendennis, who doesn't claim to be a hero but only 'a man and a brother'. From a considerable moral altitude we see the arbitrariness of social arrangements and the 'bootless'-ness of efforts to control one's destiny. Such an altitude makes possible the perpetual fun whereby a perspective is first established and then distorted, and at the same time it confines social and historical motives within a larger moral vision.

Thackeray constrains any development by his use of narrators, that is, by his management of the grammar of perspective. Beginning with his earliest journalistic sketches, Thackeray has a habit of inventing narrators like 'Samuel Titmarsh' or 'Charles Yellowplush, a Sometime Footman in Many Genteel Families'. Instead of providing 'reliable', which is to say historical, narratives of realism, these character-narrators engage readers in contradictory perspectives of the kind familiar in satire. His many journalistic 'sketches' and 'papers' – for example, 'On Going to See a Man Hanged' (*The Paris Sketchbooks of Mr. Samuel Titmarsh*, 1840) – pivot on ironic undercuts and the production of contradictions that remain unassimilable from any constant point of view or set of principles. The episodic narrative in *The Memoirs of Barry Lyndon, Esq., Written by Himself* (1844) creates terrific problems of distance and perspective reminiscent of those in Defoe. The instability of viewpoint forces us to ask questions typically raised in Swift's *Modest Proposal* or in dramatic monologue, where we are forced to see limits the speaker does not. 'And now', says the fictional autobiographer, Barry Lyndon, very much like Moll Flanders whom he resembles,

> if any people should be disposed to think my history immoral (for I have heard some assert that I was a man who never deserved that so much prosperity should fall to my share), I will beg those cavillers to do me the favour to read the conclusion of my adventures; when they will see it was no such great prize that I had won, and that wealth, splendour, thirty thousand per annum, and a seat in Parliament, are often purchased at the price of personal liberty, and saddled with the charge of a troublesome wife.

The reader knows better: that he miserably mistreats this wife who has brought him all these worthless treasures that he has so much desired (Thackeray, 1871: 241, ch. 18). This history of a poor Irish boy who, by the age of thirty, has by his 'own merits and energy raised [himself] to one of the highest social positions that any man in England could occupy' (ibid.: 122, ch. 16) certainly suppresses ordinary historical causalities.

In this fictional universe, as in Jane Eyre's, one's 'place' is more like a rhetorical *topos* than a historical site. The emphasis on chance or fate ('Fate did not intend that I should remain long an English Soldier' (ibid.: 59, ch. 4)) and on gambling suits a narrative where differences are not bases for mediation, as in history, but absolutes. Personal honour, life and death, are matters that produce rupture, not rationalization. As in *Jane Eyre*, society here is the antithesis of personal happiness, not its unavoidable context, and character development hardly figures as an issue.

Thackeray's brightest, most sparkling book is *Vanity Fair*, a novel that, like *Jane Eyre*, invokes *Pilgrim's Progress* in its governing conception. To say that character doesn't develop in this novel is to put it mildly. Each character repeats his or her mistakes for a lifetime in a comedy of errors and miscalculation; no mitigating sense of alternatives appears of the kind so evident in novels that are constructed as developments not revelations. Ultimately, and despite hopefulness to the contrary, Vanity Fair is the same in all times and places, and most change is arbitrary and unproductive. Full development of a 'self' is pointless, not to say impossible, in a howling wilderness, even when that wilderness is social. In *Vanity Fair*, society is a 'great lottery' in which one has to gamble and even the great players guess wrong, like Becky at the gambling table. The social world either has no order, or its order is so arbitrary and changeable that it cannot be a context for moral life. The episodes in this novel could be redistributed without offending any development of causality, up to and including the double ending which first offers the long-desired happy ending and then undercuts it, taunting readers with the typicality of their own desire for happy conclusions.

Thackeray's emphasis on fate and arbitrariness does not necessarily lend itself to a providential interpretation, although, as Charlotte Brontë shows in *Villette*, the very lack of earthly recompense can itself serve the cause of faith. Nor does the absence of providentialism necessarily mean the presence of history. In *Vanity Fair* the sequence is more rhetorical than historical. While the local texture of the novel often seems realistic, its framework is that of the pilgrim's progress, that is, of an episodic moral *sentence* rather than the kind of historical development essential to the production of individual selfhood. The *dramatis personae* have names whose historical properties must compete with the alphabetical, A(melia), B(ecky), C(rawley), and D(obbin). The typically opposite heroines, Becky Sharp and Amelia Sedley, have parodically parallel experiences; both are presented at court, both sink into poverty, and both end where they began, with Amelia giving her dresses to Becky. There are false bottoms in every speech (George's explanation why he should marry Amelia; Osborne's hortatory speech to Miss Rhoda), and every scene, even the terrible confrontation scene with Lord Steyne (Thackeray, 1963: ch. 53) where the compounding ironies blur any questions of guilt or innocence. Paratactic patterns thread the style; we get 'green' in dozens of different incarnations (green eyes, greengrocer, green schoolboy, green purse, Mr Green, greenhorn, dark-green carriage, green parasite, etc.), all seeming increasingly arbitrary the more they echo each other. There are unresolvable mysteries about even the most important explanations; does Becky kill Jos Sedley? Thackeray, when asked, said he didn't know. Every position, even the 'truest', can be reversed (the consistently perfect selflessness of Amelia metamorphoses when she thinks she is losing Dobbin).

The arbitrariness of all human arrangements, the lack of interesting connections between local details, continually and rhythmically point to the prevailing paradigm stated succinctly in the penultimate sentence: '*Vanitas vanitatum*! Which of us is happy in this world? Which of us has his desire? or, having it, is satisfied?' As one potentially conclusive moment after another suddenly turns sentimental or undergoes other reversal, the narrative continually asserts the arbitrariness of fate. Amelia weeps, but even in grief her attention may be divided; the greengrocer who suffers the social injustice entailed by a hierarchical class structure also collaborates in supporting that structure. And so it goes. The characteristic experience in this novel is the anticlimax. All these patterns in the narrative confirm the arbitrariness of social arrangements, of desire and satisfaction, of moral rules, and of efforts to control destiny.

The profound arbitrariness permeating *Vanity Fair* probably is one of the reasons for its continuing popularity in the late twentieth century. The novel abounds in moments where some unexpected and entirely unpredictable plot revelation produces unassimilable facts that defy mediation and explanation: Amelia dreams sentimentally of George who at that moment is lying on the field of Waterloo with a bullet in his heart; Becky, whose vigorous seduction of Sir Pitt Crawley has led to a proposal, surprises us, and him, with the confession 'I am married already'; Amelia, who resists pressure to seek help from Dobbin, finally confesses that she has already written. The novel is composed of such little emotional reversals.

The longest such episode is the Pumpernickel episode, in which Amelia is presented at court; it is a vertiginous little vignette of success, a puerile fantasy fulfilled, a glorious spiral staircase leading nowhere. Troops of happy peasants in red petticoats and three-cornered hats enjoy perpetual festivals given by the Duke and Duchess; their government, 'a moderate despotism, tempered by a Chamber that might or might not be elected', is effortless, equinanimous, even unnecessary. This episode is especially conspicuous because of its length, and consequently the break it produces in a narrative otherwise composed of short, swallow-flights of prose, but it is the same in kind; it is a kind of final orchestral statement of the same pattern of wishful fantasy so often repeated and denied in the course of the novel. This kind of narrative has its antecedent in *Don Quixote*.

The narrator of *Vanity Fair* forces readers to repeat this pattern of investment and disappointment; the novel has an almost rhythmic habit of drawing you in and leaving you stranded. The narrator's unstable detachment is quite unlike the shifting attentions of historical narrators who generally do not contradict themselves; this one changes without comment from one view of a character (of Amelia and her mother, say) to a new and very different view in the course of a single chapter, Chapter 38. The second view does not build upon the first, but completely contradicts its saccharine portrait. The lack of mediation between these conflicting viewpoints leaves the reader with a renewed sense of the arbitrariness of every conclusion, and of all social arrangements. Although nature does not trail clouds of glory here, it nevertheless underwrites the only important human connections in *Vanity Fair*; society certainly does not.

In fact, the narrator often wanders from a social particular to a moral lecture that acts a bit like epic simile. At the beginning of Chapter 38 the narrator reflects on how luck changes in this world, and how we are all 'mimes' imitating ourselves on the stage of life. From this altitude, 'the gifts and pleasures of Vanity Fair cannot be held of any great account, and . . . it is probable . . . but we are wandering out of the domain of the story. Had Mrs. Sedley been a woman of energy. . . ' (ibid.: 373–4). The rapid shift from generality to particular underscores its arbitrariness. Unlike the historian-narrator, the Nobody narrator discussed below in Chapter Two, whose distanced perspective maintains a single system of mutual relation and intelligibility, here the altitude negates the importance of the patterns its descries, except for the brooding pattern of mortality, that ultimate cliffhanger.

When the Final Revelation to Amelia of her long-dead husband's inconstancy finally 'explains' a hint dropped long before, we have forgotten dead George Osborne and the hint; it no longer matters, and nothing develops from it. Instead we get to laugh one more time at Amelia who, on cue, weeps. 'Emmy's head sank down, and for almost the last time in which she shall be called upon to weep in this history, she commenced that work' (ibid.: 658; ch. 67). The narrator keeps alive our awareness of the artificiality of the puppet show even in phrases like these. This pattern of engagement and disengagement does not permit the construction of emergent personal identities so much as it reiterates in a thousand amusing ways the same annihilation of worldly investment.

If anything durable exists outside perishable vanities and patterns of disappointed desire, it may be found in the realm of children, or in the reservoirs of undiscovered feeling and motive hinted at beneath the novel's various false bottoms. But these possibilities are marginalized in favour of the reductive cosmic pattern that affects all alike. The *carpe diem* of *Vanity Fair*, with its brooding sense of darkness outside the brightly lit show, hardly sustains a very expansive providential message. Social class snobbery, the effort to rise socially, merely separates children from their mothers and from their inheritances. Time, 'that great, grey satirist', brings no justice, sustains no development, has no memory. Instead, time undermines or erases every inscription. George Osborne's *billets doux*, trivial as they are, are more immortal than he; they survive to mock him, as do his initials scratched with a diamond on a window pane. 'Perhaps in Vanity Fair there are no better satires than letters.... The best ink for Vanity Fair use would be one that faded utterly in a couple of days, and left the paper clean and blank, so that you might write on it to somebody else' (ibid.: 182). The ephemeral nature of human life, and all its particular objects excepting perhaps the desire for immortality itself, makes the appropriate metaphor one that mocks horizons rather than opening them: vanishing ink, not the vanishing point of a common historical horizon.

Such a context is not a salubrious one for the historical development of social identity. Only two characters in *Vanity Fair* are distanced outsiders who maintain some double perspective on themselves: Becky, who sees that her successes are dull, and Dobbin, who laughs at his own inconsistencies. A reader may wish that the two people who can laugh at themselves, Becky and Dobbin, might get together; but that sort of mutuality is unavailable in the moral universe of *Vanity Fair*. The most durable thing in this novel is the doomed search for immortality in a world where everything perishes, and where momentary laughter is the highest value. We enjoy such laughter thanks to the intermittent, unstable detachment of Thackeray's narrator.

RHETORIC AND HISTORY: SEQUENCE IN THE BRONTËS, THACKERAY AND EARLY DICKENS

The narrative codes of historical and social novels, to be described fully in Chapter Two, have become so familiar that we assume them as the norm for all narrative. Historical time *is* time; what other kind of time is there? But the novels just discussed, by writers who flourished in the 1840s, do not really subscribe, or subscribe fully to the historical convention. Their sequences are not historical but rhetorical because they correspond to a pattern already well established and understood: for example, the pattern of a Christian pilgrim's progress, or the pattern of conversion. The novels that naturalize social agendas and find providential construction in history thus differ markedly from historical and social realism in their use of language, and in their entire range of technique.

Especially marked are the poetic, and non-realist, uses of paratactic images: systems of repeating thematic elements that ride along beside the syntactical progress of narrative logic like omens or shadows of another world. Such mixing of natural metaphor and conspicuous artifice conveys appropriately enough the underlying belief in a naturalized moral order that lies elsewhere than in social affairs.

In *Vanity Fair* such paratactic (as distinct from syntactic) elements reinforce the perceived arbitrariness of the human world by undercutting even its most brilliant outlines. The opening paragraph of Thackeray's novel is a triumphant case in point. Here plot commences under heavy fire from competing and arbitrary sequences:

> While the present century was in its teens, and on one sunshiny morning in June, there drove up to the great iron gate of Miss Pinkerton's academy for young ladies, on Chiswick Mall, a large family coach, with two fat horses in blazing harness, driven by a fat coachman in a three-cornered hat and wig, at the rate of four miles an hour. A black servant, who reposed on the box beside the fat coachman, uncurled his bandy legs as soon as the equipage drew up opposite Miss Pinkerton's shining brass plate, and as he pulled the bell, at least a score of young heads were seen peering out of the narrow windows of the stately old brick house. Nay, the acute observer might have recognised the little red nose of good-natured Miss Jemima Pinkerton herself, rising over some geranium-pots in the window of that lady's own drawing room.

The conventional journey here is undermined by the presence in it of a purely mathematical sequence. One day, two horses, three-cornered hat, and four miles an hour: the variousness of this catalogue does suggest the irrationality of certain classifications, although one is not sure which is the more arbitrary, the mathematical or the existential. In any case, the doubleness introduced into this sequence contributes to the sense of arbitrariness and absurdity that accompanies the voyagers just setting out.

The fun here, as in the novel generally, lies in the gap between the one order and the other, and the play of meaning that this difference opens to surprised readers. The hint that we are setting out on an important journey is accompanied by a sense of suppressed hilarity that is only increased by the emphasis on a street address which evidently has some importance in one system but none in the other, and by the potential immensity of the 'brass plate' at which the horses stop. The 'score' of young heads extends the mathematical sequence to infinity at the same time as it suggests a population; and the red rhyme between Miss Jemima's nose and the geraniums is a joke that carries a hint of trouble. There is, in short, a lot of paratactical action here that competes with and brings up short any syntactical development. This stylistic arbitrariness, along with the various interruptions of development and meaning contributed by the narrator-puppeteer, permeates the narrative and gives it its brilliance. It is entirely fitting that this novel, where nothing is balanced and where rational compensations do not occur, should begin with Becky's ungrateful rejection of Dr Johnson's *Dictionary*.

In Thackeray this style is a highly achieved, ethical result. This is not true of Charlotte Brontë's style, where even rhetorical agendas hardly justify the awkwardness, and occasionally the extreme awkwardness, of her language (for example, when Jane Eyre creeps up the back stairs with her 'victualls'; or when the Professor has 'evacuated the premises' leaving the pupils 'pondering over the string of rather abstruse grammatical interrogatories I had propounded' (Charlotte Brontë, 1987: ch. 13). Still, the Biblical overtone to Brontë's language, like that in Dickens and Thackeray, is by no means accidental; it is the language of moral *sentence*. The language of rhetorical sequences has a latitude for artificiality unavailable in novels more committed to the causalities of social and historical time.

Thackeray is a master at crystallizing for readers what is *not* said, exploiting the contrast between the actual language of a speech (some piety often) with an implicit, situational system that reverses its meanings. For example, upon discovering the surreptitious engagement of his friend, Foker, with his own sometime fiancée, Pendennis laughs that he cannot stand 'between Miss Amory and fifteen thousand a year', whereupon Miss Amory fires up: ' "It is not that, Mr. Pendennis", Blanche said, with great dignity. "It is not money, it is not rank, it is not gold that moves *me*; but it *is* constancy, it is fidelity, it is a whole trustful loving heart offered to me, that I treasure – yes, that I treasure!" And she made for her handkerchief, but, reflecting what was underneath it, she paused.' Considering the expensive bracelet from Foker that she has hastily covered with her handkerchief, the word 'treasure' suggests a usage she does not intend, and the whole situation translates her 'it's not' to mean 'is' (II: 413, ch. 35). In the whole passage Thackeray brilliantly captures the way in which Blanche's language speaks her: even to the way she half believes herself. The speech is not a self-consciously false one, but one falsified by the entire social

26

situation that gives rise to it: an insight that is conveyed without ever being stated. This satirist's reliance on an unspoken story resembles the providential novelist's reliance on paradigms like the pilgrimage or the conversion: it makes possible a kind of elaboration that goes too far for the constraints of realism.

Although Charlotte Brontë's tone is decidedly different from Thackeray's, she employs a stylistic parataxis similar to that noted in the first paragraph of *Vanity Fair*. *Jane Eyre*, for example, conspicuously contrasts red and white through a whole series of changes (red curtain, red room, red ceiling at an inn, red fires, red blood; white moon, white dresses, white furnishings at Thornfield, 'white' name (Blanche), white wedding veil, white road, and many, many more). In *Jane Eyre*, these iterative thematic elements have fairly obvious emblematic value, especially compared to the more masterly use Brontë makes of such elements in her last novel, *Villette* (1853). This novel asserts a providentialism so rigorous that it can *only* be gathered from the echoes, never from the positivities (plot, character, commentary) of the story. Here neither causality nor visionary moments support the faithful soul of Lucy Snowe who sustains her faith precisely *as* faith and without the convenient 'signs' that justify. In her little earthly city ('la villette' is Lucy Snowe's 'Vanity Fair') the social world perishes, and what remains durable is the inner and intuitive 'nature' that resiliently and apparently perversely remains true. This novel explores the thought that it is the very *absence* of worldly justice that suggests providential order: an absence that, by its very completeness, signifies the need for patience and faith (Vargish, 1985: 70–88). Even where no salvation appears, the narrative pattern of search for salvation overrides any evolutionary potential.

Style is meaning in a particularly intense way in *Villette*. The paratactic strings of images or figures – violet, shipwreck, casket, planets, nun, masked identity, walls, drowning, white – and various combinations of them intrude upon a reader's awareness as echoes from another realm of value and pattern: 'the casket' in Chapter 12 is a white box containing violets; Paul has violet eyes and an ivory forehead; a marble top table with violets appears in the place made for Lucy at the end. The considerable fabric of such echoes suggests the presence of other worlds through sheer technical virtuosity, not magic of the kind broached by the voices of *Jane Eyre*. Here the style normalizes a certain indeterminacy in experience, its difficulty in coming to rational recognitions; it creates outside the realm of rational causality a whole world where justice never seems to prevail.

The English tradition of rhetorical narrative sequence goes back notably to John Bunyan's *Pilgrim's Progress* (1678), a precursor evoked by both Thackeray and Charlotte Brontë in their novels of 1847. However 'real' the details of Christian's journey may seem, it is an archetypal journey of Everyman, taking place in a medium that is very far from the neutrality of nineteenth-century history. Obstinacy, worldliness and despair are not constitutive characteristics of an individual 'self' but, quite the contrary, personified qualities that appear as part of the external environment in which the pilgrim soul moves. The plot is as typological as the character, moving as it does from one rhetorical *topos* to another rather than in 'the quiet medium of time', as Jane Eyre puts it, and from one historical site to another (Charlotte Brontë, 1966: 443, ch. 35). Bunyan's narrative medium, his language and his temporality, in short his whole text, is very far from the neutral and homogeneous time of history; it is the qualitatively differentiated environment of a moral universe. Qualities are not 'in' Christian so much as he is in them. His journey is the straightest possible road to heaven, and any digression of the sort invited by social encounters in 'Vanity Fair' and other such rhetorical 'places' are to be avoided. Bunyan's text, which itself provided a *topos* for many subsequent novels, including *Robinson Crusoe* and *Tom Jones*, belongs to a visionary tradition with roots in medieval conventions. It is univocal. It has nothing to do with history. Thackeray's and the Brontës' commitment to this tradition inform all their novels. That is why their characters don't 'develop' in the historical sense. Jane Eyre and Becky Sharp are defined not by development but by schema that interrupt the potential neutralities of the historical medium. The religious ideal of identity derived from Christian traditions simply does not make room for the differentia of social particularity because each soul has the same value before Divinity. This religious emphasis in the construction of identity continues in good health well into the nineteenth century and, as Dickens was especially fond of pointing out, even in the midst of the crassest commercialism.

The tensions between religious and secular explanation that so galvanized nineteenth-century writers and readers appear with special clarity and brilliance in Charles Dickens' early novels. His later novels mark a shift towards a more wholly social vision: especially in *Bleak House* (1852–53) and *Little Dorrit* (1855–57), Dickens worked out the social implications of that dramatic tension between sacred and mundane so obvious in his early work. But by then there has been a sea change in his construction of social and personal life. *Bleak House, Little Dorrit* and *A Tale of Two Cities* (1859) replace the earlier, simpler, picaresque narrations with much more highly plotted ones, and by a more complex articulation of the social world. In fact, that articulation becomes his major focus in the complex mirror relations of *Bleak House*, in the dynamically converging plots of *Little Dorrit, A Tale of Two Cities,* and *Our Mutual Friend* (1864–65). By Chapter One of *Great Expectations* (1860–61), Dickens can assert that the 'identity of things' is social; and in his last novel, *Our Mutual Friend,* the play in that term 'friend' shows the degree to which he has moved from providential explanation: on one plane our mutual friend may be mortality, but on another, mutual friendship becomes the paradigm for achievable social relationships, and especially on the unifying effect of mutual friendship across class division.

The early novels, however, retain more providential and rhetorical motives. Beginning with the fabulous *Pickwick Papers* (1836–37), Dickens' early novels have the kind of picaresque and rhetorical sequence typical of so many novels before 1850. *Nicholas Nickleby* (1838–39), *The Old Curiosity Shop* (1840–41), *Martin Chuzzlewit* (1843) and *Dombey and Son* (1846–48) all work out, with greater or lesser economy, the tension between this world and the next. In these novels, the way nature and history work together is delightfully ambiguous. Those ambiguities underlie much of the fun in early Dickens, and account for much of his popularity with his contemporaries. He could appeal to readers who remained relatively secure in their Christian faith, even a dogmatic faith concerning the order of things, and yet who confronted the competing historical explanations of science and social novelists. Although he is not the only novelist to cruise the boundaries between the historical world and a moral nature, he is by far the greatest of the English novelists to do so.

The tensions between two competing constructions of individual identity – a naturalized soul, and a more historically constructed and socially circumscribed 'self' – compete interestingly in *Dombey and Son.* Published just before mid-century, *Dombey and Son* may appear to twentieth-century vision to lack structural clarity. It is an example of the providential aesthetic, and many contemporary readers simply have lost the habits that would make plain the rhetorical burden of this novel. In *Dombey and Son* the 'providential vision is pervasive and organic throughout; it shapes the novel and holds it together; it serves as a highly controlled unifying aesthetic' (Vargish, 1985: 138–9). Only by assuming Christian, and especially Anglican, doctrine can we fully understand the sacrilege of Dombey's substitution of his 'house' for the '*axis mundi*' which (in the flattering Carker's words) knows 'neither time, nor place, nor season' (Dickens, 1970: 506, ch. 37). Only the knowing reader can grasp the rampant allusions to the Book of Common Prayer in Captain Cuttle's particular transfiguration: 'Wal'r... is what you may call a out'ard and visible sign of a in'ard and spirited grasp, and when found make a note of' (ibid.: 322, ch. 23; the Book of Common Prayer defines a sacrament as 'an outward and spiritual sign of an inward and spiritual grace given unto us, ordained by Christ himself, as a means whereby we receive the same and a pledge to assure us thereof' (Vargish, 1985: 143)). To readers unfamiliar with the Book of Common Prayer, such language seems like mere 'noise'.

On the one hand, then, the providential aesthetic in the novel underwrites enactments of religious patterns and paradigms that explain many elements in the novel unintelligible in historical or evolutionary terms of the social novel.

On the other hand, both forms of providentialism in this novel, the false and the true, run up against a secular motive that is equally strong and determining and that de-naturalizes sociality. If the House of Dombey and Son is Mr Dombey's One True Church, his second wife, Edith Dombey, is the Reformation. In his second wife, Mr Dombey finds an inflexible pride equal to his; like him she has a world-centre of her own. Into Mr Dombey's univocal world of certainty, Edith introduces an absolute difference that cannot be mediated in his terms and that positively forces him to find others: terms that will accommodate the plurality of worlds and that will, in effect, produce history rather than thwart it. The whole movement of the novel chastens Mr Dombey's pride and corrects his Ptolemaic moral vision with a patently Copernican one, bounded only by the shores of death and human expressions of 'love illimitable'. Mr Dombey's view of identity, a parody of religious vision, is corrected by various perspectives that, unknown to him – outside his door, so to speak – assert the inclusive, generic identity of 'human' joy and sorrow. In Bunyan's universe, or even those versions of it found in Charlotte Brontë or Thackeray, Mr Dombey's relentless assertion of his own will might be morally correct; but in Dickens' emerging historical universe, such singleness is a destructive social evil that must be corrected or broken.

It is important to remember that providential and historical motives are not necessarily incompatible. The teleological emphasis of historicism owes a great deal to Christianity (Löwith, 1949). Providence can work through history. However, as history becomes increasingly pruned of naturalized and teleological impulses, when its explanations make room for chance, randomness and contingency, then the historical convention implies a particular narrative system, essentially a perspective system, that runs athwart 'natural' explanations of human affairs. *Dombey and Son* verges on this fully secularized historical convention, but stops short at the perfect goodness of Florence Dombey. Her 'radical, inalienable goodness' belongs to a rhetorical sequence where, typically, she 'threatens our conventional concepts of selfhood and defies even minimal requirements for credibility of character in fiction'; supernaturally good Florence 'runs afoul of our paradigms of the way people develop' (Vargish, 1985: 111). Attempts to read Florence's behaviour as ordinary, historically realistic victim-behaviour, cannot explain the novel's ending. Dickens sacrifices Florence's potentially historical identity, that of a neglected and humiliated child, to the improbably, unbelievable final reunion which sounds 'the theme of Dombey's spiritual redemption' (ibid.: 109–10). In short, the rhetorical sequence accounts for radical changes that a fully secular and denaturalized historical sequence simply would not support.

Edith Dombey, on the other hand, escapes the rhetorical sequence because she is able to differ from herself. A multifaceted, believable woman, forced by an awful mother into marital slavery, and tempered by years of self-control, she rebels very effectively against her assigned commodity function; and she not only exercises a freedom from her assigned role, showing a capacity to change that is exactly opposite to the concentric and repetitive behaviour of her husband and his toadies, she elaborately and effectively sets them up to destroy each other. Edith is consistent enough to be recognizable, yet differs from type enough to sustain a historically developed identity. And there are other characters of whom this is true: the marginal Mr Morfin who, at the end of the novel, announces his conversion from social detachment to social engagement. Initially, he says, 'there was nothing wrong in my world – or if anything not much – or little or much, it was no affair of mine'; but Mr Morfin learns from his experience to see familiar things in a 'new aspect'; the injustice he saw 'shook me in my habit – the habit of nine-tenths of the world – of believing that all was right about me, because I was used to it' (Dickens, 1970: 840–1, ch. 52). Mr Morfin's conversion, however, takes place offstage and thus figures as a rhetorical rather than a historical development.

The overriding formal assertion of *Dombey and Son* – by virtue of Dickens' deployment of those historical conventions described fully in the next chapter – is that identity emerges from and through difference, a formal assertion that makes Florence's apparently static and undifferentiated character all the more at odds with the narrative order of things. By linking different places and times into a single system of explanation, the novel formally brings together what has been divided. Two houses, on opposite sides of town, maintain the bond-in-opposition between the Carker brothers; the two mother–daughter pairs, one rich, one poor, assert a connection where the mercantile eye sees only difference; strangers turn out to be relatives. By various means the novel brings into view the human connectedness that Mr Dombey's ambition denies.

Dickens' novels play wonderfully with rift and rupture in various split structures of narration, and in the early ones the episodic plots belong to the tradition of Bunyan and Defoe rather than to the historical middling-ness of Scott and his heirs. *The Old Curiosity Shop* almost seems to insist upon duality for its own sake. On the one hand is the centripetal plot surrounding Kit and his urban cohort. Here are no expectations, no providence, but instead only disorder, force, and uniqueness: Dick Swiveller swivelling behind Sally Brass's unconscious headdress (Dickens, 1972a: 328–9), or the dervish spin of Quilp, or the various mechanicals like the little servant who has only one speech, 'will you leave a card or message?', or even the carthorse careening from one side of the street to the other grazing lamp poles (ibid.: 164). On the other hand is the centrifugal plot of Little Nell, the plot of expectation, of perspective, of the journey of hope and of the promise of providential resolve. Her journey is doomed, yet even so it counters and relieves readers from the oppression of the random, hallucinatory interludes about Kit and Quilp, just as they provide, in a kind of fascinated absorption in chaos, an alternative to and relief from the child's terrible and eventually unredeemed journey to death. This quite episodic novel does not support the systemic optimism of historical conventions, and yet it moves well away from the comforts of automatic redemption implied by a pilgrim's progress, because the pilgrim is an uncomprehending child.

Later novels insist more on the problem of mediation, and find only limited domestic solutions. In *Bleak House* there are literally two narratives, one in the past tense and one in the present, whose rifts suggest a degree of social degeneracy so insuperable that Esther's marriage hardly affects it (Ermarth, 1983: 189–92). *Little Dorrit* also conspicuously divides into two worlds without bridges, one of prisoners and one of travellers: one fixed, orderly, dead; the other fluttering, restless, even chaotic. Two worlds, two halves, two motives, two styles in an infinite and unhealed schism created by money and secrecy. In such worlds, convergences can't converge and causalities are suppressed. An aimless, fogbound quality pervades both books and belongs to a failure of parenthood on a cosmic scale. Where there is no 'natural' solution and where the social world is not yet constructed, individuals have only limited scope for success.

Increasingly the Dickens world withdraws from any naturalized moral system, and providential plot patterns fade into historical and social ones. *Dombey and Son* is again a watershed. It is precisely his social 'relation' with the wetnurse, lowly Polly Toodles, that Mr Dombey hates to admit; the relation is 'necessary' to him, but he can only acknowledge it by transforming its terms, in her case her name (he will only let her into his house under the alias, 'Mrs Richards'). Sexist Mr Dombey thinks that a girl is nothing but a 'bad Boy', and cares nothing for his daughter; he feels no gratitude to Good Mrs Brown, the poor, ugly old woman (the ultimate outcast) who returns Florence after she has been lost. Yet as Dickens takes great pains to demonstrate, it is precisely these despised relationships upon which Mr Dombey depends; they keep his first commanding hope alive, they hold the key to his revenge, and they finally keep *him* alive. In these and other ways Dickens insists here on the intimate relation of what seems remote, the social connectedness across those arbitrary lines drawn to delineate class and economic difference. Faith in the unity of the world is an old humanist idea, suggested in Dickens, as it is in Shakespeare, by the use of double plots; their convergence proves that, despite appearance, the world is unified, or at least unifiable. Increasingly in Dickens that faith finds expression in social solutions.

But Dickens does not often move beyond the personal solution to the political problem, and the larger social problems conspicuously remain. The domestic solution, for example in the marriages of Florence Dombey and Amy Dorrit, provides a frail stay against the moral disorder of London society. The separate peace of home and hearth is no match for cosmic and social dislocation; the personal solution does not go far enough. There are very few moments in Dickens like the one in *Great Expectations*, when Magwitch (alias Provis) stops playing Providence, and accepts responsibility for forging his past into its 'eternal shape' (Dickens, 1972: 441). In so doing, he accepts history over fantasy and thus becomes a free man, if a doomed one. It is the Estellas of this world – those who think they are not free (ibid.: 155) – who spend their lives living out someone else's fantasy. While nothing in Dickens necessarily detaches this historical emphasis from providential explanation, the emphasis introduces a more complex social possibility.

This compromised focus on domesticity has something to do with the irresolution between providential and secular history. Elizabeth Gaskell, whose career Dickens did much to foster, does mystify political and economic relations in her treatment of industrial strikes (Newton, 1981), but of course her vision, like that of the Brontës and Thackeray, is informed by providential considerations not Marxist ones. The promise of 'social redemption through the domestication of desire' (Armstrong, 1987: 177, 185) may be one feature of social novels that accounts for their huge popularity after mid-century; but at the same time this domestic solution was the basis for a new narrative code that served many agendas beside that of social repression. And the novels, circulated so massively in Victorian society by the lending libraries, had much to do with creating a common community of readers and sustaining it until at least 1895. The most successful of the libraries, Mudie's Circulating Library, was begun by a young man with a sense of social solidarity: detesting the trash available to him in most circulating libraries of his time, Mudie had the epoch-making thought that there might be others 'in a similar case with myself' (Griest, 1970: 19). The existence of a broad readership making new demands accounts in part for the international success of Walter Scott's first novel, a book that provides a new medium for new demands (Smith, 1984: 14).

In Dickens' work, the commitment to broadly social solutions comes late. The strong providential agenda of the earlier work remains, conflicting elements notwithstanding. *Dombey and Son* finally affirms the faith of Cousin Feenix and Mrs Chick, who believe that 'events do occur in quite a Providential manner' (Dickens, 1970: 685, ch. 51), and that 'there's a moral in everything' (ibid.: 11, ch. 2). In the providential scheme, Edith's self-sacrifice for Florence is prominent and redeeming. But there are the tragic losses, like Alice, whose sacrifice seems to redeem nothing. She is a symptom of the increasingly evident gap in Dickens' novels between providential interpretation and the sheer unredeemed evil of the world. This novel, with its wavering between the two narrative codes, establishes a problematic that guides Dickens' later books: the problem of translating intentionality from nature to society, where 'society' is constructed not as a series of 'places' in a natural hierarchy, but a self-contained and self-determining entity.

Dombey and Son, like later novels, calls 'nature' into question in the name of social conditioning. In the pivotal chapter, 'The Thunderbolt', the narrator speaks out on the *un*naturalness of what is 'natural' on the streets of nineteenth-century English cities. Although Dickens still implicitly claims that 'nature', left to itself, is good and that it is only perverted by interference, he does emphasize the constructedness of social life, for better or for worse. Society is a humanly inclusive realm where 'nature' is changed and redirected:

> Was Mr. Dombey's master-vice, that ruled him so inexorably, an unnatural characteristic? It might be worthwhile, sometimes, to inquire what nature is, and how men work to change her, and whether, in the enforced distortions so produced, it is not natural to be unnatural. Coop any son or daughter of our mighty mother within narrow range, and bind the prisoner to one idea, and foster it by servile worship of it on the part of the few timid or designing people standing round, and what is nature to the willing captive

who has never risen up upon the wings of a free mind – drooping and useless soon – to see her in her comprehensive truth!

Alas! are there so few things in the world, about us, most unnatural, and yet most natural in being so? . . . Breathe the polluted air, foul with every impurity that is poisonous to health and life; and have every sense, conferred upon our race for its delight and happiness, offended, sickened and disgusted, and made a channel by which misery and death alone can enter. Vainly attempt to think of any simple plant, or flower, or wholesome weed, that, set in this foetid bed, could have its natural growth, or put its little leaves off to the sun as GOD designed it. And then, calling up some ghastly child, with stunted form and wicked face, hold forth on its unnatural sinfulness, and lament its being, so early, far away from Heaven – but think a little of its having been conceived, and born and bred, in Hell!

(ibid.: 737; ch. 47)

This passage expresses openly the Dickensian problematic. It seems almost to grasp the existentialist thought that Hell is other people. No longer relying on a faith in 'natural' solutions apart from society, Dickens turns to society for the redemption of suffering and finds it wanting. London is cruel to the poor pedestrians who flock towards it past Harriet Carker's door and are 'swallowed up' and 'lost' (ibid.: 562, ch. 33). Greed and monocular vision in Dickens produce increasing numbers of social casualties who have no opportunity to 'mend', according to Rob the Grinder's hopeful idea. After mid-century and in mid-career, Dickens' novels no longer provide for a standing place outside the social world, however corrupt that world may be.

Despite this development in Dickens, however, he never fully abandons rhetorical sequence or fully exploits the conventions of narrative realism. He delegates the powers of historical mediation to rhetorical devices, most notably ones derived from Shakespeare. Dickens' entire oeuvre offers a fascinating instance of the competition between dramatic and narrative form. Narrative entails a narrator: a point obvious enough, yet one with immense implications. The new narrative element in historical narration includes the act of telling. This new element in nineteenth-century narrative – something absent or undeveloped in the epistolary and picaresque novels of the eighteenth century and in parodic ones from Cervantes onwards – makes possible the development of a new medium by writers like Anthony Trollope and George Eliot and other heirs of their great predecessor, Walter Scott.

Dickens' recourse to Shakespeare, however, commits him to a different direction where the narrative sequence never wholly loses its rhetorical echo. Although his narrator becomes conspicuous in occasional moral exhortations to readers, for example the one just quoted from *Dombey and Son*, Dickens' narrator does not become the Nobody, the narrative medium to be found in Scott or George Eliot or Trollope. Dickens relies much more on a series of dramatic episodes, linked together by various devices also in the style of Shakespeare. His episodes seem to take place in a spotlight on a darkened stage, rather like Fielding's similar experiment in *Amelia*. Dickens sets his narrative coordinates by Shakespeare, not Scott, with decided consequences for his narrative style.

As noted earlier, a rhetorical narrative structure can support all kinds of poetic devices that have limited function in historical narrative. Dickens' own particular version of such devices is the Shakespearian Amplified Metaphor. In *King Lear*, for example, Shakespeare introduces eyes and vision so often and so variously that Eyes and Vision begin to walk around by themselves in the play and to inscribe a realm of seeing that is larger than life; similar use is made in the same play of clothing and of other metaphors that underwrite the play's cosmic implications. Dickens often delegates the job of narrative mediation and commentary to such metaphors, using them to invoke similarly cosmic implications. The River in *Our Mutual Friend*, for example, sustains various interpretations having to do with the flow of life to death, with the washing away of detritus, with time as a river, with the difference between drowning and baptism, with play about what constitutes new life and about which world is 'the next' world.

Such metaphors work simultaneously on different levels, like the paratactic devices in Thackeray or Charlotte Brontë, amplifying each other and giving a constant resonance to particulars. In *The Old Curiosity Shop*, the going and coming from plays figures in the plot, but so repetitively that it also becomes a metaphor for life (we are always coming and going from plays), and a model for the structure of this particular novel, with its gaps between separate, almost set-piece scenes very much in the picaresque tradition of *Pickwick Papers*, and with its incessant going and coming that fulfils no plan. Other examples of the Amplified Metaphor at work are the proliferation of prisons in *Little Dorrit*, debtors prisons, and prisons of the mind and heart; the forge in *Great Expectations* as a metaphor for shaping lives as well as tools. In *Our Mutual Friend*, the world upriver, the system of locks between it and a more immediate one, the difficulty of that negotiation, all invoke passage from this world to another and better place. Part of the fun of reading Dickens comes from surprised recognitions of these metaphors. When Pip begins *Great Expectations* by literally being turned upside down, Dickens soon helps readers to grasp this as the literalized emblem of a life that is fraught with difficulty about knowing which is right side up.

The changes in the way Dickens uses these metaphors provide interesting measures of his shift between the rhetorical and historical narrative codes. The Oceans and Rivers metaphor, for example, undergoes an illustrative transformation between 1848, when he first fully orchestrates the River metaphor in *Dombey and Son*, and 1864 when he uses it for the last time in *Our Mutual Friend*. In 1848, little Paul Dombey's failing life, like a river running out to sea, is flowing away from a cruel unsustaining shore into an Ocean of 'love, eternal and illimitable, not bounded by the confines of this world, or by the end of time, but ranging still, beyond the sea, beyond the sky, to the invisible country far away' (ibid.: 908, ch. 57; also 97). Everything in *Dombey and Son*, including the Oceans and Rivers metaphor, serves a rhetorical assertion about otherworldly redemption: a rhetorical agenda that results sometimes in quite improbable characterization.

Fifteen years later, in *Our Mutual Friend*, the River is a much more ambivalent metaphor: a river where some fall in and are recovered, and also a river of death, a carrier of detritus and dust. To be caught in its flow is to be lost to meaning and value, and to be merely dead. Eugene Wrayburn, a snob and a 'drowning man' in more than one sense (Dickens, 1971: 701), has a chance to redeem his life after he is knocked injured into part of the river system. He survives this baptism, and emerges no longer the genteel snob but ready to accept redemption by love across class lines. But on the other hand, when Rogue Riderhood falls into the River where he has made his living by robbing corpses, he is brought back into the world entirely unredeemed. The amplified metaphors that clarify various redemptions in *Dombey and Son* sustain in *Our Mutual Friend* a more ambivalent vision.

Such metaphoric language in Dickens generally sustains an ambiguous relation between society and nature. Throughout his career Dickens uses nature to make social points. *The Old Curiosity Shop* moves from town to country: from the corrupt urban world where various systems have broken down and their leftovers have been collected into 'curiosity' shops, to the natural world where there is understanding and benediction for a dying child whose place is in yet another, better world. This early green world contrasts favourably with the mouldy futilities of the rotting ancestral home in *Bleak House*, Chesney Wold. But even in the latter case, the mould suggests larger social meaning.

The fullest development of the social medium found in the narrative histories of Trollope and George Eliot requires attenuation of the natural analogues and a suppression of the conspicuous construction (parataxis, amplified metaphors, signature behaviours) to be found in the Brontës, Thackeray and early Dickens. These devices serve rhetorical purposes that adjust uneasily with the agendas of historical narration. At its most complete, historical narrative establishes itself as a neutral and universal temporal medium 'in' which absolutely everything has the potential of mutual relevance to everything else within an infinitely extendable but human system. Narrative that accomplishes this, moves away from the kind of 'natural' explanation that underlies the providential aesthetic.

Around 1850 something momentous happens to English narrative. The historical convention, what is effectively a temporal version of a single-point perspective system, becomes the commanding narrative convention. Social novelists like Anthony Trollope, George Eliot, and even the later Dickens, abandon the providential aesthetic in favour of what might be called the *historical aesthetic*: an economy that constitutes time as a system of single-point perspective in which it is possible for the first time to experiment with sociality as an entity, as an emergent form.

Although novels from both sides of this divide take the form of 'histories', they differ depending on whether they maintain the neutral, homogeneous medium of time that we call 'history' or whether they do not. While for purposes of argument it is possible to distinguish between these two aesthetics – between the different discursive orders they inscribe, and between the different narrative codes they activate – in actual novels, the two aesthetics generally appear in various interesting mixtures, especially in novels of the 1840s where the construction of identity shifts unevenly between these two alternative codes. In such novels we can find both teleological and non-teleological constructions of 'history'. We can find in the same work conventions that assert a belief in 'nature' as ground and explanation, and at the same time ones that vigorously contest such beliefs. But increasingly after mid-century, Victorian novels demonstrate the ways in which individuals, taken collectively, found history as the medium of sociality.

NARRATIVE IN THE WASTELAND

Before moving on to consider historical narrative in Chapter Two, I want to follow a bit further through the nineteenth century the relation between narrative and nature. It has long been understood that nineteenth-century science, especially Darwin's evolutionary theory of natural selection, seriously unsettled religious faith for many Christians. With the dissemination of Darwin's historical explanations of species, following on from Lyell's geological history, a profound and implicit conflict appeared between scientific information and Christian dogma. These theories simply changed the description of nature in ways so persuasive and comprehensive that they amounted to an alternative account of creation. Though this certainly raised questions about religious belief, there were good answers to those questions.

But the Crisis of Faith does not depend on Darwinism alone. In fact it is quite possible to read the history of natural selection as evidence of God's work in the world: work more on the horizontal than formerly supposed, perhaps, but God's work nonetheless. Certainly churchmen lost no time in colonizing Darwin for their cause and ignoring his more radical implications. But paradoxically, the crisis of faith actually operates centrally in the Evangelical and dissenting religion that gained ground rapidly after 1800. From the Evangelical movement within Anglicanism to the dissenting sects, Victorian religion increasingly sponsored crises of religious faith as an essential component of religious experience. Doubt or even disbelief were themselves key features of religious experience, an often-necessary stage on the personal pilgrimage to God.

The vast literature dealing with this religious movement ranges broadly. Elizabeth Gaskell's novels contrast middle-class morality with working-class poverty; Charles Dickens' awfully smooth missionaries like Mr Chadband prove the limits of assured belief; Trollope's delightful Barchester novels restore religious balance by exorcising the odious evangelical, Mr Slope, and correcting the moral rigidity of the poor curate, Mr Crawley; George Eliot's *Scenes of Clerical Life* (1858) anatomize the varieties of religious experience in a country setting, and her first novel, *Adam Bede* (1859), pays tribute to the Methodist ministry that had dedicated itself to spreading spiritual comfort by spreading literacy.

It would be difficult to overestimate the importance of this religious revival to nineteenth-century English narrative (Brown, 1961). The Oxford Movement was only one of the polarizing conflicts within the English Establishment. Within the Anglican Church, Evangelicalism already had spread to high places by 1800 and had effected considerable social change. The Lord Chancellor had stopped holding public dinners on the Sabbath, Ranelagh was shut down and carriages lined the avenues to the churches instead: a novel appearance which, according to the Annual Register of 1797, 'prompted the simple country people to inquire what was happening'. In effect 'the curtain had been rung down on the old sophisticated comedy of manners, and the stage was being set for the

Victorian scene' (Quinlan, 1941: cited p. 100). By 1851 more than half of all churchgoers belonged to a dissenting and not an Anglican faith (V. Cunningham, 1975). Looking backwards from 1857, George Eliot's narrator comments in 'Janet's Repentance' that Evangelicalism was 'no longer a nuisance existing merely in by-corners, which any well-clad person could avoid; it was invading the very drawing-rooms, mingling itself with the comfortable fumes of port-wine and brandy' (Eliot, 1910: 224.) Among the several powerful effects of Evangelicalism was its levelling potential; it provided a set of public standards common for all members of the social constituency regardless of class or privilege.

But what Evangelicalism and dissenting Protestant religions contributed most to Victorian narrative was a method. The 'method' of the Methodists, for example – something that often depended on written narratives in the form of diaries and journals – involved a rigorous self-examination for inward sin, a long struggle against it culminating in a crisis, and a final 'turning' and resolution in a new sense of peace and joy that signified new life and even salvation. Similar motives appear in Evangelicalism. Loss and gain were the keynotes of True Experience. This process of self-examination literally provided a narrative structure: first for private journals and eventually for the public History that took root in nineteenth-century narrative writing and that is its greatest achievement. The history of 'turning' or conversion from one way of life to another moved from the diaries of Methodists straight into the autobiographies and novels of the nineteenth century, where it contributed both to the construction of social history and to the construction of difference between the realms of 'private' and 'public' (social) affairs.

This Protestant narrative of personal salvation, unmediated by priests or official rituals, could generate considerable anxiety as to whether or not one was saved. Aside from the few like Hannah More who enjoyed a conviction of election, the eighteenth-century Methodists and Quakers who record their experiences are almost unanimously troubled by a profound conviction of sin which must be suffered and conquered before assurance is secure. The ominous gap between subjective knowledge and universal truth is bridged by what the Wesleyans called 'experimental' knowledge, or knowledge available only through experience (Morris, 1966: 127). Earlier in the century nature everywhere justifies itself by producing the desired end point: in Carlyle, in Coleridge, in Wordsworth and in Tennyson, and in many hundreds of conversion novels and autobiographies from the most different quarters. Such plots even faintly resemble Conan Doyle's Sherlock Holmes plots, in that they produce a result that reaffirms the rationality of a unified world.

This emphasis on personal religious development could lead in quite different directions. On the one hand, the 'experimental' personal history can produce the crisis and conversion that points toward a nature divinely inspired and that confirms religious faith; on the other hand, 'experimental' knowledge can produce crisis but no conversion, and thus lead in surprising new directions that do not affirm religious faith in any traditional sense. An influential example of the former is Carlyle's *Sartor Resartus, or, the Tailor Retailored* (1833), which shows how the three-stage process of personal turning – 'Everlasting Nay'; 'Centre of Indifference'; and 'Everlasting Yea' – produces order out of Teufelsdroch's six grab-bags of ideas. Moving from original oneness (innocence), through experience of a crisis in despair, to final reconciliation with nature and the world, this conversion process makes error into truth; once the fictional editor lights upon history as a resource, he defeats chaos and 'form rose out of void solution and discontinuity'. Carlyle's professor becomes a 'seer' into nature, into the 'interior celestial Holy of Holies': a prophet of the supreme, if theologically somewhat undefined power of Life. He 'has looked fixedly on existence, till, one after the other its earthly hulls and garnitures have all melted away; and now, to his rapt vision, the interior celestial Holy of Holies lies disclosed' (Carlyle, 1970: 234, ch. VIII).

This pattern, it has long been noted (Buckley, 1951; Peckham, 1951, 1961), appears in many major works of nineteenth–century literature, and in Romantic poetry as well as in countless conversion novels. Though different in almost every way from Carlyle's *Sartor Resartus*, Tennyson's *In Memoriam* (1850) records the same process; the poet confronts material death in a universe where nature has been stripped of religious value, and represents the same progress from despair, impasse and resignation that finally triggers the saving flash of insight and allows him to pass the veil of nature and to catch 'the deep pulsations of the world' (Tennyson, 1958: 233). Narratives apparently far-removed from religious controversy or concern have the same 'experimental' narrative structure of error, crisis, and conversion. Wordsworth's *The Prelude: or, Growth of a Poet's Mind; an Autobiographical Poem* (1815; 1850) contains the three-stage process of personal crisis and turning towards enlightenment familiar from many of his shorter poems, describing how experience becomes knowledge (e.g. the 'Grotto of Antiparos' episode, VIII, in ibid.: 560–90). John Stuart Mill's *Autobiography* (1873) recapitulates a version of this same narrative, the turning point of which is the moment of resignation in which Mill renounces self-assertion in favour of powers beyond the self and outside history. Even a non-believer like Mill 'experiences' this natural pattern of redemption.

This particular narrative of successful inner life probably qualifies as one of the more fundamental meta-narratives of English speaking culture. The crisis of faith was far more than a doctrinal matter, as the popularity of confessional and conversion novels testifies. Everybody, it seems, wrote a conversion novel (Maison, 1961). Those written by churchmen often seem to be set in early Christian times, when the Church was taking its doctrinal shape. Nicholas (Cardinal) Wiseman's *Fabiola* (1854) demonstrates the power of Christianity to awaken the intellectual curiosity of heathens, particularly the Roman heroine who converts after recognizing the brutality and error of her pagan culture. John Henry (Cardinal) Newman's pagan heroine, *Callista* (1856), has the same experience, only she gets martyred into the bargain after she 'by degrees' comes to walk in the new philosophy and finds that she has a 'natural' disposition to Christian truth. The enemy in these cases is error, and is usually personified in an external mob; and faith is a peculiarly intellectual matter.

Problems develop, however, when the 'turning' does not yield anything, or produces only confrontation with a demystified nature. Many novels demonstrate a slower, unspectacular 'turning' of belief similar to Tennyson's of 'In Memoriam'. Charles Redding, the hero of Newman's other conversion novel, *Loss and Gain* (1848), desires certainty and suffers from doubt so much that his health declines. With a sublime egoism, however, he reports that 'destiny' eventually makes him a Catholic: 'come it must, it was written in heaven, and the slow wheels of time each hour brought it nearer – he could not escape his destiny of becoming a Catholic' (Newman, 1855: 206). Like Hector dragged around the walls of Troy, the (by definition heroic) fate of this sublime egotist is predestined in the nature of things. But these kinds of results appear less often as the century wears on and as a new construction of nature demystifies its processes. In any case, such struggles of faith with doubt cause chronic social anxiety in the nineteenth century – so much so that various economic upheavals look trivial compared to it.

The struggle for truth is a narrative crux during the entire century, and a primary crux of sociality. Even in novels with entirely secular and social agendas, the narrative of 'turning' appears in the structure of disillusionment and moral readjustment so common in Dickens, Gaskell and George Eliot. Beyond the canonical writers of the period, who deal extensively with these issues, there are hundreds of authors publishing thousands of novels about the crisis of faith and, increasingly, about the anxiety, even despair, resulting from the experiment. Conversion novels appear without the conversion. The structure of 'turning', together with the assumptions about nature that go with it, still appear even though the spiritual 'experiment' fails. James Anthony Froude's *The Nemesis of Faith* (1849) presents such a painfully arrested conversion experience; his character, Markham Sutherland, finds faith replaced only by an existential loneliness and grief. His difficulty in getting through the 'turning' is permanent, and he dies without reaching any affirmation; yet the pattern of search for solutions takes place in a cosmic not a social context, and Sutherland remains intensely, despairingly, insistently, nostalgic for secure faith and uninterested in more temporary or limited resolutions. He must have Truth.

Towards the end of the century, such negative conversion narratives increasingly become irresolute and even despairing as 'nature' proves increasingly unsympathetic, and Truth becomes something contestable and experimentally insecure. For example, William Hale-White's *Autobiography of Mark Rutherford, Edited by His Friend, Reuben Shapcott* (1881) describes a priest's dark night of the soul, and its aftermath.

I was overcome with the most dreadful sense of loneliness.... I was beside myself with a kind of terror, which I cannot further explain. It is possible for another person to understand grief for the death of a friend, bodily suffering, or any emotion which has a distinct cause, but how shall he understand the worst of all calamities, the nameless dread, the efflux of all vitality, the ghostly haunting horror which is so nearly akin to madness? ... I tremble to think how thin is the floor on which we stand which separates us from the bottomless abyss.

(Hale-White, n.d.: 113)

Months of depression follow. Eventually he simply outlives this 'morbidity', but the desired clarification is muted, at best, and has to do with a potentially social phenomenon, the redeeming power of human love. This late in the century one does not find the Wordsworthian faith that 'Nature wants not power/To consecrate, if we have eyes to see' (*Prelude*, XIII, lines 283–4). Nor, on the other hand, do we find the absolutist despair of Froude's pitiful hero in *Nemesis of Faith* who prefers death to uncertainty. The popular 'Mark Rutherford' always manages to maintain two voices. Though the longed-for resolution never materializes, the narrative pattern of crisis and 'turning' is retained, along with a conflicted clinging to 'natural' explanation, a deep sense of loss as scepticism ripens into unbelief, and a sense of emptiness at the lack of resolution or, as Newman put it, 'certainty'. Such impulses are pilloried in novels by sophisticated social novelists like George Eliot and Anthony Trollope, and their views continued to be echoed in the twentieth–century: 'To be right', wrote

André Gide in his journal, 'who still wants to be? A few fools'. Up through the 1890s, however, people still wanted to be 'right' in the sense of being reconciled with nature through faith.

It may be difficult for a sceptical twentieth century to grasp the degree to which the failure of religious experience and the demystification of nature affected people; not only in the nineteenth century and not only in England. One of the most powerfully uncompromising narratives of doubt is the celebrated journal of the Swiss philosopher, Henri Amiel. Published posthumously in 1881, they were translated by Mary Augusta (Mrs Humphrey) Ward into English as *Amiel's Journal* in 1885. Never a particularly popular text, this painful, uncompromising expression of unrelieved religious despair is far more radical than any of the English novels of doubt. Three years later, Mrs Ward published her own novel of doubt and 'turning', *Robert Elsmere* (1888), one of the best-sellers of the entire nineteenth century. Another piquant story of a clergyman's loss of faith, this novel shows the continuing viability of the conversion plot, at least from the point of view of sales, right up to the turn of the twentieth century.

As the nineteenth century wears on, 'nature' ceases to support the demands of faith. New social conditions make this all but unavoidable; but so does the dissemination of a demystified, non-anthropocentric view of nature. From various angles, it becomes clear that 'nature' does not support the social demands mid-Victorians wished to make upon it. The social and historical novelists went indoors, into the social arena, where human affairs could be considered under some control and where human 'nature' could provide some grounds for optimism. Those who, like Thomas Hardy or H. G. Wells, insist on staying outdoors, produce increasingly tragic and bitter narratives of human possibility. These latter writers did not even attempt to take narrative advantage of the new physical science which developed simultaneously and parallel with Darwinian biology, but which remained relatively inert as resources for social thought until the turn of the twentieth century, when modernism flourished across the cultural spectrum from physics to linguistics to painting.

At the same time as Darwinian theory was claiming public attention in its relatively genteel manner – first in private university circles, and always in accessible narrative language – physical scientists, often working outside the ordinary centres of prestige, were producing the theories of electricity and magnetism fundamental to Albert Einstein's theories of Special and General Relativity: theories that make obsolete the narrative codes that belong to *both* the providential and the historical aesthetics.

With the work of Michael Faraday (1791–1867) on electricity, the work of James Clerk Maxwell (1831–79) on the Second Law of Thermodynamics and on electricity and magnetism, and the work of James Prescott Joule (1818–89) on the principle of the conservation of energy, the focus of science shifts from biological science and narrative exposition to physical science and mathematical exposition.

The problem with disseminating these theories, even within the scientific community, was that they were not accessible to the kind of narrative exposition that Darwin uses so effectively. Biology allows the anthropocentric imagination to range very widely; it had, as Peter Morton puts it, 'something for everyone' (Morton, 1984: 224). One really cannot give a riveting narrative account of the translation of electricity into magnetism, although Maxwell's poetry sometimes comes close. No, equations are required. English culture, in fact English-speaking culture, is still coping with this initial shift towards theoretical physics, its abstraction from sense experience, and its reliance on new descriptive languages like mathematics.

Empiricism, with its long humanist habit of colonizing nature with human metaphors, remains almost as resistant to such theory in the twentieth century as it was in the nineteenth. Even in the late twentieth century, cosmic discoveries are so colonized; for example, *The London Times* describes (for what it obviously takes to be a scientifically illiterate readership) a huge cloud of alcohol discovered 10,000 light years from earth as 'the bar at the end of the universe' (*Times*, 18 March 1995: 1).

One physical theory that did lend itself to narrative construction, however, was the theory of entropy. It became explicit for Victorians in 1852 when William Thomson (Lord Kelvin) expressed one alarming implication of Newton's second law of thermodynamics: namely that a heat differential always exists in the production of work (energy moves from one, more energetic, system to another, less energetic, system; say, from a hot body to a cold one); and that eventually such energy exchange will make the universe a uniform temperature, which is a state of 'heat death' because energy thus evenly distributed and undifferentiated is unavailable for use. Every bit of work today means less energy available for work tomorrow: a troubling, if not profoundly troubling, thought for a newly industrial economy. Though the universe does not lose energy (Joule's Principle of the Conservation of Energy), existing energy becomes unavailable for work because there are no longer any of those temperature differences that permit energy to flow from one site to another.

Entropy becomes a literary metaphor for the pervasive sense of systems running down, wearing out, reaching depletion. To a society that had been attempting to reform itself into a newly inclusive democratic system, Kelvin's extrapolation provided a metaphor for system-death. Dickens' opening chapter of *Bleak House* (1853) is a well-known instance, where the 'death of the sun' becomes nature's analogue for the heat death of English feudal society, something represented in Dickens by a decayed, fraudulent, parasitic aristocracy. The metaphor haunts this novel, and Dickens' other late novels, for example in the obsession in *Our Mutual Friend* with darkness and dust.

By the time of H. G. Wells' novella, *The Time Machine* (1895), the idea of entropy has become a more familiar cosmic bogey. Wells' novella provides a cautionary example for those who attempt to incorporate a new scientific knowledge in small amounts into a relatively conventional set of assumptions. Wells' time-travelling scientist brings back from the future the dismal news that civilization and the solar system are both winding down. Reports brought back from centuries in the future show that our warm sun is really just a middle-aged star on its way to becoming a red giant. Two thousand years hence ours will be an earth no longer spinning on its axis, its oceans dead, its light fading, its oxygen depleted, and its few remaining signs of life – a fin near the shore of a red sea – 'ebbing out' (Wells, 1993: 194–9). This construction of nature could not be more unlike that of the nature novelists of early in the century; this construction of nature offers no options, no future, no hope.

Worse even than entropy in the physical universe, however, is the heat death of civilization which occurs earlier; Wells presents it as a form of cultural suicide created by luxury or, as he puts it, the unfortunate destruction of 'want and necessity'. From this vantage, the nineteenth-century effort to be responsible to all members of a newly conceived society appears instead to have been a fatal softening of civilization. Meet people's needs, it appears, and they go soft. Wells' human species, some centuries hence, has dwindled into a helpless kind of creature (Eloi) that is raised as cattle to feed the fierce, bestial rulers (Morlocks). The Eloi are beautiful and doomed, 'like the Carlovingian kings' (ibid.: 135); the Morlocks, on the other hand, are underground people, practically cannibals, and survivors. The returned time-traveller tells his fellows:

> I grieved to think how brief the dream of the human intellect had been. It had committed suicide. It had set itself steadfastly toward comfort and ease, a balanced society with security and permanence as its watchwords, it had attained its hopes – to come to this at last.... There had been no unemployment problem, no social question left unsolved. And a great quiet had followed.

The mistake, apparently, was to appeal to intelligence rather than habit and instinct; the latter are preferred by 'nature': 'Nature never appeals to intelligence until habit and instinct are useless' (ibid.: 187). This description might seem more comfortable in a skinhead manual than in a fable for the middle classes.

This message, moreover, appears in a frame-tale (ibid.: chs 1, 2, 14), while the time-traveller tells his tale in the framed chapters (ibid.: chs 3–13) over brandy and cigars to a group of male friends after dinner. Their sacred equipment (described without much irony) includes those specifically masculine items, 'libations of alcohol and reeking pipes', and their ritual power appears when 'The Psychological, to show he was not unhinged, helped himself to a cigar...' (ibid.: ch. 21). Clearly, to be normal is to smoke cigars. What is unclear is whether this after-dinner group, including the scientist, are part of the problem or part of the solution; perhaps the presence of Cigar Anxiety suggests the former.

The contradictions about values in this text are profound. On the one hand, the gentle, soft, edible people of the future are the degenerate evolutionary offspring of *homo sapiens*. But they are not strong and aggressive like the time-travelling scientist himself; they have long, tentacled fingers and are 'girlish' and soft. The bestial Morlocks who raise and eat them are worse, yet the moral of Wells' story seems to suggest that anything is better than girlish softness, security, and consequent feebleness. 'We are kept keen on the grindstone of pain and necessity' (ibid.: 76). On the one hand the story seems to discredit both literary and scientific intelligence, on the other hand to discredit habit and instinct, and then to put some questionable emphasis on pain. Are the poor, who endure more of 'pain and necessity' than the literary and scientific dinner guests, better situated for survival? Or are they only Morlocks-in-the-making?

Wells' most contradictory message is that, by feats of human intellect, shared in a single-sex, club-like society, we discover that human intellect is a precursor of irreversible degeneration; and at the same time, that by having more of pain and necessity, more of manly strength and aggressiveness, we might preserve the human species from this evolutionary extinction. Would a little less softness to the poor, one wonders, have prevented the heat death of the sun? In any case, and used variously by Dickens, Wells, and others, the entropy theory gains expressive viability as a metaphor.

But this application of scientific knowledge to social matters remains schematic and limited compared to Thomas Hardy's explorations of the agonizing ambiguities between social and natural systems. Between 1871

47

and 1895, Hardy published more than a dozen novels set in rural village life, where he maintains the analogic relation between people and nature familiar from the nature novelists, but where nature stands for pain and death. Hardy charts the decline of that very individual will so powerfully present in the Brontës' novels. Hardy's nature supports no aspiration; it merely reflects a human decline that seems very much like the entropy of the species. While Hardy does not invoke the second law of thermodynamics in his portraits of villagers, the sense of loss, decline, inertia and failure permeates his entire novelistic oeuvre.

Hardy conspicuously lacks both the faith in nature evident in nature novelists and the social solutions evident in historical novelists. Instead of social and domestic solutions we find domestic outrages, like the mother who betrays her daughter with bad advice and rejection (*Tess of the D'Urbervilles*, 1891), or the twelve-year-old who hangs himself and his siblings 'because we are too menny' (*Jude the Obscure*, 1895, VI, Chapter 2). Hardy's characters pursue their doomed journeys through 'problematic junctions, precarious crossroads' (Nalbantian, 1983: 77ff.); they wander alone; they cross paths fruitlessly or destructively. Apart from the occasional group of friends, the only organic social group evident is a mechanical legal and economic system which scarcely can be called 'social' at all and which accommodates human aspiration even less than nature does. The only social units worth anything, like the sisterhood of dairymaids in *Tess of the D'Urbervilles*, lack any saving strength.

After the social narrative that flourishes for several decades in mid-century (see Chapter Three), Hardy's narrative returns plot and character to rural villages far from urban society, and to nature. But his is a nature with no clouds of glory on the horizon. No rationality supports nature in Hardy's world; no Sherlock Holmes appears, to clear up misunderstanding with explanation and to reinscribe the law. No process of change from one life to another, however incomplete, justifies any faith in individual measures. The kind of coincidences that point to providence in *Jane Eyre* or even *Dombey and Son* – and that generally do not appear in social novels – reappear again in Hardy, but with a bitterly ironic difference: with such malign effects that they cannot be signs of providence, except some grotesque version of it. Where Hardy does suggest a Something organizing nature, it is something uncongenial to humanity.

Hardy's most brilliant portrait of nature as context is Egdon Heath, in his sixth novel, *The Return of the Native* (1878). Egdon Heath is a place where people lose their way, fail to meet, even die. It is alive and yet inhospitable. In the title of the opening chapter devoted to describing it, the heath is 'A Face Upon Which Time Makes But Little Impression'. It has a mysteriousness that remains impenetrable by, and unrewarding to, human attention. Yet at the same time Hardy describes the heath in very anthropocentric terms, almost as a screen on which is written all the pain of those who live near it. The opening description stresses the antiquity of the heath, its heroic qualities of survival, but most of all, its likeness with man:

> The place became full of watchful intentness now; for when other things sank brooding to sleep the heath appeared slowly to awake and listen. Every night its Titanic form seemed to await something; but it had waited thus, unmoved, during so many centuries, through the crises of so many things, that it could only be imagined to await one last crisis – the final overthrow...
>
> It was at present a place perfectly accordant with man's nature – neither ghastly, hateful, nor ugly: neither commonplace, unmeaning, nor tame; but, like man, slighted and enduring; and withal singularly colossal and mysterious in its swarthy monotony. As with some persons who have long lived apart, solitude seemed to look out of its countenance. It had a lonely face, suggesting tragical possibilities.
>
> (Hardy, 1978d: ch. 1)

It's those 'tragical possibilities' that interest Hardy, and that are the nostalgic keynote of his work. Like those writers for whom nature knows best, Hardy also believes in the symbiosis of man and nature; but unlike them, Hardy finds nature to be neither benign nor intelligible. It is a nature that does not answer those characters who search for justice, development, hope, even meaning. But the lack of response does not convince Hardy that there is nothing there. On the contrary, the more mysterious and complex nature is, the more it carries human qualities.

In this passage, later in the novel, Clym Yeobright, the returned 'Native', contemplates his own situation in a fir and beech grove that had been reclaimed from the heath in the year of his birth.

> Here the trees, laden heavily with their new and humid leaves, were now suffering more damage than during the highest winds of winter, when the boughs are specially disencumbered to do battle with the storm. The wet young beeches were undergoing amputations, bruises, cripplings, and harsh lacerations, from which the wasting sap would bleed for many a day to come, and which would leave scars visible till the day of their burning. Each stem was wrenched at the root, where it moved like a bone in its socket, and at

every onset of the gale convulsive sounds came from the branches, as if pain were felt. In a neighbouring brake a finch was trying to sing...

(ibid.: Book Third, ch. 6)

This language makes nature a metaphor with terrific intensity, somewhat undercut perhaps by the finch which seems a tragedy too far. The natural context echoes Yeobright's feelings and experience to such an extent that it somehow guarantees or objectifies them. In fact, the logic of this language even suggests that his feelings and experiences actually constitute nature, and that the two are inextricably linked.

In such a condition, he hardly needs the answering gaze of another person; nature itself takes that responsibility. Human 'nature' is corroborated in a natural context, not a social one, and on the whole it is a grim context. Hardy's spare language makes drama of the material universe, and leaves aside almost entirely the language of social nuance and relation. And there is little comfort in this mysterious system, if system it be: nature joins humanity in 'suffering', 'amputations', 'bruises', 'cripplings', 'pain'.

Hardy's plots generally move forward on the road, as his characters wander from place to place. Two of his most powerful and most highly achieved novels, *The Mayor of Casterbridge* (1886) and *Tess of the D'Urbervilles*, both begin and end on the road; and in both the idea that a journey might be a progress is an illusion of the characters that is blasted by their bitter experiences. The journey is no progress; where it takes them is not where they want to go, even though some kind of tragic fatality makes them go there.

What is entropic in Hardy is not so much physical nature as human nature. A wearing loss of energy plagues the characters in his later novels, which offer readers relentless portraits of the wear of change on the stubborn traditionalist (*The Mayor of Casterbridge*), the lethal drain of unacknowledged social agendas on the innocent (*Tess of the D'Urbervilles*), the conditions that make children wish for death (*Jude the Obscure*). While these are human problems, generated by human failings, Hardy situates them not in the social context of mid-century novels, but in the context of nature. Unlike the nature that supports Jane Eyre, however, this nature has a peculiarly perverse relationship to things human.

Although his social commentary is uncompromising, Hardy's narrative strategies are not particularly venturesome. He does not venture beyond the ambit inscribed by novels of doubt, and like them Hardy still assumes the appropriateness of a cosmic context for human meaning and value. His narrative sequences are correspondingly episodic and uncommitted to the social coordinations and causalities of mid-century historical novels. In Hardy, one still cries out in the wilderness; the fact that Nobody answers does not suggest that there is no one there, but merely that they aren't answering, or aren't answering on his frequency.

This is a classic defensive ploy of humanism, as Alain Robbe-Grillet has shown; a classic 'sublimation of a difference' that reunites 'man' with nature:

> I call out. No one answers me. Instead of concluding that there is no one there... I decide to act as if there *were* someone there, but someone who, for one reason or another, will not answer. The silence which follows my outcry is henceforth no longer a *true* silence; it is charged with a content, a meaning, a depth, a soul – which immediately sends me back to my own.... Should I shout louder? Should I utter different words? I try once again.... The invisible presence I continue to create by my call obliges me to hurl my wretched cries into the silence forever.
>
> (Robbe-Grillet, 1989: 60–1)

It is precisely this manoeuvre that is so powerful and so frustrating in Hardy's novels. Petrifying the universe in a 'sonorous malediction', tragedy reconciles us to suffering and loss because through them it reasserts an absent meaning. In the tragic mode, suffering is a sublime necessity, a guarantee of meaning where others have failed. 'There can no longer be any question of seeking some remedy for our misfortunes', Robbe-Grillet continues, 'once tragedy convinces us to love it'.

Yet if Hardy's plots deny any human meaning in nature, his metaphoric language and tragic sense of development continue to imply it. There is a kind of hangover from the classics in Hardy. Greek dramatic forms with their natural 'gods' lurk in the background. In *Jude the Obscure* the classics are the pre-eminent part of Jude's useless education. Greek tragedy seems a particularly inappropriate interpretive filter for a potentially absurd natural order, leaving quite aside the fact that drama is an inappropriate model for narrative in the first place, because it deals with plot and character, not the perception of plot and character. If nature is Absurd, either one can laugh about it, as twentieth-century writers, starting especially with absurdist dramatists, have tended to do; or one can cry about it, and remain nostalgic for that answering voice in nature. Hardy takes the latter alternative, maintaining the tragic relation to nature that rescues meaning for the old narrative language, even as he demonstrates the breakdown of that language.

Hardy calls into question not only the inadequacy of social usages, but the nature of narrative itself. In effect he shows the bankruptcy of the available narrative codes: both the plots of progress and turning towards truth, and also the more open-ended causalities of the social (historical) novelists (see Chapter Two). These codes all imply that lived sequences can sustain some meaningful development, and in Hardy that is precisely what we have not got. After demonstrating fully the bankruptcy of the available narrative codes, and after his last and most depressing book, *Jude the Obscure* (1895), Hardy permanently abandoned novels for poetry and poetic narrative.

These various visions of nature running down are nostalgic, even propitiatory, in the sense that they attempt to rescue meaning by means of sacrifice. But what is it that is actually running down? In Dickens it is feudal society; in Wells it is a culture of masculine energy and hardness; in Hardy it is the faith in nature as effective support for human will and effort. But does the increase of disorder in one system necessarily mean a corresponding disorder in all? Might this not be good riddance? Might not the disappearance of one system make room for the appearance of a different one? Scientific knowledge points in two quite different directions so far as opportunity is concerned; if feudalism is finally wearing out, perhaps nationalism, capitalism, communism or federalism might be gearing up.

MOVING ON

The new vision of nature emerging from science at the end of the century calls for new, even radically new, narrative strategies. In a physical universe where waves are also particles, where classical identities are in crisis, even the time and space of mid-century realism and empiricism receive redefinition. Such changes positively require experiment with narrative sequence and narrative language. The nineteenth-century English novel scarcely faced this challenge at all, and even the twentieth-century English novel confronts it with limited ambition. Right up to the turn of the twentieth century, 'natural' history can still be found foreclosing even on the experimental solutions of mid-century social novels. Novelists who eventually do experiment on any scale tend to be either foreigners or expatriates, like Joseph Conrad and Henry James, Samuel Beckett and James Joyce.

The self-conscious pursuit of abstraction evident in the major developments elsewhere in science and art remain for the most part conspicuously absent in English narrative. I want to turn here to three such innovative and roughly contemporaneous experiments in the later nineteenth century: the scientific work of James Clerk Maxwell (1831–79), the poetry of Gerard Manley Hopkins (1844–89), and the painting of Paul Cézanne (1839–1906). Each one of these giants in their field makes traditional material into something new, and does so with a kind of sheer joyousness and exuberance that, even where it is hard won, does not accommodate tragic nostalgia; each moves away from common-sense experience and moves further towards abstraction; each shows a new interest in systems and, above all, a new emphasis on the similarities or 'rhymes' between systems; and each was relatively unknown in his time for those achievements that we now regard as most monumental.

The work of James Clerk Maxwell is probably the least familiar of the three, and most in need of a substantial introduction. He was known in his lifetime primarily as an interpreter of what was already known; but he is known today among scientists as the author of 'Maxwell's Equations', the original mathematical statement of Faraday's work, especially his important 1846 paper on electricity and magnetism, that opened the doors for so much further development in science and technology. Maxwell's originality came fully into focus only after his death in 1879, at the young age of 48. Eight years later Hertz proved the existence of electromagnetic waves (1887), and Maxwell's work on electromagnetic waves became the basis of radio. His equations of the electromagnetic field led to relativity theory. His statistical mechanics was the parent of quantum theory. His creation and legislation of the Cavendish Laboratory at Cambridge encouraged scientists thereafter to work together in the interdisciplinary way he advocated (Crowther, 1935: 326).

In his own day, however, and in spite of his eminence, Maxwell struggled against a community of scientists that too often stood four square and rayless in defence of outdated mechanical models. Maxwell, a Scot, was even refused a chair at the University of Edinburgh on the grounds he wouldn't be sufficiently clear for undergraduates! He went on to occupy a Cambridge Chair (1871) and to become the founding Head of the Cavendish Laboratory, which opened at Cambridge University in 1874 and which Maxwell organized to foster science as a collaborative and collective effort. Maxwell thus suffered from the inertial force of an intellectual community in the first half of the nineteenth century in which the leaders of physics 'were still engaged on the scientific problems of an order of society preceding the industrial'. In this community, innovative scientists like Carnot, Joule and J. J. Waterston often were foreigners: foreigners in intellect and, not insignificantly, foreigners in the system of London social connections common to the then–governors of science

(Crowther, 1935: 295). Concentration of power in the City of London, and the accompanying habit of treating everything outside it – even industrial centres in the Midlands – as 'Country', ensured that the new thinking emerging from technological development remained associated with sites regarded as centres of degeneration by people like Ruskin and, more powerfully, by the naturalizing prejudices he served (Best, 1971: 50–4, 88, 95–7; Williams, 1973; Hulin and Coustillas, n.d.).

Maxwell's methods differ fundamentally from those current in the science of his day. He particularly insists on the importance of theory to the speculative power of science. He finds the intellectual state of mathematics in his time 'unfavourable to speculation' and the state of electrical science 'peculiarly unfavourable to speculation' (Crowther, 1935: 285). While there were mathematical descriptions for some of the phenomena of static electricity, current electricity and electromagnetism, no general theory connecting these types of phenomena together had as yet been found.

Maxwell produced the general theory that brought electricity and magnetism together and showed that changes in electric force would produce magnetic force. He abandoned mechanical models of 'molecules', matter and motion in favour of a series of equations that established in new terms the concept of the electromagnetic field, and the electromagnetic theory of light (Royal Society paper, 1864). He assumed that mathematical symbols were as real as, perhaps more real than, mechanisms; and so 'he escaped the chief error of the scientific philosophy of the nineteenth century' (Crowther,1935: 308–10) which was to cling to outdated mechanical models. Maxwell criticized the lassitude of British scientists who, he said, needed to develop their power to theorize in order to get past the used-up models of seventeenth-century empiricism: 'the dimmed outlines of phenomenal things all merge into another unless we put on the focussing glass of theory' (quoted in Crowther, 1935: 281)

Maxwell's paper on 'Faraday's Lines of Force' (1855–56), presented when he was aged 24, is a first step on the journey toward the wave-theory of light: a 'hydrodynamical model' of 'electrical force as analogous to the movement of an incompressible fluid through space'. Eminent astronomers of his day lived up to their limitations and rejected the theory as too 'vague and varying' when compared to gravitational dynamics and various related and more familiar theories of 'action-at-a-distance' (Crowther, 1935: 287). It was precisely Maxwell's ability to move between sciences that not only enabled him to produce a mathematical statement of electromagnetism, but also enabled him to establish the Cavendish Laboratory on principles of interdisciplinary cooperation that still remain influential. Theory is born of interdisciplinary effort; and interdisciplinary effort gives rise to theory.

Maxwell's impetus tends towards the discovery of new theories and not merely the reinscription of old ones. 'If the unification of the different branches of electrical theory is to proceed, some method of simplifying the systems of ideas in the different branches must be found so that the student can bring the chief concepts of each simultaneously before his mind.' Without on the one hand limiting thought to a particular range of physical phenomena, and without on the other hand losing sight of physical phenomena in mathematical abstraction, Maxwell encourages the theoretical scientist to look instead for what he calls 'physical analogies':

> we must make ourselves familiar with the existence of physical
> analogies [or] ... partial similarity between the laws of one science
> and those of another which makes each of them illustrate the other.
>
> (ibid.: 315–16)

This seeing of similitude, not in particulars but in systems of particulars: this is what makes possible the new experimental physics.

Scientific education itself hampered innovation because its class-bound conventions tended towards replication of received truths rather than towards experiment and adventure. One can find a classics hangover even in physics. Maxwell shines in retrospect for his playful and joyous disregard of the methodological prejudices that hampered the science of his day. Despite the difficulties posed for him by the outcomes of his own methods – and like Einstein he deeply felt the troubling implications of his own research – he did not waver in sticking either to his outcomes or to his methods. His design of the Cavendish Laboratory, which has had such influence in British science ever since, was especially successful, according to one historian, because he did not have that ancient 'prejudice against manual activity deeply incorporated in Graeco–Roman culture' to which Plato made such a 'large contribution'. This discrediting of manual labour was perpetuated to serve the power of military, religious and other 'classes that did not work with their hands':

> The medieval universities had perpetuated this attitude, which still
> persisted strongly in Oxford and Cambridge, and has not yet
> disappeared. It is an exceptionally clear example of the expression
> of class struggle in the realm of culture.... This prejudice has
> complicated historical roots and is of great social significance. The

official recognition . . . of experimental physics at Cambridge had to
be obtained in opposition to it.

(ibid.: 315–16)

Mind-binding of this sort meant that scientists like James Prescott Joule
were ignored on grounds that had nothing to do with science. 'The
comprehensive human imagination could not be nourished by Joule's
discoveries because they sprang from poisoned social sources. They arose
out of studies of engines that had been appropriated to the creation of
private wealth instead of an increase of human dignity' (ibid.: 131). The
depth of this educational refusal had influence well beyond science.
Knowledge of the engines of economic growth was actually resisted, even
suppressed, for ill-examined social reasons; and the fall in English
productivity late in the century can be linked to an English lag in scientific
knowledge (Briggs, 1983: 196–7). Conventional practices pulled in one
direction; Maxwell's method and theory and multidisiplinary effort pulled
in another.

Most important for my purposes is the vision of nature implicit in
Maxwell's work, both in his methods and his results. In his inaugural
speech as founding Head of the Cavendish Laboratory, Maxwell
explains that 'The statistical method . . . involves an abandonment of
strict dynamical principles and an adoption of the mathematical
methods belonging to the theory of probability' (Crowther, 1935:
320–31). Such methods, replacing strict measurement with statistical
probability, belong to a completely different, and perhaps a humbler
construction of nature than the prevailing one that still trails clouds of
glory into the late nineteenth century. Maxwell accepts a disunity in
nature, or at least an apparent lack of rational unity. He thus
effectually rejected the assumption that nature was unitary. If nature
is a 'book', he wrote, then perhaps it has regular pages, and the preface
indicates the end. But if nature 'is not a "book" at all, but a *magazine*,
nothing is more foolish to suppose than that one part can throw light
on another. . . . The only laws of matter are those which our minds
must fabricate, and the only laws of mind are fabricated for it by
matter' (ibid.: 281). Statements like that, implicating our measurements
in what we discover, belong to a hypothetical mental habit that can
tolerate a provisional abstraction without irritable reaching after
certainty.

Maxwell was himself something of a poet, and shows the characteristic
jouissance with which he approaches nature in an ode celebrating the
immortality, not of anyone in particular, but of 'waves in aether'.

Evolution and entropy notwithstanding, electomagnetic waves go on forever. This stanza from his ode to 'Hermann Stoffkraft, PhD' (quoted in Crowther, 1935, p. 324) celebrates the resiliance of a nature unconfined to scientific dogmas:

> But when thy Science lifts her pinions
> In Speculation's wild dominions,
> We treasure every dictum thou emittest,
> While down the stream of Evolution
> We drift, expecting no solution
> But that of the survival of the fittest.
> Till, in the twilight of the gods,
> When earth and sun are frozen clods,
> When, all its energy degraded,
> Matter to aether shall have faded;
> We, that is, all the work we've done,
> As waves in aether, shall for ever run
> In ever-widening spheres through heavens beyond the sun.

Not earth-centred, not sun-centred, not centred at all in fact, the 'heavens beyond the sun' appear in a perpetual brightness that makes earthbound entropy a merely local disaster. The very spirit of the poem is one of laughing acceptance not tragic nostalgia, because, as Maxwell says in another poem composed at the age of 21, the universe perceived at this level of abstraction inspires humility, 'crushing all that makes me proud' (*Reflections from Various Surfaces*, quoted in Crowther, 1935: 324, 282). The poem alludes to a cosmic context so vast that the conservation of energy is grounds for happy affirmation, not anthropocentric gloom. By 1895 the narrative implications of Maxwell's approach still remain to be discovered: his pursuit of 'physical analogies', his emphasis on plural descriptive systems, and his search for probability rather than determinism.

The second example of innovation is the poetry of Gerard Manley Hopkins. His work presents in a different medium that transformation of fundamental methods that Maxwell effected. Hopkins was relatively unknown in his lifetime; only after his death did people begin to realize the new opportunities his language makes available. Hopkins's poetry re-inflects English: not just by reviving archaic vocabulary, but by amplifying and diversifying the linguistic code at its root, in the sentence, the sequence, the poetic line. Such work effects the renewal and even the transformation of social codes, as André Breton (1972: 152), Julia Kristeva (1980: 133) and others have since noted. Like Maxwell, Hopkins experiments with the sheer sound and weight and quantities of English in ways that split open the iambic pentameter conventions favoured in English since Shakespeare. Like Maxwell, Hopkins sustains a level of abstraction and a corresponding joyousness that has potentially revolutionary implications for narrative sequence. Like Maxwell, Hopkins introduces an original method, especially his cultivation of the play of similitudes, or rhymes, between different kinds of systems. The two even share a reliance on religious faith as they take these new steps. Maxwell is supposed to have said that we see the invisible Christ more clearly than we would see the materially present one (Crowther, 1935:. 311). In Hopkins, as in Maxwell, we find a new vision of nature as something that is orderly, brilliant, dangerous, exciting.

For Hopkins, nature is a Heraclitean fire: it is abstract, brilliant, joyous. The language appropriate to such a vision differs from the syntactical habits of centuries, from what T. S. Eliot memorably calls that 'old Shakespe-hearian rag'. With Hopkins, to begin with, syncopation is *in*:

Cloud-puffball, torn tufts, tossed pillows flaunt forth, then chevy on an air-built thoroughfare: heaven-roysterers, in gay-gangs they throng; they glitter in marches.
Down roughcast, down dazzling whitewash, wherever an elm arches,
Shivelights and shadowtackle in long lashes lace, lance, and pair.
Delightfully the bright wind boisterous ropes, wrestles, beats earth bare
Of yestertempest's creases; in pool and rut peel parches
Squandering ooze to squeezed dough, crust, dust; stanches, starches
Squadroned masks and manmarks treadmire toil there
Footfretted in it. Million-fueled, nature's bonfire burns on.
Hopkins, from 'That Nature is a Heraclitean Fire...'

There is little left here of iambic somnolence; little left of the rhyme that anchors a line. Alliteration closely wraps some syllables, then lets them loose in a different rhythmic patter: 'torn tufts, tossed pillows flaunt forth / then chevy on an air- / built thoroughfare'. The end-rhymes are uneven, lost in the turmoil (abbaabac); meanwhile rhymes appear along each line, and dissolve, as if the words are moulting: 'crust, dust; stanches, starches'. This nature, however, is redeemed by the hope of the resurrection, which compensates the 'indig | nation' of death:

I am all at once what Christ is, since he was what I am, and
This Jack, joke, poor potsherd, patch, matchwood, immortal diamond,
    Is immortal diamond.

But even before the final affirmation, that redemption appears in those parallels, those rhymes, those facets, those multiplied patterns in things.

Physical analogies materialize not just in nature but in language itself: in 'shivelights and shadowtackle'; in the almost geometrical possibilities which appear in 'manmarks' and 'Footfretted'; and most of all in new rhythmic economies, like the one in 'Delightfully the bright wind boisterous ropes, wrestles, beats earth bare'. Sound and rhythm multiply, escape the line, shoot in various directions simultaneously, creating linguistic fields.

Hopkins's play with radical new forms of interruption, of rhythmic variation, has important implications for narrative sequence. Separation and difference are not fatal to unity in Hopkins's sequences, but essential to it. His alliterations deflect the thetic, productive, syntactical sequence sideways, into varieties of rhythmic counterpoints where new linkages appear in the linguistic element itself. The sliding evolutionary relationship, where one thing merges imperceptibly into another, is cut and cropped by abrupt changes in register and interval. Sound meets silence; a kinetic pause generates an imbalance and a patter of rhymes that, in turn, suggest unusual connections where none had appeared. It is like a verbal hypothesis, energetic with unexpected linkages. Nature, in fact, 'is a Heraclitean Fire' that contains perpetual life. As Maxwell puts it, 'waves in aether, shall forever run / Through ever-widening spheres of heavens beyond the sun'.

Hopkins called the geometry of nature 'inscape'. His journal from 11 July 1866 contains this descriptive comparison of oak, cedar and beech trees:

> Oaks: the organisation of this tree is difficult. Speaking generally no doubt the determining planes are concentric, a system of brief contiguous and continuous tangents, whereas those of the cedar wd. roughly be called horizontals and those of the beech radiating but modified by droop and by a screw-set towards jutting points.

Hopkins's inscape exists well beyond common-sense experience and beyond so much ready-made formulation. He seeks both the detail, and the abstraction that makes the detail brilliant. He notes the 'prismatic' colours of clouds, the 'planes' and 'tangents' of tree species. 'All the world is full of inscape', he writes in the well-known journal passage, 'and chance left free to act falls into an order as well as purpose: looking out of my window I caught it in the random clods and broken heaps of snow made by the cast of a broom'. Not because the clods fall in *a* single pattern, but because repeated parallel curves rhyme. Braids, meshes, flutings, king-fishers, tufts, dragonflies, pillows: the pattern of things in plurals. On the whole, Hopkins avoids anthropocentric descriptions of nature or any ultimately tragic sense of life. Hopkins's affirmation of 'an order as well as purpose' faintly echoes Conan Doyle's (Sherlock Holmes's) affirmation that there's 'a pattern and a purpose in it'. But instead of unfolding the material causalities of detective fiction, Hopkins seeks a different kind of abstract pattern: the union with tension in it, the rhymes between things apparently different, the echoes between coral and leaf. Beauty and Brilliance in Hopkins's nature are far too potent for ordinary detection.

The third and final example of innovation appears in painting, but not in English painting. In the 1870s, when Maxwell and Hopkins are working in England, the painters exhibiting are Alma-Tadema, Rossetti and Burne-Jones, of whom it could be said that they, too, like Maxwell's and Hopkins's contemporaries, re-inscribed old forms. Narrative painting that forms the mainstream in nineteenth-century England has its headwaters in the Renaissance. Even the pre-Raphaelites, whose programme was to seek the opportunities evident *before* the Renaissance, do not appreciably innovate technique or medium even as they seek surprising pictorial subjects. In Paris, meanwhile, Degas, Manet, Cassatt, Morisot and Monet understandably overawe their nearest English speaking competitor, James McNeil Whistler, an American. (Elie Faure's *History of Modern Art* dismisses all these Anglophone painters: Burne-Jones 'is only a sentimental Mantegna entangled with a Botticelli infected by Puritanism. Rossetti shelters his chlorosis under the aegis of the Platonic aesthetics'; and Whistler is 'the prince of amateurs' who 'arranges with sagacity his grays, his blacks, and his pinks' (Faure, 1937: 188)). The empty spaces and obliquity of Degas, and the figural flatness of Manet, are already well beyond English painters.

But even the French Impressionists were insufficiently aware of the innovative pictorial technique that most looks forward to the breakthroughs of the Fauves and Cubists. From the mid-1870s on, Paul Cézanne transforms the technique of painting. Though Monet, Pissarro and other painters knew his work, it was not shown (except for one or two canvases) until 1895, the year of his first one-man show in Paris organized by Ambroise Vollard. Cézanne's technique of ' "modulating" colour, applying it in small, graded units' (Theodore Reff, in Rubin, 1977: 48), materializes a new kind of pictorial space where the depth of single-point perspective gives way to relationships of line and colour. Often these relationships are quite dynamic, like those in *Nature morte avec pommes* (1895– 8, Museum of Modern Art, New York), where a drawn patterned curtain participates in vectors that threaten to cross out of the frame altogether on one side and that are contained at the opposite side of the canvas by monumental verticals. Cézanne's colour sometimes absorbs line entirely. His backgrounds characteristically come forward, his space flattens, his objects appear in relationships that are powerful to the point of distortion.

By these and other means, this artist moves perception of the world beyond common sense, or at least what a Renaissance pictorial tradition had trained to be common sense. For example, his still life, *Nature morte au panier* (c. 1888–90, Musée d'Orsay), so radically modifies the perspective system of representation that the objects seem about to whirl off-centre and spiral away from the ground, defying gravity. His 'modulating' technique seems to remove weight from objects and to require active intervention by viewers. In one of his portraits of his gardener, *Vallier assis* (c. 1905–6, Tate Gallery), this hatching effect does not so much present the object as it guides the eye to fill in the object by perceiving sheer colour, intensity and relation.

Cézanne simply departs from the illusion of neutral space so powerfully important in realist painting right through Impressionism. Instead he presents a world of torque, fluidity and transparency. His late watercolours have been described as 'prismatic universes' (Reff, in Rubin, 1977: 13). For example, his *Etude de feuillage* (1895–1900, Museum of Modern Art, New York) presents a kind of dynamic among planes in light that has rightly been called 'kaleidoscopic' (Geneviève Monnier, in Rubin, 1977: 114). The large empty spaces that he leaves in his canvases produce a new kind of pictorial space, one far removed from the immense, neutral space of single-point perspective. By making a new kind of space available in painting, Cézanne tranforms the method of his day and provides an impetus for modernism.

The last English painter to achieve anything like this kind of powerful re-direction of the very tools of pictorial art was J. M. W. Turner, who died in 1851. Despite his vestiges of early classicism, Turner remains above all interested in that medium of sight, that atmosphere, that 'light' which increasingly becomes his subject. His works from the 1840s, for example *Mountain Landscape* (c. 1840–45) and *Seascape with Storm Coming On* (c. 1840), or even *Sunrise With Sea Monsters* (c. 1845), are almost entirely abstract representations of space as pure atmosphere, as pure medium of light. In Turner the rationalized faculty of sight that belongs to the scheme of single-point perspective begins to lose its coordinates in the physical world. Looking backwards, Turner's emphasis on 'light' as opposed to space seems preternaturally forward-looking. Certainly French impressionists sojourning in England during the Franco–Prussian war had had the opportunity to study his work. English painters, on the other hand, either did not or could not follow Turner's direction.

Maxwell, Hopkins and Cézanne all develop the *tools* of their arts beyond the terms of long-standing traditions. Where are the comparable innovations in English narrative? George Meredith grasps the spirit of science as few nineteenth-century novelists besides George Eliot grasp it; but Meredith's actual achievement does not alter the historical narrative code fundamentally. After *The Egoist* (1879) his narrative style suffers from density and obscurity, as if straining to sustain by linguistic means alone the civility he champions so eloquently in earlier novels, from *The Ordeal of Richard Feverel* (1859) to *Beauchamp's Career* (1875–6) and in his 1877 *Essay on Comedy*. Some find in his poetry more clarity concerning the links between aesthetic and scientific ideals (Cosslett, 1982: 101–31). Like Meredith, Thomas Hardy uses the available narrative conventions ironically – for example, the development that does not develop in *The Mayor of Casterbridge* – but he does not really experiment very radically with the basic grammar of perspective and sequence that he inherits from earlier novels, and neither do his contemporaries. It is worth more than passing note that these two of the most important late-century English novelists, Thomas Hardy and George Meredith, both shifted between novels and poetry, in Hardy's case giving up novels altogether after 1895.

During the last quarter of the nineteenth century, other kinds of imaginative invention, particularly technological innovations, diversify exponentially the social conditions that novelists write about, in some cases altering the very basis of perception. The national telephone service organized in 1890–91 permitted people to speak invisibly to each other. From the mid-1880s and 1890s people could hear music and speech imported into their own rooms, first through the phonograph and then through Marconi's wireless (1896); and they could go to the cinema (1895) to watch a sequence constituted artificially by cutting and appearing to equal realism at the business of presenting life-'like' images. Physical experience differed as well in terms of sheer mobility alone. The British railway system was developed by 1870 to a point where it remained for more than a century. In the thirty years between 1850 and 1880, three million Britons travelled extensively outside their home country: two million to the United States and one million elsewhere around the globe. The first flight was to come in less than a decade. Cartography and exploration, once the lone venture of heroes, had become part of ordinary experience.

Such statistics at least suggest the overwhelming alteration introduced by technology into the basis of every formulation, including social definitions. By 1895, 'sixty years since' (to use Walter Scott's subtitle from *Waverley*) is a very long time ago indeed, not just in terms of social and political life but in terms even of the common-sense experience that putatively supports conventional thinking in science and art. It was a period of intense political and social experiment. The social and historical novelists of mid-century contributed more than a little to legislative efforts towards social justice: for example, Parliamentary legislation widened the franchise among men, improved the legal status of married women, increased the access to university education for non-Anglicans and non-males, and based Civil Service careers on competitive exams – something Asa Briggs has called 'the one great political invention of Victorian England' (Briggs, 1983: 226, 205ff.). Yet this buzz of experiment and adventure does not seem to inspire similar activity among novelists.

The sense of cultural depression in late nineteenth-century England has been often mentioned, and certainly it is obvious in a nostalgic and tragic writer like Thomas Hardy, whose parting shot in narrative, *Jude the Obscure* (1895), may be the greatest downer in literature. Certainly some end-of-century malaise can be associated with economic depression in the 1870s and with a new stasis in the Empire, where Britain no longer enjoyed easy industrial supremacy, where renewed war in France made peace seem less secure, and where new nationalism and tariffs in Europe gave new priority to a much older and more rapacious view of colonies (Benians, 1925: 282). Still, these economic motives do not account fully for the cultural conservatism that hampers development of new methods and forms. There was economic depression in Britain in 1846–47, and an international crisis of representation at the same time, and yet there seemed to be none of the cultural malaise that appears to hamper late-century efforts.

English novelists tend not to find joy in narrative experiment, and turn like Hardy and Meredith to other forms, or simply re-inscribe, with what in the hands of lesser novelists might be called a vengeance, reduced examples of the historical narrative that had been put to more exploratory uses in mid-century. For example, at the same time that writers like Hardy, Gissing and Conrad are all examining the problems of living with social and moral uncertainty, Kipling 'is *celebrating* the fiction of an absolute control that finds its political justification in the idioms of imperialism'; his *The Light That Failed* (1891) 'is written looking down a gun-barrel' (Poole, 1975: 23). Such conservative reaction against the experiments with narrative codes interferes with social renewal.

Outside England, various Russian, American and French novelists experiment at different speeds with the historical narrative codes familiar in mid-century, producing work based on various epistemological, even metaphysical, challenges: a certain gap of insufficiency between practice and meaning in Dostoevsky; a Jamesian emphasis on digression as an experience in its own right; a hyperbolic swelling in Zola's material universe; a confrontation with the absurd in late Flaubert (Nalbantian, 1983: 132). Such hints of late-century decadence can be viewed in an international perspective as a necessary preamble for modernism, a movement that took place in Europe earlier and with more vigour than in England. In fact it is arguable (Hynes, 1990) that, by enlisting the arts in the war effort, England decisively crippled its access to the general movement of modernism that found European expression in Kafka, Picasso and Einstein (Vargish and Mook, forthcoming).

The most radical experiment with narrative style in the English novel appears in the work of Joseph Conrad, a Polish expatriate who wrote in English well before he took up residence in England. In 1895, the year Hardy published his last novel, Joseph Conrad published his first (*Almayer's Folly*), the first of his many experiments with how European values survive where there are no enforcers, and in cultural settings at the margins of European civilization. Conrad's technical innovations are moderate enough compared with those of Kafka or even the later Joyce, but his experiments with the perspective system of historical and social narrative correspond to his steadfast refusal to find meaning in nature. The step towards seeing nature as neither meaningful nor meaningless, but simply absurd, takes Conrad one giant step away from the tradition of English narrative that persists through the century in one form or another. In Conrad, nature is 'purely spectacular':

> The ethical view of the universe involves us at last in so many cruel and absurd contradictions, where the last vestiges of faith, hope, charity, and even of reason itself, seem ready to perish, that I have come to suspect that the aim of all creation cannot be ethical at all. I would fondly believe that its object is purely spectacular; a spectacle for awe, love, adoration, or hate, if you like, but in this view – and in this view alone – never for despair. Those visions, delicious or poignant, are a moral end in themselves. The rest is our affair.
>
> (Conrad, 1947: 713)

Conrad's nature does not cooperate with human effort, as it does in Meredith's *The Egoist*, and Conrad's nature is not tragic, as it is in Hardy's novels. The heart of darkness is entirely human in all its expressions, from London terrorism (*The Secret Agent*, 1907) to the outcast life of various Asian jungles (*Victory*, 1915). The beliefs that sustain social life in Conrad are merely protective lies about a material universe that is humanly unfathomable precisely because it has no depth, no inherent transcendence. The centre is not the centre as early as *Heart of Darkness* (1902). Conrad's technique is correspondingly experimental, especially his emphasis on the figural elements of art, on the production of striking, opaque images, and on the rifts and even irreparable separation between one viewpoint, one attitude, one culture and another.

But Conrad is almost over the horizon of Victorian fiction. What one misses in late-century novels is a narrative innovation comparable to Maxwell's law or Cézanne's images or Hopkins's poetic line, especially when new constructions of nature made such innovation not only possible, but necessary. Even original experiments with subject matter, like Sarah Grand's delightful and unconventional treatment of gender and so-called 'nature' in *The Heavenly Twins* (1894), does not fundamentally alter existing narrative codes. This novel in fact anticipates the continuing vitality of historical narrative conventions in the twentieth century, primarily as a means for exploring intractable social problems. But despite such specialized uses, the uneven and broadly conservative development of the narrative medium in late-century England testifies to the existence of cultural impasse.

2

THE IDEA OF HISTORY

PROLOGUE: GETTING COORDINATES

Historical narrative is a convention of considerable abstractness and artificiality, but one that masks those characteristics. It will help to focus that abstraction during the following discussion to have in mind a single metaphor for the problems addressed in the historical code: a travelling metaphor having to do with the condition of roads. There are two very different systems of British roads: the interlinked system of motorways on the one hand, where a road keeps its identifying marks – its name (usually a number) and its geographical direction – as it crosses indiscriminately from one region to another. The motorways belong to a more-or-less single network, like their predecessors, the canal and railway systems of the nineteenth century.

Local roads, on the other hand, are defined by local circumstance, and they change identity accordingly. No sooner has a traveller set out in a certain direction on a road with a particular name than the direction and the name change without notice, according to motives that are entirely mysterious to all but the local traveller and that remain entirely current and determining. Backroads submit to no coordinating system. They run at tangents to the points of the compass till such points all but vanish from awareness. There is no overall set of coordinates that explains relationships on backroads, and that one might use to negotiate the choices that continually arise between this turning and that one.

Functional knowledge of local byways, whether physical or social ones, remains inaccessible to summary at any significant level of generalization. Only those bent on changing places would want a system of coordinates applicable equally in all places. The discontinuity between this bit of the road and the next troubles no one with local knowledge; and who would need more general, more abstract knowledge except, perhaps, a foreigner? If someone must ask the way, perhaps they ought not to go there. Such relentless emphasis on the local has its strengths in a kind of value-immanence – in concreteness, tradition, preservation, replication, continuity – and its limits in parochialism.

What the metaphor of motorways expresses in spatial terms, this chapter will explore in terms of time. Like space, time can be local and finite. Such was the medieval construction of time; such is the post-modern construction of time. In between, however, for several centuries between the Renaissance and twentieth century, we have humanist time, the time of history and project, the time of Newton and Kant, the common denominator time 'in' which all things share a potential for mutual relevance. Translated into social and narrative terms in the nineteenth-century historical novel, this construction of time is the exception, not the rule, even in Western literature. Marcel Proust, for example, is not a humanist historian; he makes time into a dimension of space in this recollection of the church at Combray:

all these things made of the church for me something entirely different from the rest of the town; a building which occupied, so to speak, four dimensions of space – the name of the fourth being Time – which had sailed the centuries with that old nave, where bay after bay, chapel after chapel, seemed to stretch across and hold down and conquer not merely a few yards of soil, but each successive epoch from which the whole building had emerged triumphant...

(Proust, 1928: 46)

The building is not 'in' time, in the sense that things are 'in' history; it is more the other way around. Time is 'in' the building. Time is a dimension of *it*. For Proust, the consequence is a sense of tradition whose weight 'conquers' sequence and difference. Proust conveys a sense of time that is not historical: the sense that time is private, personal, limited; that materiality and space modify time or, in other words, that time is a dimension of place.

This Proustian time is not the abstract medium of Newton, of Kant, not the cosmic neutrality 'in' which identity can be perceived serially; it is not the medium that made empirical science possible. Instead this localized awareness of the past suggests a nearly ahistorical kind of temporality: one almost typological in its insistence on replicating local arrangements rather than changing them. And such localized awareness of time means that the differences between one locality and another remain unmediated, complete, absolute: unavailable to measurement by a common set of coordinates of the kind implied by the terms 'society' and, above all, 'history'.

Nineteenth-century social novels seek precisely the common denominators, the common horizon that we find absent in Jane Austen or the nature novelists discussed in Chapter One. In social and historical novels, relentless locality is always a problem because it thwarts any sense of human mutuality and insists upon a single and a narrow construction of what 'the human' might be. To keep one's 'place' – either geographical or social – obviates to a significant extent the need to negotiate identity among others and thus to conceive of 'society' in the largest sense. The social novels of mid-century literally construct historical time as they experiment with the possibilities of constructing from various parochialisms a new sort of social order.

For better or worse, historical time requires individuals and groups to consider their situation in a very broad context indeed, in some cases the context of millions of geological and biological years. In their histories of the earth and of species, Lyell and especially Darwin establish and give prestige to one of the most powerful common-denominator abstractions invented by Western culture since the Renaissance: the abstraction of historical time. This is the construction of time that nineteenth-century historical novelists bring home to millions of readers: a common-denominator time that offers an opportunity for mediating those social differences that, in local time, simply seem absolute. This narrative construction of time makes headway in England only against the resistance presented by powerful sense of place, similar to the kind described by Proust and borrowed from religious and feudal tradition. The chief contribution of the nineteenth-century novel is precisely the construction and dissemination of the historical narrative code and its particular accompanying values: its ethic of mobility, its emphasis on emergent form, its reliance on mediation, its assertion that identity is series-dependent, and above all its construction of a neutral medium 'in' which all events have mutual relevance.

Historical, which is to say social, novels produce two constructions that still, more than a century later, seem universally familiar, or 'natural', to Western European cultures: first, the construction of time as history, that is, as a medium: something neutral and homogeneous, not local and finite; and second, the construction of society as an entity with characteristic features and identity, and not merely a rung or 'place' on a cosmic hierarchy. Both these common-denominator abstractions work to override the multitude of local definitions, or parochialisms, discovered everywhere in English society by Victorian novelists. This chapter deals with the construction of historical time; Chapter Three deals with the construction of Society as an entity.

CONSTRUCTING HISTORICAL (SOCIAL) TIME

Historical time is, above all things, *neutral* time. It is a medium that does not interfere with measurement and project. This kind of temporal abstraction, where 'time' is everywhere and nowhere, has incalculable importance to the development of institutions which have continuing functional value in Western and democratic societies, especially to empiricism in science, and to representation in politics and in art. The widespread, functional acceptance of time as a neutral medium 'in' which things happen may be so familiar to twentieth-century readers as to seem 'natural'; but it is not natural, and has only recently come to seem so. In fact, such abstractions as 'history' and 'society' in their democratic, all-inclusive senses, made slow and contested headway in English narrative even during the nineteenth century, and still cannot always be taken for granted.

The claim that we construct time takes some getting used to. Most citizens of Western democratic societies take 'time' for granted as a universal. But our 'time' is not Homer's time, fractured by directives from the gods, nor Augustine's essentially phantasmal time. Our time is the time of history and project, the neutral time of Newton and Kant 'in' which causalities unfold and entities subsist. Looking backwards from the late twentieth century we can create what Herbert Butterfield calls a 'gigantic optical illusion' of 'history'; we see it running its neutral course, a kind of cosmic motorway, from the origin of the world to the present day, including in it everything from Homer to holographs.

The danger of such an optical illusion, as Butterfield once reminded historians, is that it can act as a blinker or filter: not only influencing our interpretations of the past but, more potently, masking the function of those interpretations in the present. '[We] lavish vast areas of print on researches into some minute episode' and yet 'come to our fundamental ideas in the most casual manner possible', devoting to them 'only the kind of thinking that is done in asides'. For example, 'it is astonishing to what an extent the historian has been Protestant, progressive, and Whig, and the very model of the 19th [sic] century gentleman', and to what an extent since about 1800 this historian has contributed to the development of European nationalism, even 'romantic nationalism'. Such unexamined practices can have ominous implications: 'It is possible for historians to mislead a nation in respect of what it might regard as its historic mission' (Butterfield, 1963: 5, 23–4; 1969: 30).

Even for those who try to be methodologically alert, it still may come as a sort of epistemic shock to realize how recent is the broad common assumption of historical time as a 'natural' condition – a common medium stretching to infinity 'in' which individuals exist and events take place. It is an epistemic shock to realize that this historical convention is not only completely absent in ancient Greece or medieval Europe, it is by no means commonly held even in 1800. Homer did not inhabit our history, nor did Augustine or even Henry VII, if by history we mean the convention that asserts the existence of a common time, a neutral medium in which interesting comparisons can be made between things widely separated.

In the following sections, the term 'history' and 'social time' are used almost interchangeably. Of course the one term applies overtly to a medium while the other seems to invoke an entity; but the medium and the entity depend upon each other entirely. History *is* social time. Social time is history. The very idea of society as an entity depends upon the historical convention 'in' which 'it' can be perceived according to a particular grammar of perspective. The two live or die together, just as do those other symbiotic twins, 'the subject' and 'the object'. The social novel constructs, codifies and explores historical time; it exploits a particular grammar of perspective, translated from space to temporality where its implications for sequence can fully appear.

The construction of historical time in nineteenth-century realist narrative corresponds precisely to that construction of space in realist painting achieved several centuries earlier. In both cases, the apparent focus on realist objects or subjects has distracted attention from the fact that what such art represents are the media of modernity, neutral time and space. To attack realism for being too materialistic, as even nineteenth-century critics have done, is to miss the point of the realist art. The most recent such attack is instructive because it makes my point inadvertently. Roland Barthes attacks what he calls 'classical Dutch realism' in general, and the 'vacant church interiors' of the Dutch painter, Saenredam, in particular. Barthes criticizes these pictures as examples of almost mindless materialism:

> Saenredam painted neither faces nor objects, but chiefly vacant church interiors, reduced to the beige and innocuous unction of butterscotch ice cream. These churches, where there is nothing to be seen but expanses of wood and whitewashed plaster, are

irremediably unpeopled, and this negation goes much further than the destruction of idols. Never has nothingness been so confident.... He articulates by antithesis the nature of classical Dutch painting, which has washed away religion only to replace it with man and his empire of things.... Behold him, then, at the pinnacle of history, knowing no other fate than a gradual appropriation of matter.

(Barthes, 1972: 3–4)

In this description Barthes establishes firmly the fact that he has quite missed the whole point of Dutch realism. It is not the materiality of the objects – their sheen and sheer instrumentality – that such pictures chiefly represent. What they represent is precisely space, just as realist narrative represents time: but space and time constructed as neutral, as homogeneous – in short, as media in which mutually informative measurements can be made. Everything depends on that. These media are the common denominators of the human world, the media of modernity in a post-medieval world. The material objects merely support and specify that construction. It is precisely the emptiness of Saenredam's interiors that calls attention to the existence of that space, that common atmosphere, that unified world. *Of course* such pictures show empty space; that is their whole point. The material 'in' it merely acts as a support or carrier for the powerful, overarching generalization about space and relationship. Saenredam's use of architectural elements to sustain this construction of space has a long and distinguished history reaching back to the Quattrocento, when painters like Piero della Francesca used them to specify a then-original construction of space.

Like the painter, the historian represents a medium that holds out powerful possibilities of generalization and control. These include the political and practical possibilities. It can be argued that representation in art has a cultural function very similar to representation in politics: that both belong to the same cultural epoch; that, in short, democracy is the realism of politics in the sense that it is the single-point perspective system of politics. (Of course, to say it is 'realist' is not to give it any special priority, but just to say that it conforms to a particular convention; but more of this later.) Its political ideology coordinates all viewpoints into a single system; even its physical arenas are amphitheatres for aligning individual perception centrally. This convention is simultaneously an ethic and an aesthetic, the key tenet of which is the idea that any variety of perspectives still can converge in one horizon, one common medium, one and the 'same' world. Everything belongs to a single system of relationship and measurement.

For all practical purposes, the nineteenth century popularized historical thinking, including all its definitions of sequence and identity. History
is a convention, like any other: a product of collective and imaginative
effort to solve or defer certain problems. While habitués may regard this
particular construction of time as the only one, it is nevertheless far from
being universal and is in fact a fairly local and fairly recent invention of
Western Europe. It is thanks in considerable measure to writers of the
nineteenth century that we now take history for granted. Although the
Renaissance, and especially Erasmian humanism, contained the seeds of
modern historical thinking, its full dissemination awaited the nineteenth
century. At the end of the Middle Ages the idea was simply too radical to
unfold its implications easily or at once.

The idea of history is radical in 1500 because its totalized system of
explanation tends to compete with religion. This potential of historical
conventions emerged slowly. The nineteenth century materialized that
potential and disseminated it so broadly that it became common sense.
Initially instrumental in spatial and mathematical languages, this representational convention – this discourse of perspective – was conducive to
the growth of empirical science during the seventeenth century and of
technology in the eighteenth, and conducive also to the reformation of
religious and political discourse in England beginning with the Tudors.
The Reformation, or at least the 'transalpine' Reformation in the Nether-
lands and England, had a humanist basis that imported into religion itself
this grammar of perspective. The Quattrocento was well past by the time
this new grammar made possible the neutral time and space of empirical
science and Newtonian laws, not to mention Kantian imperatives. The
full mathematical implications of these representations did not appear
until 1630 in France, and the political and social implications – the
political development of the idea of representation, for example, and its
translation into conventions of representational time – were still taking
shape in the eighteenth and nineteenth centuries (Ermarth, 1983: 1–92).

For whatever reasons, Europeans in the nineteenth century were able
to write into existence a new historical narrative of social identity,
beginning with the astonishing achievement of Sir Walter Scott (1771–
1832) who, for nearly the first time, treats the social order as an evolving
entity, rather than a cosmic site for picaresque actions. While history of a
kind can be found in Gibbon's epic of Roman history, in Jane Austen's
last writings, in Carlyle's histories, and in all of Scott's novels, historical
codes are still exceptional in English narratives around 1800. Even as
late as 1850 such thinking is still being contested both in fictional
narrative and in science. What happens during the nineteenth century,

especially from around 1850, is that historical thinking gains broad cultural acceptance.

The key to the idea of history – it cannot be said too often – is neutrality. History is not essentially a matter of chronology, or of sequence, or of causality. Medieval chronicles have chronology, for all their elisions and magic. Sequence can be found in rhetorical and rhythmic narratives as well as in historical ones; in Homer and Milton as well as in Trollope. And Aristotelian causality operates quite cheerfully in the most ahistorical medieval philosophy and theology – and for that matter even in some twentieth-century literary criticism where Aristotelian four-fold causality is shamelessly inflicted upon unsuspecting young minds.

What above all does distinguish historical time from other constructions of temporality is its *neutrality*. Unlike the time of God, or the time of kings, history is the time common to all. Homogeneous and universal, historical time is not end-stopped or riven by divine agency; it is a neutral, open, unproblematic medium – at least hypothetically. Because it is neutral historical time acts as a universal common denominator, a categorical imperative, a constant by which all else can be measured.

Neutrality is precisely what we have not got in the narrative code of conversion narratives discussed in Chapter One. Narratives of personal 'turning' use history, but only in order to do away with the need for history. The pattern of experience leads not just to a limited personal solution, but to Truth, after which history is unnecessary. 'History' is a personal definition, not a collective medium, and after truth destroys error the personalized 'history' comes to an end. The autobiographies of John Stuart Mill and John Henry Newman, so different in values and commitments, are both very similar on this point and in their narrative terms. Both are histories to end history.

Newman explains the 'meaning' of his conversion from Anglicanism to Roman Catholicism by turning from doctrinal argument to 'the history of my mind', and his religious search for a still point ends when he finally has 'no variations to record' (Newman, 1956: 17, 192, 227). Mill's historical phase of life ends in a little apocalypse, after which there is no more history to tell: 'no further mental changes to tell of, but only, as I hope, a continued mental progress; which does not admit of a consecutive history' (Mill, 1924: 155). Even where the particular conclusion cannot be clearly enunciated, and the indefiniteness of Mill's solutions, like that of Carlyle's 'Life' in *Sartor Resartus*, has drawn considerable comment (Letwin, 1965: 318), the narrative convention of personal 'turning' operates to contain the potential messiness of change in a conclusive pattern that brings history to a full stop. These life stories do not treat history as the neutral medium sustained by the perspective system of history. Like Proust's church, such narratives make history a *finite feature* of individual life rather than a *neutral context* for it.

Neutrality in the medium is precisely what single-point perspective produces. Temporal realism, or history, organizes – one could say rationalizes – the faculty of consciousness in much the same way that realist painting, with its commanding perspective system, organizes (or rationalizes) the faculty of sight. By this convention all perspectives, whatever the variety, still converge in one horizon, one common medium, one and the 'same' world. History is a temporal form of Saenredam's realism. It provides for readers a construction of the world similar to that of the painters who, in the Renaissance, fully exploited for the first time a grammar of spatial perception governed by single-point perspective techniques.

This grammar of single-point perspective is far more than mere technique, however, and it has had influence well beyond the Quattrocento painting and architecture where it first appeared. In prior centuries, William J. Ivins, Jr, has argued, it had been precisely the *lack* of a grammar of perspective that accounted for 'much of the failure of classical and medieval science'; and it was the presence of that grammar that made possible the instruments of projection and rationalization that supported cartography and exploration, a new astronomy, and eventually empirical science, not to mention representational government. So there was much more than religious ornament or even political symbolism at stake in those church frescoes of Masaccio, and in Brunelleschi's plans for the Florentine Duomo. The technique of single-point perspective made possible, for the first time, an exact duplication of spectator awareness: an image of the world 'like' it looked to an individual spectator, so that one could mentally walk around the object, taking it in serially. Such techniques were essential to scientific description. Before them, no image 'could be exactly duplicated' because there was no 'grammatical scheme for securing either logical relations within the system of pictorial symbols' or correspondence with the *appearance* of objects in space (Ivins, 1973: 8).

Because visual art presents simultaneously what must be grasped over time in narrative, it is easier to see in painting how this grammar of perspective produces a formal agreement, as Alberti's diagrams show, out of the convergence or *formal consensus* of all possible perspectives. The single vanishing point testifies to that agreement; it enforces it. At the same time, and even more powerfully, this formal agreement, this consensus, literally constructs the neutral 'space' of Quattrocento realism. It is the singleness of the horizon, the lack of disagreement among vanishing points, that permits neutral space to materialize.

The same thing happens in historical narrative during the nineteenth century, although the serial potential of single-point perspective becomes more emphatic than it is in painting. Historical narrative makes neutral time materialize by coordinating all past moments into a single, temporal horizon. Maintained from a vantage ever in the future of the action, the historical narrative always reflects backwards over a gap in time, mediating it. The very existence of a meaningful interim – between then and now, between one act and another, between one thought and another – means that potentially a mutual relevance, a buried affinity can emerge between events that points to a single system of explanation. The more fully a writer explores the powers of the past tense, the more substantial is the neutrality of the temporal medium, the more unified the world.

Tense, not person, is the key to history; one can write history in either the first or the third person, but never in the present tense (Ermarth, 1983: 88–9). The mutuality, the 'consensus', the formal agreement not to contradict, aligns all possible moments into a single stream, a single system of explanation. 'Once upon a time' always suggests a link between then and now, a linkage made possible by a common system of organization. Historical narrative thus guarantees the neutrality of time by rendering it unitary. The more fully a novel exploits these powers of the historical convention, the stronger is the assertion of a common world: the crucial humanist and empiricist assertion that there are not two or more times – one for God and one for man, one for him and one for her, one for them and one for us – but only a single time common to all. Such novels do not create a *perspective* so much as they create a perspective *system*. The time thus constructed is *neutral* because 'in' it, past and present can reflect upon one another without reference to or interference from any other system of explanation. It is neutral because (hypothetically) it provides a common denominator for everything.

Given the immediate effects of narrative realism, or history, such abstraction may seem out of place. And realism, like any other convention, is an hypothesis, a way of producing relationships, and as such it is, like any convention, abstract and arbitrary (not 'natural'). But realism compounds its abstraction by masking it. Ostensibly historical narrative, like Quattrocento painting, simply re-produces the world as it appears to spectator awareness. But there is nothing 'simple' about it, especially given the fact that, for most of world history, art has made little or no concession to that spectator awareness which realism both exploits and underwrites.

Historical narrative exploits fully the power of the past tense to recover everything, absolutely everything, into a single system of temporal relationship, a single system of explanation. The characteristic historical shift in perspective moves from an inclusive 'future' position relative to the events narrated, backwards to a series of more limited perspectives which it incorporates into a larger sequence and, implicitly, into a structure of interpretation and significance that exceeds any particular moment and that is visible only in hindsight. This hindsight is an immense new power in narrative. Just as in realist pictures implied perspectives are infinite, so in historical narrative a number of possible and potentially infinite perspectives support the construction of a common medium.

The objectivity of the narrative thus depends upon a systematic collection of voices. What is called 'the narrator' acts as a specifier of that system; the narrator is a kind of administrative function. This implied spectator, positioned indefinitely at some point in the future of the narrative events, coordinates them through the power of the past tense into a single system of mutual relevance. This mutuality testifies to the neutrality or all-in-common-ness of the medium 'in' which all events take place and thus, by a characteristic circularity, at the same time and by the same gesture, constructs that temporal medium. The 'consensus' of realism in time and space lies in this formal agreement, or formal system of non-contradiction, and not in any content. That formal consensus establishes, *not* this or that truth, but the neutrality of the medium, the neutrality of time. It may seem that this neutrality or in-common-ness of time, this 'historical' medium, makes collective agreement possible in the first place. What I'm arguing, however, is the reverse: that collective agreement of a formal sort – the achievement of a single-point perspective system in time – is what makes 'history' possible.

A final and crucial point about historical narrative concerns what has been called 'the narrator' but which is really a sort of administrative function in narrative. The term 'narrator' suggests, comfortingly but falsely, that the narrative hindsight can be referred to an individual, and it thus seems to calls attention to and validates the individual perspective. In effect such a reading of the narrative function in question trivializes it, and masks the existence of the perspective *system*, with its manifold abstract powers. Identifying this system by its specifying function alone ('the narrator'), obscures the system's most powerful function, which is to render time neutral, homogeneous and infinite. This time, like the neutral space of pictorial realism, is the medium of modernity; it makes possible mutually informative measurements upon which representation depends, in politics as well as in art. In neutral time, for example, events in Bosnia and events in England, or even Uruguay, are not events in alternate, parallel universes as they would be in Einstein's time or Aristotle's, but instead events in a common time, a shared universe, a system of mutual influence and dependence. Temporal neutrality is a deeply humanist formulation of time; its assertion of human solidarity; its implicit extension of powers by relay from one mind to another, one memory to another. Individualizing this narrative function naturalizes it, and thus trivializes its powers (Culler, 1975: 200–1, 134–9). If we cannot give up 'the narrator', we should at least, as I have argued elsewhere (Ermarth, 1983: 65–92), speak of the narrator as 'Nobody'. When the narrative function that maintains single point perspective is individualized – taken to be 'the historian', or 'the narrator', or worse, 'the author' – the personalizing gesture naturalizes the whole convention by assigning it to individual intention. Its very power of unifying the world disappears from view. Once that is done, whatever appears in the text of, say, *Bleak House* or *Middlemarch* or *The Egoist* need not be considered as an expression of a certain grammar of perception common to a culture; it can be put down to this, that or the other writer and to their biography, including the history of their times; it can be ransacked for information that then (somehow) 'explains' the narrative.

But historical narrative functions in quite a different way. Regardless of who is the novelist, the narrative voice of history, with its powers of interpretation, bridges the gaps between things, between people, between groups, between events, and even between conflicting parts of individual people. The crucial feat of mediation is formal, and consists in its apparently neutral inscription of history as the common (and neutral) medium of social experience. The mnemonic reflex – that reflex of the past tense always evident in every description and every 'quoted' conversation – remains the most important function of such texts. It is the function that maintains time as a constant, and thus as a potential for connection across the kind of silence and limitation with which most characters struggle.

The reader still with us will by now be longing for examples. More extended ones appear in the next section, but here some short examples of the historian-function will show how it formulates all times as constituents of a single medium. We can begin with a small instance of comparison between text from two different novels. Each shifts from one temporal perspective to another:

But now that he had done the deed he found himself forced to look at it from quite another point of view.

and

He thought that he disliked seeing one who had mortified him so keenly; but he was mistaken.

These passages from Anthony Trollope and Elizabeth Gaskell are formally interchangeable; each could appear in the other's novel, or almost any social novel of the time. Trollope's narrator speaks of his character, Adolphus Crosbie, in *The Small House at Allington* (Trollope, 1991: 268; ch. 25), and Elizabeth Gaskell's narrator speaks of her character, John Thornton, in *North and South* (Gaskell, 1973: 239, II, ch. 4) in exactly the way that all historical narrators speak of characters. It seems simple, even obvious. Yet the gesture specifies an entire system of relatedness and promise. Each passage encloses a private present tense in a larger past-tense recollection. What is 'now', for Adolphus Crosbie or John Thornton, is 'then' for readers who are granted the unique power of such novels, the power of historical hindsight. Each sentence thus involves a double temporal moment: the limited present one and the larger one in which it can be interpreted, and in fact *must* be interpreted. The coordinating narrative hindsight, located at an arbitrary point in the future of every 'action', literally constitutes the historical medium. Like these small examples, an entire narrative incorporates, without contradiction, all possible viewpoints, all mental moments, all sequences into a single system of explanation and relationship. The singleness of the perspective system guarantees the neutrality of time and thus the universal relevance of the forms and laws that emerge 'in' it.

Any historical narrative is such sequences writ large. It aligns a series of such moments into a single temporal sequence, into a time common to all events, that is, a common time. Far from being a simple property of the physical universe, this common time is an imaginative creation of considerable power and uniqueness. It can be deployed in different ways. Dickens and Hardy, for example, tend to push towards the limits of history, viewing society from its margins and shifting perspective in ways that are more staggering than that which we find in the two passages just quoted. George Eliot and Trollope emphasize the fine-grained quality of negotiations between a private mind and a public social situation. But all thoroughly historical narrative traces the human project, not from here to eternity, but over hairline cracks in consciousness and over boundaries between near neighbours and between times.

The presiding vantage point of consciousness in historical novels operates not by proceding chronologically, but as consciousness does, by zig-zagging back and forth 'in' the neutral time that, *by this very gesture*, the narrative creates. The common temporal medium is thus saturated at every point with consciousness. While the power of historical conventions to mediate between widely separated instances sometimes is named 'the narrator', that title utterly excludes from our awareness the most important and most powerful function of this mediation: that it literally *constitutes* historical time in the novel. The mediating function enables time to pass. It produces not consciousness *of* historical fact, but literally the constructed medium which makes the perception of such measurable, collatable 'facts' possible in the first place.

The more a novel tests this power of history to recover everything, however disparate or apparently contradictory, into a common time, the more triumphant is the final assertion of integrity and rationality in the human order of things. In all such novels, the narrative, merely by recognizing differences in condition or view, contains it in the historical sequence. When Charles Kingsley's impoverished London boy, Alton Locke (*Alton Locke, Tailor and Poet*, 1850), ventures out from the vast city one day, he looks over a fence into a landowner's estate and sees for the first time a green field. The surprised child sees a world different from his accustomed one. But the reader, with the privilege of hindsight, recognizes a moral link in that very separation between the child's poverty and the landowner's wealth. The reader 'knows' that such deprivation should not exist, should be mitigated, ameliorated, ended; and in that knowledge mediates the very gap that the narrative discloses.

Take one more limited example of the narrator, this time in George Eliot's *Middlemarch, A Study of Provincial Life* (1871–2), speaking of one particularly disagreeable marriage: 'Poor Lydgate! or shall I say, Poor Rosamond! Each lived in a world of which the other knew nothing' (Eliot, 1956: ch. 16). This statement, by virtue of the same act, both describes a gap and bridges it. It is a mediate presentation of consciousness that inscribes, in the very act of noticing these characters' failure, the common condition of which they know so little. This typical step in a historical sequence shifts perspective in order to unify the world. A good motto for this historian function would be this line from the poet, Mark Strand: 'We all have reasons for moving. I move to keep things whole'. As Elizabeth Gaskell put it in *Mary Barton* (1848), always 'there is another side to the picture' (Gaskell, 1987: 64, ch. 6). These feats of mediation constitute not just the historical narrative but, much more powerfully and more importantly, they constitute the historical medium: the time common to all. This narrative function is a mediation – some might say 'sublimation' – of a difference; it embeds every moment into a structure of significance so comprehensive that (hypothetically) nothing and no one is left out. Even though the attention to particulars masks the abstraction of this realist convention, still its most compelling functions do operate for readers at a high level of generalization.

Historical narrative conventions thus maintain a formal 'consensus' or perspective system that re-enacts in modern form the principle of non-contradiction so deep in the Western psyche. Its 'agreement' is not about anything so trivial as good and evil, but about whether or not the world is One. This consensus remains the most powerful feature of the historical narrative convention. As a single-point perspective system, history constructs a world where common agreement is by definition unavoidable. The single vanishing point testifies to that agreement; it enforces that agreement. Lack of agreement – the kind found in postmodern or medieval art – would simply mean the destruction of that neutral medium, the space or time, 'in' which the objects of realism and history appear.

If the single-point system wavers, more than one system of relationships may appear, and a contradiction threatens. In a painting, for example, if the single-point system does not govern all relationships then the world looks literally 'cracked', contradictory, not-One, as it does in those early Renaissance paintings, where two different vanishing points seem to govern different parts of the painting; or as it does in Escher prints. If the temporal sequence of a narrative often slips into the present tense, contradictions can accumulate to a point where readers lose the privileged vantage point inscribed by the historian-function and essential for grasping the 'meaning' which the historical sequence customarily unfolds. Too much present tense threatens the neutrality of the medium and thus the singleness of a world lacking a common denominator in time.

Dickens and George Eliot routinely use such present-tense moments to indicate some liminal phase of the narrative, either at some margin of inhumanity, or at the reader's doorstep. Most accomplished novelists make rhetorical points with such slippages; in fact, present-tense addresses to the reader regularly punctuate historical narration. 'Amazement sits enthroned upon the countenances of Mr. and Mrs. Lammle's circle of acquaintance' (*Our Mutual Friend*, III, xvii); 'This is what I undertake to do for you, reader' (*Adam Bede*, II, i); 'It is so pleasant to have a friend who possesses the power of setting a difficult question in a clear light' (*Mary Barton*, ch. 5); and (most famously) 'Reader, I married him' (*Jane Eyre*, final chapter).

The writer who wants to suggest that the entire structure of human connectedness is threatened can introduce the present tense as a kind of marker of the limits of the common medium and the common world. Describing in *Adam Bede* the narcissistic flirtation by the young squire with the dairymaid, George Eliot shifts to a mythic present:

> Ah, he doesn't know in the least what he is saying. This is not what he meant to say. His arm is stealing round the waist again, it is tightening its clasp; he is bending his face nearer and nearer to the round cheek, his lips are meeting those pouting child-lips, and for a long moment time has vanished. He may be a shepherd in Arcadia for aught he knows, he may be the first youth kissing the first maiden, he may be Eros himself, sipping the lips of Psyche – it is all one.
>
> (Eliot, 1968: ch. XIII)

But of course it never is 'all one', and the consequences in this case will be bitter enough. The historical narrative, which then resumes its past-tense perspective ('There was no speaking for some minutes after'), goes to work constructing those mediations that offer the prospect of future resolution even where local resolution fails.

Similarly Arcadian, if more idyllic, George Meredith describes in *Richard Feverel* the meeting of two lovers destined to thwart the System by which the hero's father raised him:

> Away with Systems! Away with a corrupt World! Let us breathe the air of the Enchanted Island.
>
> Golden lie the meadows: golden run the streams; red gold is on the pine-stems. The sun is coming down to earth, and walks the fields and the waters.... He calls her by her name ... Pipe happy Love! pipe on to these dear innocents!
>
> (Meredith, 1984: ch. XIX)

The shift out of the past tense does more than merely signal a break from the world of common concerns and social time; it brings into focus by contrast the existence of that neutral medium that the past tense maintains. Because they are 'in' that time, it is clear that this present tense idyll is aberrant and cannot continue.

In later Dickens novels such present-tense shifts indicate some inhuman shallowness. For example, the chapters in *Our Mutual Friend* that describe the Veneerings are all in the present tense. In *Bleak House* Dickens splits historical time itself, dividing the novel into two separate, interleaved narrations each bearing only half of the historical function. The past-tense recollection belongs to Esther Summerson, whose vision is not broad enough to include herself and whose brutally limited history makes it difficult for her to function as more than a receiver; she is an agent without the power to act. The present-tense narrative, on the other hand, has the broad vision that would normally belong to the Nobody narrator, but it sees without memory and thus without the power to interpret, much less to intervene; it 'sees' like the eye of a camera, but has none of the meanings produced by hindsight. The point in the riven and fallen social world of *Bleak House* is that organic social relationships cannot survive where hindsight is divorced from overview (Ermarth, 1983: 181–97).

George Eliot's narrative routinely and rhythmically ends up in the reader's present, as with these well-known examples from a single page of *Middlemarch* (Eliot, 1956: ch. 20):

Our moods are apt to bring with them images which succeed each other like the magic-lantern pictures of a doze . . .

Nor can I suppose that when Mrs. Casaubon is discovered in a fit of weeping six weeks after her wedding, the situation will be regarded as tragic . . . we do not expect people to be deeply moved by what is not unusual . . .

As it is, the quickest of us walk about well wadded with stupidity. . .

The early months of marriage often are times of critical tumult – whether that of a shrimp-pool or of deeper waters – which afterwards subsides into cheerful peace.

These moments of pause simultaneously threaten and highlight the power of historical narrative. It matters little whether the present tense appears rarely or often, so long as it does not fundamentally disturb the main business of the historical narrative, which is to prove that human variety all belongs in one medium and one world. The fact that there is always 'another side to the picture' means that the human world is enlarged to infinity. That is why the endings of novels fully exploiting the historical convention always seem provisional and arbitrary; they are simply one moment more in an infinite horizon.

The 'historical' novel thus has everything to do with a particular construction of time, and nothing essential to do with antiquarian subject matter. This point is worth a moment's attention, because usage of the phrase 'historical novel' has tended to emphasize precisely period costume. By the present definition, however, *virtually all nineteenth-century social novels are historical novels* because they exploit fully the powers of the past tense. Although some among those novels make special use of formally historical material – say, the beheading of Charles I, the battle of Culloden, the Renaissance, the French Revolution, the state Church, or the railways – that material does not of itself make them historical novels.

Historical novels that do make such special use of historical material often focus on traumatic moments in political and cultural life: especially the process of religious and political change that established the libertarian culture so valuable to a prosperous nineteenth century. John Henry Newman's *Callista* (1856) or Cardinal Wiseman's *Fabiola* (1854), both in early Christian settings, enable their authors to focus on prejudice against Catholics; Trollope actually invents a Bill of Disestablishment of the English Church as part of his fictional experiment in *Phineas Redux* (1873–4). The political turmoil attending the Renaissance is the context of George Eliot's *Romola* (1862–63); the beheading of Charles I figures in Henry Shorthouse's *John Inglesant* (1881); the French Revolution, and by comparison the English Peace, contextualizes domestic affairs in Charles Dickens' *A Tale of Two Cities* (1859).

This historical habit can be traced most importantly to Walter Scott; for example, the eighteenth-century wars of succession in his *Waverley, or One Hundred Years Hence* (1814) provide an opportunity to consider the politically charged idea that, in a unified Britain, all points of view require accommodation. His novels focus on those political differences that Britain, in order to *be* Britain, simply had to mediate. But such novels are not primarily rhetorical narratives; they are histories that use particular details, whether remote or familiar, to show that everything is mutually related 'in' time, and to show how the laws of historical and social development appear in and can be derived from local detail. The historical novelist cares about the emergence of identity and the conditions of that emergence, not the antiquarian details of a past era for their own sake.

Not surprisingly, then, the same issues to be found in such antiquarian novels usually can be found in the rest of an author's work. The historical material in *A Tale of Two Cities* functions, as social conditions often function in Dickens, as a background of social chaos against which shines a foreground of saving (presumably socially saving) negotiation, for the sake of domestic love and between men from different sites on the social spectrum; the story of Sydney Carton's sacrifice for love has the same chiaroscuro, looming, urban presence, the same rude mechanicals, the same great descriptions of travelling that characterize other Dickens novels. George Eliot's *Romola* links background events in Renaissance Florence, particularly the negotiation between religious, political and intellectual powers, to private dramas of betrayal and self-deceit; but the public effects of private narcissism, the inner processes of self-betrayal, and the consequences of choice are the same in this setting in the dawn of modern society as in her later novels.

What makes such novels historical, again, is not their dated material. They are historical because they exploit the past-tense narrative's full powers of mediation and projection; because they constitute a common time in which for the first time a single, human world can be treated experimentally, in itself and not in a 'higher' providential scheme. Comparison over wide periods of history, so the convention goes, yields the laws that govern personal and social forms, and thus the power to predict and even control those forms as they evolve in the future. The point of using antiquarian subject matter is to demonstrate as dramatically as possible the continuity of the present with the past and, therefore, the universality (i.e. the 'naturalness') of the laws of social experience: a point that is emphasized by antique dress but not determined by it. If currency of subject matter were determining, we would no longer be interested in books like Trollope's *The Way We Live Now* (1874–5) or George Eliot's *Daniel Deronda* (1876). What made these two novels 'contemporary' in their time was their use of a grammar of perspective. Particular subject matter simply specifies in a particular way that historical convention.

Historical narrative answers a need for mediation that is particularly acute in the nineteenth century. The loss of faith in cosmic unity, the new horizons opened by geological, biological and physical sciences, the uncertain enterprise of achieving social unity during a nineteenth century haunted by revolution elsewhere, all cause upheaval in the very basis of social order and create a need, even an anxious need, for new forms of mediation. History, with its social face, is one answer to that need, providing a mediation between past and future that reformulates in new terms age-old problems of identity and relationship. The ancient religious problem of mediation is historicized and becomes a social problem. The convention of historical veracity develops such prestige that it becomes a prime means for conveying messages to young readers, even though, as some commentators have noted, veracity itself was not always important (Grafton and Jardine, 1986: 220; Rowbotham, 1989: 152).

This narrative continuum, then, in which consciousness, time and language mix inextricably, literally *constitutes* historical time in the same way that single-point perspective literally constitutes realistic space in Renaissance painting. This can be a problematic point to grasp, not because it is so difficult but because it is counter-intuitive. It is, to put it in other terms, a representation of God's time as Newton conceived it; even now for many of us this just *is* time, and we have trouble seeing it as something constructed and, therefore, fragile and itself vulnerable to historical mutability. In multitudes of narrative sequences nineteenth-century narrative constructs historical time by reuniting all temporal perspectives in one sequence to create single-point perspective in time. This narrative continuum that binds together time and consciousness, this historical medium is the narrative equivalent of pictorial realism. A realistic narrative is by definition a historical narrative. The sequence literally threads together a whole series of moments and perspectives into one system and one act of attention.

The commitments that this narrative convention entails run very deep, in part because of a promise implicit in realistic convention: a promise of almost superhuman powers of generalization and objectivity that will enable us to subsume or eradicate whatever is inexplicable or mysterious. In a convention that extends to infinity the rationalized powers of human attention, no atrocity need remain unexplained, no mystery unsolved, no mistake unrectified. Some may remain unexplained; but they *need* not. The medium of creation extends potentially to infinity, or as far as our own creative courage may take us. Realism's link with humanism is nowhere more evident.

Keeping in mind the analogy with Dutch realist (and for that matter Renaissance realist) space, we can formulate as follows the crucial principles for constructing historical time:

1 History, the temporal form of realism, is a grammar of perspective whereby it becomes possible, through a consensus of views (like that visible in single-point perspective painting), to construct not objects but a medium: a neutral, homogeneous time analogous to the space of Michelangelo and Raphael. It is the time of Newton and Kant, the time of empiricism and history. What it takes to construct this medium, and therefore this kind of identity, is that founding consensus of views evident in single-point perspective systems, where every point of view implicitly agrees with every other in the sense that they all view the 'same' world.

2 Only in such a medium is it possible to perceive (i.e. to construct) 'objects' in the modern sense. From planets and starfish, and from 'self' to 'society', the objects of realism and history emerge in a series of manifestations, 'objectified' by the fact that they belong to one, not several, systems of explanation. Instead of seeking identity as a medieval historian would have done in the exact congruence

between one case and its prototype (Ermarth, 1983: ch. 1), the modern writer looks for identity in the series that at the same time seems to 'produce' identity. And as each little history is embedded 'in' a larger series, and ultimately 'in' history, that single-point perspective system in time thus literally objectifies the world.

3 The tantalizing circularity of such a convention requires attention. This supposedly objective world is itself constructed by the very perspective system that supposedly views it. Even more tantalizing in the temporal version of single-point perspective is the ambiguous inseparability of time, consciousness and language: never any one without the others.

The interest of historical and realist narrative lies in the abstraction that rationalizes perception. It asserts a communality or mutual relatedness across all time as a kind of promise that every act takes its place in a larger structure of significance. Despite appearances to the contrary, history does not focus on this or that object (individual, encounter, town, promise, act, event) but instead on the construction of a neutral medium for which those objects are only the carriers. The primary 'object' represented in historical narrative is, like the space represented by Saenredam, the time that is common and neutral. 'In' these media of modernity it becomes possible to make mutually informative measurements between things apparently unrelated to each other, and thus to consider the entire world as a single arena of relationship. What is being represented in nineteenth-century narrative, then, is nothing less than the power of representation itself. The abstraction of history lies, not in the particulars which populate it, but in the temporal medium they occupy; and in the assertion implicit in such media that the world is one system of mutual relevance. To have brought history to this state of importance was the work of centuries, but by 1850 almost all literate people had absorbed it.

MEDIATE POWER

The power of the temporal medium, its mediating capacity, has a fascinating double life in narrative. Putatively neutral and 'natural' as air, the time of history nevertheless appears in narrative as a phenomenon of language and consciousness. The events that readers of historical narrative interpret are themselves events of interpretation. In historical narrative all events are events of awareness, of articulation, of language. The interpolated narrative medium becomes itself an object of focus and attention, a function to be dealt with, a feature of the world.

As the last section suggested, the interest of historical narrative lies in the shift from one perspective to another: the shift that constitutes the neutral temporal medium. As the vantage shifts constantly in time from one position to another, the reader enjoys the delicious slide from perspective to perspective that gradually but surely aligns disparate and apparently conflicting variety into a single sequence of time and consciousness. What the narrative represents is this mediation.

A shift of viewpoint is not in itself new to nineteenth-century fiction; we find it rampant in Sterne and Richardson and throughout the eighteenth-century, where the preferred narrative sequence lacks precisely the coordination, the grammar of perspective that historical narrative confers. Eighteenth-century novels consisting of letters or journals prevent from forming the crucial hindsight that maintains the rationalized system of historical relationship. In epistolary time, relationships get scrambled, letters get forged or lost. Twentieth-century narratives from *Ulysses* onwards often also have similarly unmediated sequences that require readers to perform for themselves the crucial interpretive act of mediation between one viewpoint, one moment, and another.

But in nineteenth-century historical narrative that very mediation – that crucial negotiation of the shifts in viewpoint – is *itself* represented in the text. With 'meanwhile' clauses, witty commentary, and full orchestration of the grammar of perspective, historical narrative oversees the steps between one moment and another, and thus maintains the mutual relatedness of all the world. Situated in the middle distance, the floating abstraction, the Nobody narrator that remembers impersonally but in detail, enacts an extended invisible community of consciousness in time, a community that extends to the reader. This power of rationalized consciousness, putatively 'in' time, actually constructs time as the neutral medium we have come to take for granted and that is far, far more powerful than any personalized narrator.

It is precisely this medium that distinguishes the nineteenth-century social novel from the work of a writer like Fielding. Fielding's historian-narrator in *Tom Jones*, for example, declares his crabby idiosyncrasy in much the way Sterne's narrators do, but the world the reader negotiates belongs not to any mediation provided by this reader-accomplice, but to a highly artificial, even geometrical plot based on epic style and calculated with almost mathematical regularity. Three books, corresponding to Departure, Journey and Arrival, each contain two volumes of three sections each, exactly balancing episodes so that, for instance, Section

Two opens with Sophia pursuing Tom and ends with Tom pursuing Sophia. The author uses interpolated tales and other frame devices to bring the narrative frequently to a 'dead halt' (Goldknopf, 1972: 134) in order to emphasize symbolic, not historical values.

This is Cervantes, English style; and a glorious book it is. But it is not historical narrative. Trollope reflects on this consideration concerning Fielding, when he says that the plot of *Tom Jones* is 'almost perfect' but that, nevertheless, 'good plot . . . is the most insignificant part of a tale' (Trollope, 1993: 115). What Trollope finds important is the proportion that ensures that each subsidiary plot, each part and character, shall 'take their places as part of one and the same work – as there may be many figures on a canvas which shall not to the spectator seem to form themselves into separate pictures' (ibid.: 217). Fielding's experiment with the mediate powers of the narrator makes his *Amelia* an oddly fascinating novel; but that is not where Fielding's greatness lies (a similar point could be made about Thackeray's *Henry Esmond*).

'The narrator' is really only a name for the most powerful function of the historical convention: one that – it bears repeating – precisely can *not* be individualized. Always in the future of every action simply by virtue of the fact that every action in the past tense has already happened, and at the same time always present and always realized in every narrated moment, 'the' so-called narrator is really a discursive function that maintains the link between now and then: a function that maintains the single-point perspective system in time. This function of the narrative language literally represents consciousness collected into a commanding structure of mutual awareness and significance. The consanguinity in such narrative between time, consciousness and language only serves to emphasize the oneness of the world: the faith that all consciousness is potentially consciousness of 'the same' world; that all languages are but dialects of a common human power of exchange.

The narrative style is thus a kind of promise of extended power through solidarity. In spatial terms, the implication is that, if we were not too limited, too busy, too lazy, or too old, we could see everything simply by moving around infinitely in space; but given human limitation we rely on the sights seen by others, their testimony, their satellites, their camerapersons, to supplement and extend what we can see. The same implication holds for consciousness in time; if we were not too busy, too lazy, or too old, too mortal, potentially we could become conscious of everything without ever leaving our chair, so exchangeable is consciousness and so infinite its time.

In novels, then, the grammar of perspective works through the mediating function of what has often been naturalized as 'the narrator' but which is not so individual a function as that term suggests. Occasionally this power takes on individual features to express a prejudice or speak in the first person, but generally it appears as a reflex of the past tense, as the power to include all narrative voices in a single, common temporal horizon. Neither Godlike nor consistently individual, the narrative perspective vacillates inclusively in a middle range of possibility. This feat of mediation itself, and not the more particular descriptions that support it, constitutes the chief representation of the historical and realist text. And an heroic feat it is, in the face of the prolixity and apparent chaos of the social and human world, to assert that this world is one.

While we take the historical medium for granted when we read a realistic novel, what we are really doing is accepting and confirming the humanist belief – and it is no more or less than an arbitrary and breathtaking act of faith – that our powers of collective agreement literally make possible historical continuity. In the realistic medium, a contradiction is merely an incompletely grasped relationship, and one that implicitly may be resolved at a higher level of understanding. The consciousness required for transcending particulars in this way is everywhere in general and nowhere in particular: linked with individual awareness at various points but always exceeding them. The power of this consciousness is Nobody's power: at once human and unspecific, present but not individualized. In realistic novels our sense of a network, a system of relationships, a balance between parts of an immense and complex and always changing social entity, emerges precisely in this reflex from one moment and one consciousness to another. The narrative sequence of realism literally engenders the very consciousness that interprets it (Ermarth, 1983: 65–92).

Before turning to particular narrative passages, one final comment about the profundity of this nearly invisible narrator-function. This complex treatment of perspective embodies the collective awareness of a culture, perhaps even the self-consciousness of the species, but in any case an invisible community of awareness that, in each novel, transcends the particular moment at the same time as it finds expression there. This blend of consciousness, time and language does not belong exclusively to any character or even to the historical author; the entire range of narrative awareness constitutes it; its narrative expression is precisely Nobody.

In social novels the mediating function of this 'Nobody' narrator takes on crucial importance, even to the point of becoming the main representation of the text. Take, for example, the following passage from Trollope's *Barchester Towers* (1857). Here the Nobody narrator directly addresses one of the characters, the virtuous Mr Harding: a man so timid of confrontation that he cannot even bring himself to speak to his own daughter the few, obvious words that would clear up a rapidly compounding misinterpretation concerning her civility to the odious Mr Slope. Eleanor, for her part, intensely dislikes Mr Slope, but local gossip has her on the brink of wedlock with him. Mr Harding cannot bring himself to ask her directly. The narrative characteristically alternates between perspectives, including Harding's view, and Eleanor's, as well as a more distanced one. At one point, as if in exasperation, the narrating voice addresses the character of Mr Harding directly:

> Ah, thou weak man; most charitable, most Christian, but weakest of men! Why couldst thou not have asked herself? Was she not the daughter of thy loins, the child of thy heart, the best beloved to thee of all humanity? Had she not proved to thee, by years of closest affection, her truth and goodness and filial obedience? And yet, knowing and feeling all this, thou couldst endure to go groping in darkness, hearing her named in strains which wounded thy loving heart and being unable to defend her as thou shouldst have done!
>
> (Trollope, 1982: 274, ch. 28)

This is what those seeking to personalize the narrative function would call 'authorial intrusion'. An apostrophe of this nature would be considered a 'break' if one was thinking of such narrative in terms of plot; but here such a turn of language and consciousness is merely another position in a sequence which at once establishes the unmediated gaps *between* one perspective and another and, at the same time *and by that very act*, links those same, disparate perspectives. After giving Mr Harding a shake, the narrative then returns to its normal and more neutral business of representing Harding's viewpoint ('He wanted to believe her incapable of such a marriage') and of commenting on it ('Nothing but affection could justify such fickleness, but affection did justify it').

In context, such a passage has all the additional force given it by compounding plot lines and anticipations, in which various mistakes require correction and various conflicting versions must be reconciled so that the social ceremony of Barchester can be renewed. Where a particular point of view becomes too insistent or immoderate it develops sufficient energy to threaten the community; then it must be colonized or, in radical cases, exported, as in the case of Mr Slope's evangelical stringency or Madeline Neroni's suffering and laser-like perceptiveness. All the points and counterpoints of awareness, the reflex of each character's mind at each stage of the sequence, together with the independent narrative voice that addresses Mr Harding, all are perspectives coordinated by the single, abstract, historical reflex. Just as all spaces are coordinated as one space in Saenredam, so all times are one common time in Trollope, one common system of explanation for a common world.

The excerpt from Trollope also reveals how complex a perspective-consensus can be in language. The quasi-Biblical vocabulary and rhythms of the apostrophe provide a voice that certainly is not the voice of the final distanced comment, nor even of Mr Harding's normal speech: but rather closer, perhaps, to the archaic Biblical language that belongs to communal tradition and that may be one reason why he is so entangled in his mind as to be unable to see to the end of his nose. This language offers an especially good example of how the narrating consciousness represents a character's possibilities – potentials of that particular mind that might be realized if only some of its crippling habits were loosened. With its power of distanced hindsight, the historical narrative here creates a kind of aura of awareness that Mr Harding himself could and should reach, and even would expect himself to reach. Both in the Biblical language, and in the more capacious past-tense narrative that encloses it, the very language invokes perspectives that belong not to this or that individual, or even to a focalized narrator, but to a potentiality of the system that is at once realizable and as yet unrealized.

Such multilaminations of perspective in the narrative language, and the ironies and undertows of interpretation they momentarily create and abandon, account in large measure for the distinctive pleasure of reading historical sequences. The centripetal pull of the historical mediation contains the centrifugal propensies of various perspectives and produces a harmony not unlike that of a symphonic ensemble: the more specialized the voice, the richer and more complex the final harmony. The possibilities of poor timing, stray motives, and sheer numbers of episodes (nineteenth-century social novels are almost always very long), sustain various dissonances and conflicts that keep the harmonies and resolutions from being easy. This tension is at least partly responsible for the kind of chronic, low-grade risibility that so often accompanies such historical narration.

Because we have become so accustomed to taking these conventions for granted, it is worth considering another, similar example of stylistically complex narrative perspective. This one comes from George Eliot's *Felix Holt* (1866), and describes Esther Lyon through a sliding perspective in a way similar to that of the passage just discussed. The language performs a sort of *glissando* that operates unpredictably between various vantage points, ranging from one so favourable as to seem close to the character's own at her worst, to one very critical of her, and including ones in between.

> Her own pretty instep, clad in a silk stocking, her little heel, just rising from a kid slipper, her irreproachable nails and delicate wrist, were the objects of delighted consciousness to her; and she felt that it was her superiority which made her unable to use without disgust any but the finest cambric handkerchiefs and freshest gloves. Her money all went in the gratification of these nice tastes, and she saved nothing from her earnings. I cannot say that she had any pangs of conscience on this score; for she felt sure that she was generous: she hated all meanness, would empty her purse impulsively on some sudden appeal to her pity, and if she found out that her father had a want, she would supply it with some pretty device of a surprise. But then the good man so seldom had a want – except the perpetual desire, which she could never gratify, of seeing her under convictions, and fit to become a member of the church.
>
> As for little Mr. Lyon, he loved and admired this unregenerate child more, he feared than was consistent with the due preponderance of impersonal and ministerial regards.
>
> (Eliot, 1972: 159–60, ch. 6)

In this passage there is no dialogue, so the language 'belongs' to the narrator, but within that range that narrator is neither single nor still; instead it is a function of language and consciousness, ever-present, ever-mediate, ever-multiplied. Various perspectives require mediation: the dangerously narcissistic viewpoint of Esther Lyon at her worst; the uncritical attitude of the adoring father who yet sees her failure at least partially; and the critical perspective of Esther's own behaviour which here belongs to 'nobody', or to that collected power of the narrative system – the collective awareness – for which Felix Holt sometimes speaks. A kind of aura of possible awareness accompanies even the narrowest consciousness, shadowing it with wider possibility.

This language is both personal ('I cannot say that she had any pangs of conscience on this score') and not personal ('Her money all went'). Such language can move attention within wider or narrower regions of intelligence or irony with a mere turn of phrase – as, for example, with the 'irreproachable nails': a phrase that incorporates Esther's own trivial pride in her manicure with some ineffable criticism. Such narrative does not step off the edge of the social world, as Dickens sometimes does when he points to eternity; this moves outward only as far as history will allow ('she saved nothing from her earnings') and then turns down the lane of Mr Lyon's mixed fears concerning his own affection, which he doubts is consistent 'with the due preponderance of ministerial and impersonal regards', and does so in a language that has the stalwart but somewhat airless earnestness of Rufus Lyon's gentle orthodoxy.

Recorded as the past tense, each sentence communicates that what 'is' the case has, from the wider vantage point, already happened and thus already taken its place in a commanding structure of significance. This formal possibility George Eliot thoroughly exploits by attending to the way that consequences of actions shape our ability to act. Close to a character's mind but not identical with it, the narrative continuously creates a kind of aura for characters consisting of what they are and what they might be, and an assertion of relationship between the one and the other. At the widest angle, the narrative inclusiveness asserts that, however different or apparently unrelated particular events or persons may seem, they are mutually relevant because, for better or worse, they belong to a single system of relationship, a single system of explanation and, perhaps, are capable of being mutually conscious.

In both Trollope and George Eliot, then, the language and the sequence ask us to attend not to events and characters but to the perception of events and characters – in short, to the act of historical attention. We cannot properly call it 'the narrator' because in effect it is a power of supervision, even surveillance, that by definition attends the grammar of temporal perspective (historical narrative), as it engages us in the act of narrative mediation, the pleasing slide of consciousness from one site to another in an apparently infinite range of 'human' awareness. Once that narrative medium is put into question, as it is in twentieth-century narrative, once we start asking after the motives of a Trollopian narrator, we are in the world of the underground man and Humbert Humbert. But the nineteenth–century historical function does not have that opacity precisely because it is not personalizeable. Even at its most personalized moments, such as those when Dickens' narrator speaks, as if from nowhere, the ultimate pronouncements of social failure ('Dead! my lords and ladies, Dead!'), the voice specifies not a single perspective, but a perspective system. All historical novelists provide this medium in varying ways.

This medium George Meredith explicitly identifies as what he calls the Comic Spirit: a floating presence of consciousness existing quite apart from individuals. It is a power of culture: a kind of civilized medium for social awareness contrasting with the barbarisms of the class system. It is distinctly and explicitly gender-neutral. Described in his 1877 *An Essay on Comedy*, and deployed explicitly in *The Egoist* (1879) as well as implicitly in many of his other books, the Comic Spirit is the power of seeing differences between a limited horizon and a wider one. This cultural 'emanation' calls attention precisely to the narrator-function, which is to shift unceasingly from one parochialism to another, mediating between them and providing context and second perspectives to what would otherwise be absolute, 'natural', timeless as Proust's church at Combray. Some peoples, says Meredith (speaking in this case of the Germans) may not see 'the sly, wise emanation eyeing them from aloft'; but peoples who are truly civilized possess a kind of cultural aura, or discursive power, that arises from two essential conditions: the presence of intellectual interest, and equality between the sexes. No society without these is truly civilized.

This 'wise emanation' is neither individual nor personal, as the inadequate term, 'the narrator', implies. It is a power to view oneself and one's situation from more than one viewpoint:

> You may estimate your capacity for comic perception by being able to detect the ridicule of them you love without loving them less; and more by being able to see yourself somewhat ridiculous in dear eyes, and accepting the correction their image of you proposes.

This Comic Spirit depends absolutely upon intellectual development, and upon equality between the sexes: 'a society of cultivated men and women is required, wherein ideas are current, and the perceptions quick, that he may be supplied with matter and an audience. The semi-barbarism of giddy communities, and feverish emotional periods, repel him; and also a state of marked social inequality between the sexes' (Meredith, 1956: 53; 42; 3). Like the historical narrator, The Comic Spirit is a medium constituted specifically by the joining together of what a segregated society puts asunder. Meredith, who certainly was not oblivious to the social functions of class, insists that it is gender segregation, not class division or, in his day, race division, that lies at the root of cultural failure.

The capacity represented by the Comic Spirit in Meredith exactly resembles the 'Nobody' narrator, except that it appears more in spatial than in temporal terms. But the powers are the same: the power to recollect not just this or that life, but collective life; a power at once human and at the same time abstracted; a power that is systemic, not personal. Considered temporally, it is the power of hindsight always present in historical narrative that guarantees the present will evolve manageably into a future. Seeing more widely and keeping several trains of thought together in one sequence, the 'Nobody' narrator is a capacity of a social entity, something that in the nineteenth century is being experimentally tried.

Dickens shows in the narrative experiment of *Bleak House* the dangers of segregating the two functions of history. In this novel, the powers of historical Nobody narrative are divided between two separate narrations, one with a capacity for oversight but no memory, and the other with a memory but insufficient oversight. The narrative itself creates a fractured condition that is replicated and echoed in every corner of a moribund society. For the social entity to function *as* an entity, the whole structural and narratological implication of *Bleak House* announces that these two capacities must work together. Otherwise, the social entity cannot function. The two dispositions of historical narration, oversight and recall, are necessary to produce the representational effect: the perception that everyone lives in one and 'the same' world. Segregation of any kind, whether by gender or economic power, effectively gives the lie to this power of representation.

The historical medium begins to attenuate in novels toward the end of the nineteenth century. In George Gissing's novels, say, for example, *The New Grub Street* (1891), there is an almost Dickensian sense of time running out, and yet the sense of temporal connection between events often becomes quite tenuous: lost in the endless series of mismatches and misconceptions that plague those trying to live a deep life in a shallow world. Even though his scenes and voices are particular enough, it is difficult to 'locate' them in terms of a meaningful sequence, even though the historical convention as he uses it still continues to assert their relationship. Thomas Hardy still uses this narrative system, though ironically or tragically.

Because its purpose is to connect what fails of connection, historical novels positively emphasize rifts to be healed and gaps to be bridged. Without breakdowns in communication owing to individual stupidity, inexperience and corruption, the historical convention would have no room to show its power to connect. The business of historical narrative is precisely to overcome such failure. Dickens especially exploits class division for this purpose. 'What connexion is there', asks the narrative voice, between the orphan boy sweeping the slum crosswalk and the beautiful, haughty Lady Dedlock (*Bleak House*); between the snob and the stranger (*Our Mutual Friend*); between a criminal and a boy attempting to get ahead in the world (*Great Expectations*)? His novels exist to show the connections between these, and in general the human connectedness of the social world. It is in the very splits between high and low, poverty and wealth, motion and rest, that we can discover the unity of the social entity. All historical novelists pursue these problems of social connection; some, like Dickens and Mrs Gaskell, take up a vantage point at the margins of society and at the limits of time, others, like Trollope and George Eliot, pursue them from vantage points well within the range of social experience.

It is worth recalling here that mid-Victorian realism is exceptional in the history of narrative (Alter, 1975), and that this historical convention was *not* common even among novelists early in the mid-nineteenth century. In fact, history was regarded as something of a non-starter even in the 1850s when Trollope, carrying a manuscript to a publisher, was advised: 'I hope it's not historical, Mr. Trollope?' he said. 'Whatever you do, don't be historical; your historical novel is not worth a damn' (Trollope, 1993: 101). Even in mid-century, historical narrative structures had to be justified. Trollope's work did much to change that. So did Mudie's Circulating Library, a very large portion of whose stock, perhaps as much as half, was historical writing either as history, biography, or novels (Griest, 1970: 20–5, ch. 3).

Up until mid-century the popular narratives of the time rely on parody and satire, or invoke gothic magic, or rely on the picaresque, or are patterned by sequences already well established and understood – as, for example, a pilgrim's progress. These are not narratives that require a neutral temporal arena. There is no history in *Wuthering Heights*, a novel where a reader has a hard time finding out what time it is. For example, after a fairly intense close-up series during the first half of the novel, the first Catherine dies and twelve years disappear from view; they are simply mentioned, and the narrative continues as if twelve years ago was yesterday. Several years pass unremarked during two pages describing young Linton Heathcliff's misery, and then one year takes forty pages. Even these calculations are made with difficulty, and generally readers find it virtually impossible – and in the end boring – to determine the kind of systematic relationships that would allow them to say that one event takes place at roughly the 'same' time as another. But, of course, time has no importance at The Heights, either in characters or between them; time alters little. The puerile attempts of Lockwood, a potential narrator, to mark the time seem increasingly parodic: a desperate gambit of an uninteresting man to control what is uncontrollable. There is no history here.

Nor is there in Thackeray. His habit of inventing narrators, for example, tends to swamp historical perspective; he uses perspective in the manner of satirists to fracture everything rather than to construct a common medium in which the emergent forms of social life might become apparent. In *Vanity Fair* these Thackerayan narrators in turn constantly introduce third parties not involved in the action: a possible rich aunt ('I wish you would send me an old aunt. . . . ' (Thackeray, 1963: 87, ch. 9)); or fashionable news ('When my friend the fashionable John Pimlico, married the lovely Lady Belgravia Green Parker. . . . ' (ibid.: 152, ch. 16)); or a family named Jenkins ('What is Jenkins? – we all know – Commissioner. . . . ' (ibid.: 350, ch. 36)). The net effect is to annoy and confuse a reader who, as one student put it, is 'trying to determine who is a character in the novel and who is not'. This cast of extras do not fill in a common horizon, as they do in George Eliot's or Dickens' novels; on the contrary, the variety has a deliberately distracting and digressive influence. It belongs to the realm of parodic undercut and satire, not the realm of historical possibility. Such narrative refuses to readers the 'distance' that history grants. Instead, readers constantly find themselves yanked into the text and asked to arbitrate, rather than merely to view arbitration.

The historical convention allows for an immense range and variety. George Eliot's history involves a rhythmic shift of attention that stays 'well within the range of relevancies', but conceives of that range in the broadest terms culturally; Dickens' narrative perspective remains at the margins of the social world, mainly the English social world, and his holism is focused much more consistently on the issues of wealth and class. History moves in minutiae in Margaret Oliphant's hands, sometimes so slowly as to generate impatience. Elizabeth Gaskell's histories tend more towards episodic vignette than dramatic tension. History in George Meredith is saturated with consciousness and comic spirit. Anthony Trollope holds steady at a middle distance in the centre of one social class. Thomas Hardy's schizoid narrative perspective alternates anxiously between distance and immersion in a world where the middle range must often be forfeited.

But in all historical novels the central effect remains the same, as a shifting perspective repeatedly enacts connectedness in time and thus brings into being the common order of things, with its causalities, its recoveries of the past, its projections of the future. This mediating consciousness, a phenomenon of time and language, literally constitutes history even as it appears to take it for granted. The ambiguities, problems and paradoxes of the historical convention are considerable. History is the most deceptively palpable of abstractions (Ermarth, 1992: 25–44). One way to express the distinctive paradoxes of historical thinking is to say that its relativism is absolute. It allows no possibility of relativity in the scientific sense. Single-point perspective creates a neutral and infinite medium so inclusive that it amounts to a categorical imperative. The idea of history allows for no bounds, no difference; it claims universality; it even may become assimilated with cosmic time which is 'natural'. Yet historical time is constructed of 'founding subjects', as Michel Foucault called them, and belongs to a particular phase of European culture.

The bonding of time and consciousness in historical narrative is yet another of its mysteries that we have scarcely attempted to fathom. And another is the problem of teleological motive which, because of Christian antecedents, seems hard to avoid in historical thinking even though hypothetically it allows massively for the action of chance. The idea of progress is one such teleological expression, where historical process is defined as the fulfilment of some implicit 'structure'. A final problem is the one raised by Lyotard (1988: 63–5) in his critique of the consensus vehicle as a 'terrorist apparatus' determining who speaks and who keeps silent: something that forecloses on radical difference by claims to universal inclusiveness; as Chapter Four will suggest, such claims to inclusiveness are in many cases demonstrably false.

The historical convention's paradoxes are not easily sorted, especially not by historical novelists, and especially not when the convention itself acts so successfully to mask its own artificiality. Such ambiguities and problems, while they raise logical difficulties, also account for the staying power of that humanist grammar of mediation that underlies the historical narrative. Humanism has immense powers to recover everything, however disparate and contradictory, into its formal consensus, its agreement that the world is One and thus rationalizeable (Robbe-Grillet, 1989: 51). Such thinking lends itself to democratic political thought; it also lends itself to imperialism of the sort that determines to spread the benefits of civilization from one place to another, 'Imperialism was an assertion of the right of Government over other lands and peoples, and behind this assertion, in the last resort, lay a theory of human destiny, and interpretation of history' (Cobban, 1966: 327): not just a theory of the progressive superiority of British ways however, but also, however paradoxical the results of imperialism made it, a theory of the solidarity of the human species.

One assertion made by the historical convention that should be kept in view here is its assertion about language. The question of whether English is a common language, and common to whom, is a deeply political question, and not just in England but also internationally, as the empire requires more input and attention. Historical texts assert that language, like time and potentially even consciousness, is a common denominator, a medium shared among the most disparate individuals. Language is a 'common' medium in various senses: it includes the language of common people, in all its rich variety of dialect and inflection; and language is common in the sense of shared, a property that belongs to everyone in spite of local sub-definitions. Dickens, Gaskell and George Eliot incorporate into this common medium dialects of urban poor or Midland farmers; Trollope includes specialized class inflection, like the drawl of the aristocrat or the nuance of the conversation that exerts power. But the inclusive historical narration asserts that these different dialects not only belong in a common language, they *constitute* the common language: that the shared language, like the shared world, is constituted by such differences, not by their exclusion. This runs entirely athwart the hierarchical construction of 'society' that creates local communities, clubs, clans by means of exclusion, not inclusion.

The emphasis on historical time as a common medium seems to have been a largely European phenomenon in the nineteenth century, not an American one. We find it in the novels of Stendhal, Balzac and Flaubert, of Tolstoy and Turgenev, of Trollope and George Eliot. But we do not find it in the novels of Hawthorne, Cooper, Melville or even Mark Twain. The dark romances and allegorical stories of Hawthorne and Melville are portentous and riven by mysterious, often evil, forces outside of social control. Their 'Nature' is a constant preoccupation and source of energy, albeit sometimes destructive or ungrounded energy. The medium of common life, in the form of realist and historical narrative, had to rest its claim on the meagre achievement of writers like William Dean Howells. The sensibility to which this mythic narrative appeals is religious and apocalyptic. In it, Carlyle continues alive and well, living in Boston Massachusetts. Their space and time seem more like those of medieval cosmology than those media of modernity constructed according to a grammar of perspective and serving humanist agendas. For all its documentary and theoretical confirmation of democracy; for all its inscription of narratives of common weal implied in the powerful political documents written between 1776 and 1840, the United States continues to produce novels that fracture the very grammar of temporal perspective, and that disturb the very neutral medium of historical time that supports the notion of a common weal in the first place. One clue to this apparent oddity, a democratic society without the media of common public function, can be found in the naturalizing language of the revolutionary documents of the 1770s, where the rights of 'man' are asserted to be 'natural' and 'self-evident'. This does not encourage citizens to think of themselves as constituents of a common weal so much as claimants on a treasury stored up, either in heaven or in 'Nature'.

The historical novel enacts the socialization of consciousness. The mainstream Victorian novel inscribes, codifies, explores, and generally rubs into the grain of discourse this collected medium, this consciousness indistinguishable from collective historical memory. History is a social medium, a blend of time and consciousness and language, that provides the very basis of social order. Novels represent only one specification of the historical grammar of perspective. In the political ideas of John Stuart Mill and the Reform Parliaments, in the work of physical scientists like Lyell and Darwin, we can find the same discursive strategies at work: similar ideas of sequence, identity and relationship. But by far the most widely shared exploration of this discursive possibility was historical literature like novels, autobiography, and social and political histories of everything from feudalism to the French Revolution.

EMERGENT FORM

An essential premise of the grammar of perspective is that identity is series-dependent: not just revealed in a series (epistolary novels like Richardson's *Clarissa* do that), but dependent upon the collected result of a series. The identity of a person or a society, that is, of any entity in time, exists only in, and nowhere apart from, a collection of mutually inter-dependent expressions. The more various the expressions of the entity, whether individual or social, the more powerful is the generalization (the identity) that informs and unites them. Identity that emerges only serially, like a cone from conic sections, has a potentially dynamic quality that Victorian novels exploit to the tenth power. All forms of identity are emergent forms, necessarily generalized and abstracted from particulars. When identity thus floats between particulars, and can only be discovered comparatively and serially, then the moment has arrived for the Victorian social novel with its endless evolutionary experiments.

Such novels gain their momentum and suspense from questions about mutual relationship in a shared, common world. What is the relation between the coddled boy and the failed husband in Meredith's novel, *The Ordeal of Richard Feverel* (1859)? What is the relation between the young lady at the roulette wheel and the passerby who observes her, in Chapter One of George Eliot's *Daniel Deronda* (1876)? What is the relation in Trollope's *Phineas Finn* (1869) between Phineas Finn, MP for Loughshane in Ireland (Chapter One), and Lady Laura Standish of a good English family (Chapter Two)? The mutual relevance of these particulars, as of all details in the shifting course of a historical sequence, becomes clarified only gradually. The results remain in suspension as the yet-unclear forms emerge.

This confidence in the deep structures of social discourse, and faith in their possible mutations, support a range of cultural experiments in the nineteenth century: from social legislation, to biological and theological speculation, to painting, Victorians explore the possibilities of emergent form. Historical novelists attend especially to the ways in which past actions formulate present ones, limit them, direct them. As has just been indicated, they support the narrative medium by shifting perspective so as to consider the ambiguities of half-formed subjects and groups in-process. George Eliot's narrative sequences anatomize how individual choices constitute and alter identity. The identities she has in mind are not only individual characters but also whole social groups, and in fact the very existence of society as an entity. In *Middlemarch, A Study of Provincial Life* (1871–2) we watch not only the evolution of Dorothea Brooke from a state of selfless ignorance, and the consequences of sexist carelessness in Dr Tertius Lydgate, but we witness as well more broadly distributed forms of social experience: different ways of waiting for death, different kinds of temptation, different cases of love problems. All her novels emphasize the encounter between systems, the surprise influence that determines a course of events. Certain social developments follow from the moment in *Adam Bede* (1859) when the artisan shifts his standing with the local squire by knocking him down. In *Daniel Deronda* (1876), social determinations follow from the crossing of paths between the English gentleman and the Jewish visionary. In these and other ways the historical series produces those cumulative, emergent abstractions called 'individuals' and 'society'. The characteristic multiple-plot structure that divides historical novels (Garrett, 1980) allow writers and readers to look for precisely those moments where personal choice modifies the collective future.

Trollope, in his *Autobiography,* wonders whether his efforts to portray character over several novels will succeed with ordinary readers:

> It was my study that these people, as they grew in years, should encounter the changes which will come upon us all; and I think that I have succeeded. The Duchess of Omnium, when she is playing the part of Prime Minister's wife, is the same woman as that Lady Glencora who almost longs to go off with Burgo Fitzgerald, but yet knows that she will never do so. . . . To do all this thoroughly was in my heart from first to last; but I do not know that the game has been worth the candle. To carry out my scheme I have had to spread my picture over so wide a canvas that I cannot expect that any lover of such art should trouble himself to look at it as a whole. Who will read

Can You Forgive Her? Phineas Finn, Phineas Redux, and *The Prime Minister* consecutively, in order that they may understand the characters of the Duke of Omnium, of Plantagenet Palliser, and of Lady Glencora?

(Trollope, 1993: 168–9)

One gets splendid and enjoyable glimpses of character in each novel, but it is possible fully to *see* his main characters, especially in the Palliser series, only by seeing them through a series that lasts over several novels. The identity of, say, Phineas Finn, MP, appears in his Irishness, in his lack of independent wealth, in his political ambition, in his changing attitude towards women, and eventually in his learned ability to set limits to his own ambition. What Phineas Finn turns out to be is not inconsistent with what we first see, but not evident there either. His various choices and actions are the constituents of what can be perceived as a single form or identity only in the end.

More than most novelists, Trollope characteristically carries over his developments and his characters from one novel to another. In order fully to appreciate Mrs Proudie's death in *The Last Chronicle of Barset* (1867), in all its humour and poignance, one really must know the first of the six Barchester novels, *Barchester Towers*, published ten years earlier. The emergent form in the six Barchester novels, the identity in question, is a rural, English, clerical community, just as the later 'Palliser' novels treat the Parliamentary community in London, aristocratic and arriviste alike. Individual developments constitute that 'form-of-the-whole', but the society as an entity, or as a system of practices, is what Trollope is anatomizing. An individual character like John Eames first appears as a raw but determined country lad in *The Small House at Allington* (1864); but in *The Last Chronicle of Barset* he demonstrates the advantages of his determination as he defies failure and begins to rise in a London world where we at first expect him to fail. Meanwhile, his rival, the slick Adolphus Crosbie, gets what he wants and ends a failure. The emphasis is all on change, on the mutual relations that produce change, and even on the dangers of stasis. The charming Lily Dale stays the same, and the long sequence shows the deep limitations of certain kinds of changeless constancy.

Historical narratives belong to a variety of cultural expression that depends upon a belief in emergent form. Similar discursive agendas can be found elsewhere in the period: in serial publishing, which came into its own in the nineteenth century; in evolutionary, especially Darwinian, science; in the new historical theology; and in narrative painting.

Whether its material is animal, mineral or spiritual, the historical identity is an abstraction, a 'form of the whole' (Whitehead, 1938: 112; Ermarth, 1983: 22–4) that cannot be perceived in any one case, but only in a series of cases.

Serial publication expresses the vast public interest in serial form. This publishing format declares by its very nature the evolutionary possibilities of sequence. Dickens, following on from Walter Scott's example, made a huge financial success from his early episodic narratives, beginning with *Sketches by Boz* (1835–36) and *Pickwick Papers* (1836–37). Serial publication became *the* form of Victorian fiction, more important even than the famous 'three-decker' (named after a kind of battleship). Dickens not only exploited serial publication himself, he urged it on contributors to his journals. Some, like George Eliot and to an extent Trollope, disliked the format; but like it or not, most novelists submitted to it in one form or another (eight volumes, monthly parts). And such publication was not just an English phenomenon; Flaubert, Tolstoy and Henry James join Elizabeth Gaskell, Hardy, Kipling, Reade and the rest of the Victorian novelists publishing in parts.

Much has been made, with justice, of the ways in which the serial format inhibited writers or determined their production (Hamer, 1987; Hughes and Lund, 1991). But the ubiquity and insistence of the format can be read another way. The very idea of mediation evidenced in historical writing may have been inspired by the episodic format of the novel in letters, the most popular narrative form of eighteenth-century novel and evident well into the nineteenth century in epistolary and picaresque novels. In any case, the inspiration for the serial form was broad and cultural, and not limited to the success of a single novelist, even one so influential as Dickens. Even published as single volumes, Victorian novels must still be taken in bits, because they are almost universally composed of relatively short chapters. Despite significant differences in authorial style between George Eliot and Hardy, Gaskell and Meredith, still the process of reading them is virtually the same in each case, being a process of adding incrementally to a single picture, one encompassable a bit at a time. The 'whole' picture unfolds its order, as Trollope says, one element at a time. Serial publication need not be explained by local phenomena; it suits the conditions of discourse in the nineteenth century.

Charles Darwin's evolutionary theories, circulated from the 1840s onwards, were a most powerful Victorian confirmation that identity is series-dependent. By historicizing the explanation of nature, Darwin changes the way human beings are defined. No longer products of special divine acts of creation, no longer heroes and heroines in a providential universe, human beings take their marginal place in Darwin's millennial processes, resting in unvisited tombs and even discovering hereditary ties with apes. Even allowing for the caution that Darwinism was not the only Victorian interpretation of time and development (Bowler, 1989), Darwin's work demonstrates the historical convention at its most powerful and commanding, extending the serial development of forms so far beyond locality that they appear always in process and without imaginable origin or end.

The ground had been prepared before Darwin, in large part by Charles Lyell's *Principles of Geology* (1830) and Robert Chambers's *Vestiges of Creation* (1844). Historical explanations of the earth's creation and development, while not necessarily presented as conflicting with Christian explanations, nevertheless offer an alternative cosmic story with considerable scope and explanatory power. The earth itself turns out to be an emergent form, evolving over vast millennia in ways that could be explained scientifically. It is thanks to this Victorian thought that twentieth-century children have been able to undergo the previously unknown Dinosaur Phase of development. It is also some thanks to these predecessors that Darwin had a prepared public when he finally published his celebrated histories of species that detonated in every part of nineteenth-century British culture. Darwin's *The Origin of Species*, somewhat reluctantly published in 1859, and his *Descent of Man* (1871), demonstrate that the forms of life, especially of human life, are not fixed permanently by God, but are emergent, mobile, even unstable. To readers accustomed to local definitions, a most unsettling feature in the work of both scientists and in the work of science generally, is their requirement to generalize on a grand scale. The essential stories that Lyell and Darwin tell require the mind to put local detail into larger patterns that, on the local level, are invisible and abstract. Such patterns belong to specialized knowledge of embryos or of the earth's crust. The telling similarities between individuals are internal, not external (Darwin, 1968: 427, 397, 400). Observation requires to be aided. What is visible does not tell the story; it must be aided by comparisons over time, even millennial periods, which is the only way commanding and evolving structures become evident.

Darwin's ideas are familiar enough not to require summary, and his influence has been substantially explored for more than a decade (Cosslett, 1982; Beer, 1983; Morton, 1984). What is important here is the way his ideas about emergent form gained prestige and currency from already prevailing narrative forms, and in turn codified those forms in new ways. Gillian Beer has shown how Darwin brought into scientific currency certain explanatory tools derived, not from science, but from literary narrative, and particularly how his metaphoric language transfers values back and forth between the natural and the social world.

For example, the Darwinian idea that rarity is a precursor to extinction raises questions for culture, whether or not culture operates like nature. If marginalization ('rarity') is the prelude to extinction among all other species, that may appear to sound an ominous knell for the poor, the disenfranchised, the colonized, who were increasingly marginalized because of changing social and economic patterns; the idea might even suggest that the eradication of cultural marginals is 'natural'. If cultural marginals are seen by implication as 'natural' candidates for extinction, then it would not be surprising to find them actually disappearing under the attentions of British colonial power – this happened to certain aboriginals subjected to the scientific attention of Victorian anthropology – without there ever being a link made between that attention and that extinction (Stocking, 1987).

While Darwin's own attention to moral questions, primarily in the *Descent of Man*, is brief and unsatisfactory, his *method* easily becomes a metaphor for cultural forms of life because he uses the same grammar of perspective, the same emphasis on the common instead of the idiosyncratic, the same assumptions about emergent form and material law used by realist artists since the Renaissance, and in his own time by historians of culture beginning with the particularly popular historical novels of Walter Scott.

Darwin's work can lead in different and even contradictory directions, as his contemporaries were aware (Morton, 1984: 32, 224). On the one hand, there is much that is conservative in his language, especially in the *Descent of Man* which is full of crossover applications from ape sexuality to human ethical and gender relations (Darwin, 1979, II: 318, 328). On the other hand, Darwin's deployment of the idea of emergent form looks in quite revolutionary directions. Despite his analogical vocabulary, the material processes he describes are without explicit moral dimension. By insisting that everything takes its form historically he insists on changeability (stasis means extinction), and he allows for the complete alteration of identity. A single characteristic can lead to 'irreversible biological revolution' and even, as one species evolves into another, 'a forgetting of initial conditions' (Prigogine and Stengers, 1984: 128–9). It is precisely such forgetting that becomes the mainspring of the narrative in Hardy's novels (Beer, 1989: 13).

These moves beyond equilibrium structures potently qualify certain influential Enlightenment treatments of sociality and of economy even as they gain currency in nineteenth-century discourse: for example, Adam Smith's 'equilibrium analysis' of wealth (Robbins, 1935: 68). To the extent that Darwin insists on the open-endedness of the historical process, and allows for the role of chance in its functioning, his work contests the definition of a steady-state universe where everything can be described in terms of initial states and laws of motion.

With the profound, even fecund circularity that belongs to the historical convention, Darwin's work shows that the forms of nature – and by potential analogy the forms of social existence – belong integrally to a world that they in turn rely upon; that they continually transform the world even as they constitute it. The potential permanently to forget initial conditions balances in Darwin with the fact that the laws of change never change. His is a single, interrelated system of natural selection that operates according to fixed laws and that remain the same from one millennium to the next. Even though whole species become extinct, the system remains the 'same system' (Darwin, 1968: 448–50, 397, 400). In its scope, if not its details, the system almost resembles a religious one in that it treats a historical and humanist construction of time as a universal and (hence) a 'natural' condition.

My next instance of faith in emergent form is narrative painting, the mainstream English pictorial tradition of the nineteenth century. Narrative painting is not in itself a particularly English phenomenon; the heroic canvases of French painters like Gericault (d. 1824), David (d. 1825), and Ingres (d. 1867) lead on directly to the Establishment art of nineteenth-century France. For example, James Tissot's (1836–1902) painting of *The Departure of the Prodigal Son* (*Le depart de l'enfant prodigue*, Petit Palais) appears in the 1864 Salon. The picture may be read left to right, as the prodigal leaves his family on his way across the central dock to a ship on the right. Using the same architectural elements to be found in Italian painting four hundred years earlier, Tissot constructs the single-point perspective illusion; the water and the far-off meeting of sky and sea maintain the sense of horizon so ingrained in the grammar of perspective that continues prominent through the nineteenth century in England. Here there is no Impressionist concern with light and the conditions of perception. Instead, the picture re-codifies the values of perspective painting using Christian allegorical material and antique dress. This is the narrative tradition which literally refused to show the Impressionists, thus prompting them to show themselves in 1864, as the Salon des Refusées, and the rest, as they say, is history.

This mid-century narrative painting belongs to a tradition stretching back to Alberti's *istoria*, the ideal of a realist art that expresses in one massive, explanatory moment an entire political or legendary story. By 'history' Alberti meant capturing on canvas the heroic high points of culture and, by implication, the processes and sequences that produced them. In these terms, 'historical' events could include not only the beheading of a king, a battle, the trial of a martyr, but also such typological 'moments' as the death of Christ or miracles like the Annunciation. For centuries, the Christian story was *the* story, and thousands of painters used elements of that story. But the controlling code in such painting has nothing to do with subject matter, which can range easily from the botanical to the miraculous. Content is not the issue in realism, whether in narrative or in painting. The issue is the construction and exploration of neutral time and neutral space, the media of modernity.

Narrative sequence is implied in pictorial single-point perspective systems from the beginning. Appreciation depends on the eye taking in various perspectives, implicitly moving from one to another, literally collecting them within the single point system. Narratives multiply in the delightful *Virgin and Child* by Pinturicchio (Bernardino di Betto, 1454– 1513; Philadelphia Museum of Art). The Child is writing the testament; hieroglyphics border the virgin's robe; three trees appear in the background; in the distance one sees the flight to Egypt; there is even a perilous gap between foreground and background that, though consistent with realistic (single-point perspective) space, seems rather to threaten it. But the potential gaps and failures of this 'realist' space are recovered. The Christian miracle can and does take place in the space of this world. The éclat of putting the religious story into a medium devised on the basis of individual spectator awareness only adds to the charm of this image, as of so many like it. The longevity of this Albertian and Renaissance tradition is astonishing. It began in some Florentine churches over six hundred years ago and, for many, it still remains the norm of good visual art.

Nineteenth-century English narrative painting uniquely exploits the narrative potential of this long-established pictorial tradition. Unlike Europe, where history painting declines 'precipitously after 1855' (Eisenman, 1994: 225), England developed the form after about that time, and as an alternative to the Romantic nature painters from Constable to Turner who treated nature as a site or emblem of social activity, an example of which is Turner's 1844 painting, *Rain, Steam, Speed – The Great Western Railway.* Domesticated narrative painting, shorn of the heroic qualities of David or Ingres and focused on domestic subjects, is practically an English specialty. Here the heroic achievement lies not in the capstone act of a single mythical figure, but in the achievement of social coherence. Of the multitude of examples, Willam Powell Frith's (1819–1909) *Railway Station* (1862) is a masterpiece of the genre. Frith's worldliness and attention to domestic detail differs from the Pinturicchio's calmer scene; but the pictorial convention, including its narrative potential, is the same.

This picture of the departure platform at Paddington Station shows a common social space full of narratives: a crowd of people in various stages of preparation for travel, one weeping farewell, one kissing her child, another checking a bag: a very middle-class scene, with porters, a dog, various kinds of baggage and of dress; with likenesses of Frith's own family, of the art dealer who commissioned the work and of two well-known detectives of the time portrayed in the act of arresting a well-dressed man; behind them, the waiting train, an engine of mobility and speed; and all of this, a frozen moment of actual time, with its proliferating, potentially chaotic details, collected on the platform under the station's high ceiling arches and hanging electric globes. This overarching internal space takes up half the picture and frames the human community, collected temporarily by the wish to travel, even as particular destinations differ.

This picture, too, is full of narratives, full of implied sequences all contributing to the expression of a single social moment. It is a masterly evocation of the implied sequences that single-point perspective in space had always implied and that Alberti glorified as *istoria*. The eye is asked to 'read' a variety of narratives that, nevertheless, constitute a common social entity. The epic and heroic individuals of the Renaissance are replaced in Frith by the social group, albeit an almost exclusively middle-class group right down to its criminal element. What is heroic here is the social entity itself, not any of its particular, constituent figures. Not only is this an entity on the move, it is an entity *because* it is on the move.

Other well-known narrative painters from this period are Holman Hunt (*The Light of the World* and *The Awakening Conscience*), John Everett Millais (*Blind Girl*), and Ford Maddox Brown (*Last of England*). Their canvases yield considerable narrative meaning. The artists make domestic or religious points, some attempt medieval effect, but none appreciably modifies the controlling perspective system. In pre-Raphaelite paintings the intensity of the colours and images gesture in the direction of flatness, though generally they fail to flatten. It is always useful to remember that there was no Salon des Refusées in England. While these English painters, and those mentioned in Chapter One (Alma-Tadema and Burne-Jones), were working in England, and while Tissot and his ilk were working in France, Impressionism was developing its parallel course, its first exhibition taking place in 1874. Impressionism is interested in light, and in the ways it varies perception. The Impressionists' emphasis on perception at the expense of objectivity – at the expense, that is, of the relational accuracy made possible by single-point perspective – took radical directions in the work of Manet and Degas, the latter himself originally a narrative painter (for example 'Semiramis Constructs Babylon' (1860–61)). After Impressionism it did not take long for painters in France to deconstruct the realist medium, to deny its neutrality. Thereafter, at least in the work of the most creative painters, the grammar of single-point perspective is dismantled, the medium of realism and consensus is a thing of the past. English painting only turns in this direction conspicuously in the work of J. M. W. Turner (d. 1851), who had finished working by mid-century (see Chapter One, pp. 60–61).

Another instance of historical faith in emergent form appears in nineteenth-century theology, in a movement towards historical explanation that had immense influence on nineteenth-century religion. Historical theology, the so-called Higher Criticism, emphasized the historical condition of Christ, of Christianity, and of the Church and all its dogmas and documents. Religious explanation itself is subjected to the narrative codes of history. The Higher Criticism had begun in France in the eighteenth century and was carried on in the nineteenth chiefly by German theologians and philosophers whose key works were translated into English by Marian Evans, soon to become 'George Eliot'. In the twentieth century they have been important to existential theologians like Karl Barth, Reinhold Niebuhr, Paul Tillich and others. David Friedrich Strauss's historical account of Jesus, *Das Leben Jesu*, published in 1835–36 (Marian Evans's translation, *The Life of Jesus*, published in 1846) was so controversial that it simultaneously prompted the offer of an appointment for Strauss at the University of Zürich and a public outcry that prevented him from accepting it. Even more seminal was Ludwig Andreas Feuerbach's 1841 treatise, *Das Wesen des Christentums*, the translation of which (also by Marian Evans) was published in England in 1854 as *The Essence of Christianity*.

In England these sensational first works by relatively young German writers inspired considerable interest because of their social as well as their religious implications, and not just among specialists. A ribbon-manufacturer in Coventry, Charles Bray, published in 1838 *An Inquiry into the Origins of Christianity* showing that the life of Jesus Christ and the spread of his religion were consistent with historical and natural explanation, and that neither depended on miracles. Bray's sister, Sarah Hennell, published a number of works on related subjects, and her brother-in-law, Charles Hennell, published a well-disseminated work on *The Philosophy of*

Necessity; or, the Law of Consequences as Applicable to Mental, Moral, and Social Science (1840). These English versions of the Higher Criticism treat religious issues in social and philosophical terms by treating them historically. While this was a shock to some, it seemed to others to rescue religion from dogmatic catastrophe by showing what Feuerbach calls 'the anthropological essence of religion'.

Feuerbach's radical step, and one that leads in an entirely different direction from Marx's social vision, was to reverse the direction of Christian thinking about human life. Christian tenets, says Feuerbach, are nothing less or more than projections of human aspiration and value. To say 'God is Love' really is a way of saying that love is our highest value, that 'Love is God'. This anthropological approach to Christianity systematically submits doctrine to comparative, one could say interdisciplinary, treatment.

Feuerbach argues that theological Christianity, because it depreciates human differences and homogenizes the human 'essence', effectively subverts sociality. Because it considers all individuals to be essentially alike, theological religion actually extinguishes the qualitative difference between one individual and another; it treats human differences negatively.

> Between me and another human being there is an essential, qualitative distinction. The other is my *thou*, – the relation being reciprocal, – my *alter ego*, man objective to me, the revelation of my own nature, the eye seeing itself. In another I first have the consciousness of humanity.... But morally, also, there is a qualitative, critical distinction between the *I* and *thou*.... But Christianity extinguishes this qualitative distinction; it sets the same stamp on all men alike, and regards them as one and the same individual, because it knows not distinction between the species and the individual: it has one and the same means of salvation for all men, it sees one and the same original sin in all.
>
> (Feuerbach, 1957: 158–9)

Feuerbach even claims that 'the idea of man as a species, and with it the significance of the life of the species, of humanity as a whole, vanished as Christianity became dominant' (ibid.: 160). This is because the 'characteristic doctrine of the universal sinfulness of man' in effect extinguishes any possibility of recognizing humanity as a species, because it constitutes human identity by levelling differences between individuals (ibid.: 155). Instead, Christianity promotes a kind of exaggerated hero worship; it effects an 'immediate unity of the species with individuality', concentrating 'all that is universal and real in one personal being'. This makes 'God' a 'deeply moving object' and an inspiration to imagination, whereas the idea of 'humanity', on the other hand, 'has little power over the feelings because humanity is only an abstraction' without the personalized quality, and a degenerate one at that.

Viewed in historical context, then, the outcome of Christian doctrine is to negate individual difference and thus to negate the very principle of sociality. Christianity, he says flatly, 'does not contain in itself the principle of culture' (ibid.: 160). If all individuals are conceived as *essentially* alike in mortal sin, then emphasis on the differences between them have no particular value, or worse, a negative value to the extent that a difference is a distraction from the religious essence of man, which is single.

Feuerbach's alternative, anthropological (and cultural) definition of identity reverses the emphasis of doctrinal religion. Culture maximizes difference. 'Doubtless the essence of man is *one*', says Feuerbach, anticipating Sartre by a century, 'but this essence is infinite; its real existence is therefore an infinite, reciprocally compensating variety, which reveals the riches of this essence. Unity in essence is multiplicity in existence' (ibid.: 158). In other words, *to secularize difference is to reverse its value.* Where theological religion depreciates difference, anthropological religion maximizes it. The anthropological 'essence' of the human species is the sum total of its expressions, nothing less. Its so-called 'essence' is plural.

Feuerbach concludes that species-awareness – the identification of oneself with an inclusive 'human' group – depends to an extent on historical and anthropological thinking about culture and about religion. To be conscious of oneself as human is to recognize oneself as a member of this infinitely differentiated sum of individuals which is the species. The essential unity of this species lies in its *existential* multiplicity. In history, what individuals have in common is the condition of being different from other human beings. Always emergent, always exfoliating in different directions, the 'human' species is a potentiality always in the making, a creature that is the sum of its expressions, the ultimate emergent form.

An important social implication of this work is that the doctrine of human sinfulness encourages negative social relationship, especially encouraging envy and resentment instead of love and charity. Religion, in this view, trains people to think that everyone is essentially alike (in sin) and so to regard unique achievement as threatening, and grounds for suspicion or resentment. This is a subject, as Chapter Three will discuss, that John Stuart Mill takes up as well in his essay *On Liberty* (1859). The very 'excellence' or superior accomplishment that makes a person stand out makes her or him vulnerable to religious intolerance. Culture, on the

111

other hand (to the extent that it is free of theological interpretations), reverses this effect; culturally, each individual is constructed *as* a cultural difference.

The most interesting emergent form to emerge in nineteenth-century English narrative is the form of society itself. Victorian society, as has often been noted, has a uniquely developed sense of historical difference. For various excellent reasons, nineteenth-century readers had an intense awareness of their historical uniqueness, of their difference from the past. Because of industrialization and related changes, practically every aspect of their lives had changed: where they lived, how they organized their day, what they used as money, how they travelled. As one commentator summarizes it, 'conditions in this island changed from those of a mainly rural and mercantile community, governed chiefly by a landowning aristocracy, to those of a predominantly urban and manufacturing community, tending towards pure democracy' (Robbins, 1952: 170). Well, perhaps not quite *entirely* pure. Innumerable journal articles announced and explained this sense of belonging, more or less unanimously, to a historical moment rather than, as in feudal society, to a hierarchically differentiated and 'natural' place.

In the first decades of the nineteenth century this sense of society itself as an emergent form informs the continuing debate over the identity of the era. 'The spirit of the age' and the 'signs of the times' occupied many columns of journals across the entire range of public opinion. Influential early examples of the genre were published in 1829 by Thomas Carlyle and Robert Southey, and in 1830–31 by Thomas Macaulay and John Stuart Mill. The debate was often acrimonious and illogical. David Robinson protested in 1830 to the fictional editor of *Blackwood's Magazine*, 'Christopher North' (whose columns were alternately written by John Wilson, William Maginn, Thomas Hamilton and William Blackwood), that the phrase 'spirit of the age' was merely the 'slang of faction' dedicated to the subversion of important values like religion and morality, the master–subordinate relation and (presumably following on from master–subordinate relations) harmony among classes. The estimation of the new age was often dismissively negative, but what matters for present purposes is that, regardless of opinion, all such essays recognize historical difference as the key to social definition.

This sense of historical difference has vertiginous possibilities for paradox, such as the use of historical analysis to denounce history. Such flavours appear extensively in a series of YMCA lectures on 'The Age We Live In'. One lecturer, the influential Evangelical minister, Revd John Cumming (pilloried by George Eliot in an 1855 *Westminster Review* essay), informs his 1847 audience that the millennium is at hand, the evidence for which is the mixture of good and evil through the ages of Man from Adam to Napoleon; this perennial evil he reviews in a style of runaway *amplificatio* before offering his parting advice, which is: be Protestant, and independent in mind. The same lecture series offers the Revd Hugh Stowall the opportunity in the same year to explain the negative tendency towards extremism in the spirit of the age; he recommends that faithful Christians strive 'in this emergency' to be living examples, that they pray for humility, the Queen and Parliament, and that they 'hide [themselves] . . . until the indignation be overpast' (Stowall, 1886: 73–4). These talks use a sense of historical difference as a basis for denouncing history (certainly avoiding its methods) and for codifying dogma.

The new age is often lamented, whether its spirit belongs to the Oxford Movement or something more intangibly social. In 1844 Richard Horne in his essay on *A New Spirit of the Age* concludes that Dickens represents the 'entire spirit' of an age of social morality and (using a quintessentially historical convention) he argues that this spirit is undermined by a few untouchables, like historical novelists, and Pusey, the proto-papist. Less hortatory and far less conservative, even Frances Power Cobbe (1864: 486) laments the manners of the new age, the emptiness of which she evokes with a particularly charming metaphor, an older style of social conversation. 'We *talk* now – we never *converse*. . . . How really *delicious* a thing it was! How – when its atmosphere had once wrapped us round – we felt ourselves expand in it, as sea-anemones do in warm and sheltered caves, where there is no chance of a breaker ever disturbing the surface!' Sarah Grand, some decades later, takes a different perspective on this social 'wrap'; it is precisely the chief obstacle to progress. At Fraylingay, in Grand's *The Heavenly Twins*, 'after it was certain that you knew the right people, pleasant manners were the only passport necessary to secure a footing of easy intimacy' (Grand, 1992: 54). This 'easy' intimacy, her novel shows, is generally based on ignorance and exclusion: beyond agreeable manners, a matter mainly of knowing who someone knows. In such a climate – Cobbe's 'warm and sheltered caves' looked at from another perspective – the poor women of Grand's novel are coddled and 'protected' literally to death.

Others describe the same cultural events as achievements, focusing mainly on technological advance and economic practices, but they, too, emphasize the emergent qualities of society itself. In a *Fraser's Magazine* article on 'The Age We Live In' (1841) Antonio Gallenga (under the pseudonym 'L. Mariotti') claims that 'the Spirit of the Age is Steam; its philosophy is material', and he somewhat confusedly arrives at the idea that we should explore this new age, which is variously an age of Education, of Works, of Words, of Opinion, of Toleration, of Peace, of Uncertain and Unsettled Government, of Party Spirit, and of Railroads. And, finally, an anonymous essay in *Fraser's Magazine* of 1851 illustrates, by comparison with the eighteenth century, 'the superiority of our own times' with regard to peace, commerce, communications and capital accumulation; above all the writer singles out competition and 'the natural law of supply and demand' for encouraging the cheapness that 'lies at the root of all civilization' (Anon., 1851: 8, 13). This sense of inhabiting a society essentially different from anything in the past is especially acute in mid-nineteenth-century writing. Whether the editorial opinion was for or against it, everyone seemed to agree that the spirit of the age rendered the historical moment uniquely marked, and the society contained in it at any given point uniquely identifiable.

Historical narratives capture that sense, so broadly evident across a varying cultural range, that whatever things are now, they could always be otherwise. 'The fiction of the age makes little sense unless the reader supposes he [sic] is watching men and women make decisions which could be otherwise' (Watson, 1973: 78); and this contained potential largely accounts for the apparently inexhaustible interest in historical narratives shown by nineteenth-century readers. In Darwinian science and historical novels, as in the mid-century social and political theory discussed in Chapter Three, attention is focused on the unreduced tension between individuals and the collective (literally collected) social order. Those 'social' problems that call for conscience and choice can only be described and defined if they are treated as mutually informative in the first place. The same could be said of Darwinian development and Philosophical Radicalism: they explore the way chance and choice determine outcomes. The compelling interest in them all arises from the sense of tributaries joining a common stream of development, and from the sheer *experimental* fact that, given the operations of chance and choice, it could have been otherwise.

In one sense, literary history is the most complex of all instances of emergent form because it takes the social intangibles into account. Emergent identity and the form-of-the-whole may be easy enough to understand when we are talking about geometric forms, where conic sections demonstrably produce a clear form-of-the-whole, or when we are talking about the millennial evolution of species. But things become horribly complex when we are talking about social identity; here the slices of 'life' now require definition of precisely that 'whole' environment formerly explained by special creation and separately described. In addition, novels subject this complex material to aesthetic demands. Rationalizing social awareness is not easy to do; it is a continuing project of mid-century narrative.

One witty, anonymous Renaissance painter had these problems in mind when he or she demonstrated that it was possible to construct an 'Ideal City' but impossible to people it. In each of two similar paintings called *Ideal City*, an architectural scene appears in perfect single-point perspective but containing little or no sign of human life (Palazzo Ducale, Urbino; Walters Gallery, Baltimore). What emerges from the perspective system is only the architectural system itself. Life is messier than that. A 'self' may change for better or worse. An event may point in at least two directions. Does the individual identity emerge as a gendered, or a political, or an economic entity? If all three and more, what is its status *as* an entity? Does society itself qualify as an entity, a 'human' whole? If so, does a common human species imply a universal social entity, common to all humanity, or social orders common only to national or linguistic communities? Narrative art gives freedom and play to this complex of problems in ways that are economical and imaginative. Such writing plays a considerable role in the mid-century effort to construct a new kind of society. Such questions invigorate the narratives of the nineteenth century between 1840 and 1890, and in certain reincarnations invigorate narratives still.

3

SOCIETY AS AN ENTITY

PROLOGUE: THE SYMPHONY

Nineteenth-century changes in corporate order take place on such a scale that they are hard to encompass without a wide horizon and the help of analogies and metaphors. I will begin this chapter with a small version of the kind of change in corporate order that the chapter pursues more at large. An event in musical history provides a parallel logic to that taking place on a far more complicated scale in nineteenth-century social change.

During the nineteenth century, valves were added to the trumpet. This event simultaneously changes not only the individual instrument, but also the ensembles in which it participates, and the kind of music that could be written for such instruments and ensembles. Prior to this change trumpets had limited capacity for cooperating with other instrumental voices to produce orchestral melodies. Trumpets with no air holes or valves could not play complex melodies or vary the pitch much beyond the notes of a single key. Consequently trumpets were used for fanfares, or to add brilliance or vigour to a moment of ensemble performance; this is true even for Bach's Second Brandenburg Concerto, whose high trumpet parts are written for the valveless trumpet. These instrumental limitations also influenced the kind of music written for trumpets. Because its range was too limited, few solo works were composed for the instrument and those few were confined to the difficult high end of the register. Once the trumpet gained valves it could modify instantaneously the sounding air column to play any pitch in its range, and thus to play melodies (Ledbetter, 1993).

In the nineteenth century, then, the trumpet becomes a more specialized voice, one that can better cooperate with a lot of other specialized voices to produce the single, composite sound of symphonic music, with its comprehensive melodic, as distinct from polyphonic, development. The modified instrument simultaneously becomes more specialized and more embedded in a group. And the trumpet is only one case. Many modern symphonic instruments are late eighteenth- or early nineteenth-century inventions; for example, the grand piano, the trombone and the oboe are more specialized descendants of the harpsichord, the sackbut and the shawm. Multiplied many times over, such newly specialized instrumental 'voices' produce a new composite sound, a new kind of orchestral group, and a new kind of composition. In music, as elsewhere, increased specialization, or individuation, produces a new kind of corporate entity.

Compared with earlier music, especially music in the polyphonic tradition, the development of symphonic music shows a decrease in the independence of any particular musical line. The sonata form, as Charles Rosen (1971) has explained it, achieves developmental composition by sacrificing independence in the musical line. Earlier music, by contrast, and this includes the baroque, calls for relatively small musical ensembles where timbre and blend can be maintained: no tubas along with the flutes. In still older, more polyphonic traditions – back all the way to the motets of Josquin des Pres – each musical line is relatively independent of the others: vocal and instrumental parts remain resistantly, pleasingly (and to borrow a phrase) 'heterogeneous to but in sight of' each other (Kristeva, 1980: 132–5). The listener's pleasure depends on hearing the play between carefully maintained qualitative differences of timbre, pace and voice. The fragile quality produced by the old instruments in small ensembles also contributes to this effect and to its characteristic pleasure.

Greater individuation among instrumental voices develops in tandem with classical symphonic ensembles, beginning especially with Haydn (1732–1809) and Mozart (1756–91). These differ in magnitude and in kind from the instrumental voices required to perform motets, cantatas and fugues. The instrumental sections of a symphony orchestra do not stand alone. Where the polyphonic musical line remains relatively independent (Spitzer, 1963: 39–44), the symphonic 'parts' – those assigned to violin or percussion or woodwind sections – make little sense independent of the whole to which they contribute, a fact verifiable at any practice session. The specialized part, combined with others, produces a single sound composed of strings, woodwinds, tympani and the rest. The relationships between these voices change but in ways that are much more *mutually* constrained than in pre-classical music. No instrumental section ever develops the kind of independence found in the separate parts of a polyphonic motet.

In the work of Beethoven, Brahms, Schubert, Mendelssohn, Wagner,

Liszt, and the rest of the still-current musical canon, the nineteenth century thus develops ground laid in the later eighteenth century by Haydn and Mozart. The more specialized and various instruments become, the more textured and unified becomes the corporate sound they produce. Even between composers like Haydn and Beethoven (1770–1827), two near contemporaries at the turn of the nineteenth century, one can hear very different influences and agendas. Haydn's architecture can be heard within a fairly short sequence, and the smaller sequences build larger ones that very much resemble each other in kind. The spatial analogy seems somehow appropriate in speaking about Haydn's music; it is precisely its local balancing act that makes such classical music so pleasant.

In contrast to Haydn, Beethoven's music requires suspension of formal anticipation, and a good memory, as the small constituents incrementally constitute large and differentiated sequences (Rosen, 1995). A temporal model seems more adequate to this form; it does not exist as architecture so much as development. Analogy with historical form has even been suggested (Kramer, 1990: 23) in the description of 'secondary expressive doubling' in music as being a 'musical equivalent of the past'. Where Haydn's musical line seems still in touch, however remotely, with polyphony, Beethoven's musical line pushes convention to the limit during the course of long, complex sequences. Beethoven's music is much more abstract, in the sense that its overall form emerges slowly and often tests the limits of convention. One must keep in mind the emergent form. The suspension of harmonic resolution, the tensions created by structural instability, or dissonance, lead inexorably (and almost always) to resolution.

The symphony, both as ensemble and as composition, thus constitutes a new version of corporate order in music. Its claim on attention and its capacity to give pleasure arise from the ability of this diverse ensemble to speak as one. A common tempo and a common harmonic framework ensure that strains and tensions in the system of harmonic relationship remain resolvable, concordable.

The social parable in this musical event has to do with the reconstruction of society as a corporate entity, and with the way narrative undertakes in its own medium a similar reformation of corporate order. The interest in a social novel, though it may seem to lie in its increase over earlier novels of individuation in character and event, actually arises from the affirmation that such individuation and variety entirely serves the construction of a single system of measurement, a single, common human world, a single system of historical and social explanation, and especially the assertion of society as a single entity.

Like the sonata form, the social (historical) novel perpetrates and then resolves instability and dissonance among its constituent elements – elements that have been redefined by this very project. The development in a symphony depends upon a new specialization of instrumental voice and a newly unified, harmonic enterprise. Similarly, the development in a social novel depends upon a new range and specificity of individual awareness that constitutes a social entity treated as such in English narrative for the first time.

The more 'Nature' after Darwin comes to look like a battleground, the more Society becomes the primary context for human life and even a protection from nature. Social and historical novels develop a vision of the social entity conspicuously different from the economic system developed from Adam Smith and pilloried in fictional capitalists like Dickens' Merdle and Trollope's Melmotte. The very grammar of perspective in social novels by definition includes everything in its human discourse, including the economy and 'the market'. What co-exists by definition co-responds. Of course there are one or two anomalies and difficulties in the programme (see Chapter Four), but it is important to be clear that the social, which is to say the historical, novel experiments with quite new definitions of sociality.

Historical and social novelists, in a word, rethink the role of difference in the social order of things. This subject has already been approached in Chapter Two with discussions of Darwinian science and historical narratives. Without 'nature' as a justification for distributing difference hierarchically, the whole definition of corporate order requires rethinking. This rethinking appears broadly across the entire range of cultural expression, of which novels are but a part. From science and music to narrative and politics we find experiments with new forms of specialization and consequent adjustments in ideas of order.

Increasing attention to systemic arrangement, as the symphonic analogy suggests, depends upon increasing attention to individualized function and is not inimical to it. Each detail, and each individual, has a constituting role in the general definition or social form-of-the-whole. Just as the specialized functions of organisms constitute both a species, and also a larger ecosystem in which species flourish or fade, so in political theory the new thinking involves exactly this relationship between constituent and entity. This new relationship John Stuart Mill explores in his great essays *On Liberty* (1859), *Considerations on Representative Government* (1861), and *The Subjection of Women* (1869). In social narratives, novelists by the hundreds experiment across the whole range of social circumstance with this new relationship between individual voice and collective identity. What is at stake is nothing less than a shift in the way an entire culture constructs identity. The expressions of new corporate relationship in the nineteenth century are deeply embedded, broadly prepared, and diverse.

This chapter deals, first, with Victorian political explorations of a new corporate identity; second, with the competition between social and economic versions of that identity; and finally, with treatment by three historical and social novelists of the differences that increasingly constitute society.

IS THERE SUCH A THING AS SOCIETY?

The twentieth-century Prime Minister, Margaret Thatcher, once outraged public conscience by declaring that there is 'no such thing as Society'. The comment flies in the face of a humanist tradition that still remains the mainstream for Europe. It is the tradition that allows a Member of Parliament to speak in 1992 of the BBC as 'the voice of the nation, speaking to itself'. It is what allows the opposition Labour leader of 1994 to raise the banner of 'mutual social solidarity' and 'civic society' (Channel 4 news interview by Jon Snow, 8 December 1994). Anxiety about the dissolution of this public identity may even be what prompts a BBC radio commentator in 1995 to say that British society needs Royalty because 'we need someone to interpret the nation for itself'. Civic solidarity remains basic to modern political discourse.

To believers in that discourse Margaret Thatcher's remark might seem merely another insult to the collectivity from right-wing conservatism. She has a point, however, although probably not the one she intended. The point is that the modern sense of society as entity, as something independent of natural or cosmic explanation, does not have broad dissemination until well into the nineteenth century. Until then 'natural' and providential explanations of human affairs, including certain well-known economic variants, override the perception of society as an entirely human construction whose flaws must be rectified by human intervention. 'There were *societies without the social*', as Baudrillard claims, 'just as there were societies without history'. There is more to this than what Lionel Robbins once called French 'stunt anti-rationalism' (1939: viii). Baudrillard, I take it, means that both history and 'the social' are particular constructs for particular cultural moments, and that it is quite possible to experience time and to carry on social life (what he calls 'society') without them. Given this perspective, Baudrillard makes sense when he speaks of the 'extreme gibberish of the "social sciences" ' with their testimonials to the ageless existence of 'the social' (Baudrillard, 1983: 67–9).

If history (the convention) and society are relatively recent constructions, so is 'the market system' and the 'profit motive'. Robert Heilbroner makes the case as follows:

> The profit motive, we are constantly being told, is as old as man himself. But it is not. The profit motive as we know it is only as old as 'modern man'.... The idea of gain ... is as modern an invention as printing.

(Heilbroner, 1980: 30–1)

Like History and Society, the 'profit motive' is anything but a 'natural', which is to say universal 'human', disposition. If the profit motive is 'only as old as "modern man"', and if, as Foucault and others have argued, the modern idea of the 'human' species is about the same age, then both 'man' and 'the profit motive' are only about three hundred years old. The same may be said for 'the market'. Market-*places* may be old; but the market-*system*, which '*is a mechanism for sustaining and maintaining an entire society*' is a fairly recent invention, as new as the humanist conception of the species 'man', as new as 'the profit motive', and as new as the idea of gain conceived in terms of capital.

In sum, the idea that society is an entity evolving in time belongs to the same fiction that creates 'man' as a humanist species identification, and that creates both capitalism and its 'market'. The nineteenth century inherited from the Enlightenment several powerful ideas that are intimately related, and that inform its literary, political and social narratives for at least two hundred years: the idea of 'the market'; the idea of 'the profit motive'; and the idea of society as an entity, autonomous from nature, humanly constituted, and governed by laws. These powerful assumptions, sometimes working together and sometimes in opposition, provide the growing points which social novelists explore (Heilbroner, 1980: 22, 25).

The idea of a unified, inclusive social entity has been attacked by Foucault, Baudrillard, Lyotard and others, as primarily a disciplinary mechanism. The key term of opprobrium (popularized by Foucault) is 'panoptic' – a term for the surveillance mechanisms of a centralized culture (in the prison, the hospital, the school, the military camp) that curb individual initiative and difference – literally the power to differ. The critique has some validity, though it applies better in some contexts and in some national traditions than in others. But when, as often happens, the authors of such critiques omit to consider the temporal aspect of these new developments, and to consider the positive as well as negative political implications of that temporal aspect, then they seriously limit their own relevance.

For those interested in these powerful and suggestive arguments (Foucault, 1977; Baudrillard, 1983; Lyotard, 1988) it should be said that the 'panoptic' space objected to is precisely the space that makes possible *any* idea of social unity in the sense being explored in the nineteenth century. 'Panoptic' space is the neutral medium that, like its temporal counterpart, makes possible the definition of society as being a system managed by people in the first place, and not a series of ledges in a Christian God's cosmos. As with Barthes's essay attacking the 'empty' space of Dutch realism (see Chapter Two, pp. 70–71), these discussions by Foucault, Baudrillard and Lyotard override a crucial distinction between the humanist construction of space and time in which so much has been possible – including the opportunities for critique exemplified by Foucault, Baudrillard and Lyotard – and extreme versions of that humanist construction represented by the panoptic prison.

It seems especially important to guard against extremist or totalizing extrapolations from the assumption, stated explicitly by Lyotard, that, because it never fulfils its promise of inclusiveness, the centralized perspective or 'consensus' construction is a 'terrorist apparatus' (Lyotard, 1988: 63–66). The infinite space and time of history, realism and consensus may be 'terrorist' for those who are excluded without acknowledgement from the consensus (see Chapter Four); they may be 'panoptic' in Foucault's sense, although who is *in* the tower remains a question – maybe Nobody, as described in Chapter Two – see pp. 76; 86–94. Still, since the Renaissance these media have also been the media of democratic institutions and empirical science, both demonstrably liberating discursive ventures. The social critiques by Foucault, Baudrillard and Lyotard have substantial value, especially for habitual humanists and dyed-in-the-wool empiricists, and for anyone who wants to grasp the fundamental postmodern reformation of these essentially Newtonian assumptions; but we must be careful not to carry them, as Mr Brooke says in *Middlemarch*, 'over the hedge'.

So the answer to the question, 'Is there such a thing as society?' is this: 'There is if enough of you believe there is'. Society as an entity, constructed from multitudes of individual subjects or social instruments, arises as an article of collective cultural faith; it is a work of imagination; it is an artefact of collective belief; it is not at all 'natural'. There are more and less optimistic ways to view this state of affairs. In Baudrillard's view, the contract society does not exist: 'there is no contract, no contract is ever exchanged between distinct agencies according to the law – that is all sound and fury – there are only ever stakes, defiance, that is to say something which does not proceed via a "social relation" ' (Baudrillard, 1983: 68–9). His claim that 'things have never functioned socially' means that, to him, the nineteenth-century exploration of that construct was a delusion of rationality, an illusion produced by the grammar of perspective in the service of certain quite primitive agendas.

The present study argues that the nineteenth-century position is more optimistic than Baudrillard's, but not necessarily different in kind. Mid-nineteenth-century social novelists and philosophers are willing to agree that society is a construct. Most social (historical) novels are construction sites. The novel is not merely a reflection, it is an agent of social integration (Blake, 1989: 135–6). Social and historical novelists experiment with making harmonic relationships from the problematic negotiations between constituencies. But these narratives, by virtue of their grammar of perspective, nevertheless treat the idea of society – a common social world analogous to the common physical one – as an inspiring hypothesis: a possibility demonstrably preferable to the tribal condition of 'stakes' and 'defiance' to which, long before Baudrillard, Walter Scott and others had objected. While mid-nineteenth-century social novelists were aware that society was an hypothesis, they believed in human power to make ideas incarnate and thus to 'realize' them beyond the realm of simulacra.

The most interesting emergent form of the nineteenth century, then, is 'society' itself. By the middle of the nineteenth century the very term 'society' has changed its meaning from longstanding and more traditional usages. Well through the eighteenth century (and of course in scattered instances still in the twentieth) 'society' kept its feudal connotation: a small group of the well-born and well-behaved at the top of a 'natural' hierarchy. By the mid-nineteenth century, however, the term 'society' has been transformed, and a new referent has emerged: an autonomous 'human' entity composed of the entire range of social groups and constituencies. Nationalist adjectives could be appended (English society, Italian society), but powerful as these differences were, they did not modify the underlying humanist recognition of a species solidarity. By the late twentieth century Society has become an immensely useful explanatory construct, often in upper-case to indicate its objective status, and sometimes favoured in student examinations and essays as the First Cause of much that might otherwise require further explanation.

The word 'public' changes its value correspondingly. Formerly merely specifying an opposite to 'private', after the seventeenth century 'public' refers to a single organized or extended community such as 'Christendom' or 'Europe'; after the eighteenth century 'public' refers to the human race. The British locution of 'public' school belongs to the feudal phase of the word, in which 'private' families send their children out to be educated at sex-segregated ('public') schools rather than bring in tutors ('private') to accomplish the educational job; but in this locution 'public' has nothing to do with most of the world which, the implication goes, know nothing even of the distinction between 'private' and 'public'. This construction of 'public' is an index of feudalism; it indicates with a certain circularity that the 'public' is anything outside the domestic households of the wealthy or upper classes, but to the extent that this external realm remains relevant *to* the wealthy or upper classes. The existence of a *res publica*, something belonging to a common order of things that transcends clan organization altogether, never enters this equation at all; it might as well belong to another solar system.

By the mid-nineteenth century, most readers and virtually all novelists writing in English – except perhaps the resistant Bulwer Lytton and a few Americans – understood 'public' to mean a common world shared by everyone, however problematic the terms of sharing might be. The 'social' in this modern sense, and certainly the rationale for it, was invented in the late eighteenth century, largely in France and the United States, with impetus from the Philosophes, the Federalists, and Rousseau. England's equivalent republican phase had appeared precociously nearly a century earlier, and was largely eradicated after twenty years by the so-called 'Glorious Revolution' – certainly a malapropism to anyone weaned on Franco–American political thought. But even Enlightened Franco–American political thought still appeals to 'nature' for its founding generalizations. It remained for the nineteenth century, and largely through narrative, to explore the social implications of those previous political and economic experiments.

While revolution abroad made the English think anew about the nature of social constituencies, there were other influences closer to home that carried social experiment into specialized political and social arenas, particularly by utilitarians, with their newly inclusive agendas, and their heirs, the so-called Philosophical Radicals. It was England's peculiar situation to have lost its seventeenth-century chance at a democratic republic, but to have had a set of nineteenth-century social novelists and political philosophers who hypothesized about a kind of society that was made possible by republican revolutions that had very largely been carried through elsewhere, and not in England.

The changing view of nature described in Chapter One fosters the emerging experimental sense in the nineteenth century that society is a system in its own right. Thousands of social narratives exploring new social possibilities depended on a critical new sense of separation between society and 'nature'. If science had demystified nature, it had also outlined a blank place on the map where belief and value operate quite apart either from material process or from magic. In an 1858 review of books on scientific subjects, Sir Henry Holland concludes that the scientific spirit of the age reaches only to the doorstep of sociality. 'The only honest conclusion from scientific work', he writes, 'is that man is of an entirely 'different order of things' than the physical universe (Holland, 1862: 16). Such views are no wonder in a time when nature was proving no easy ally to any kind of faith. When phenomenal rarity is only a prologue to extinction, human definitions of value obviously belong to a 'different order of things' from the millennial moral moonscape glimpsed in Lyell's and Darwin's vision of physical nature. Under pressure from such visions, the human borders close against a material cosmos no longer spiritualized and thus no longer hospitable to qualitative value. Like a planetary body condensed from a cloud of cosmic dust, society appears in nineteenth-century narrative as an entity, and no longer as a hierarchical collection of sites in a 'natural' order. Such a construction provides a new horizon of definition for individual and collective life.

Charles Dickens is fond of showing that the social entity either moves as one or it does not move at all. Somewhat less apocalyptically, George Eliot treats society as a kind of open-ended network of possibilities. But in either case, 'society' is all-inclusive. That is the key premise of the social and historical novel. Society is one thing, not many: a single system of mutual interdependence and mutually informative relations. This emergent form, Society, can be perceived because, for the first time, it is conceived as being 'in' time – 'panoptic' time if you will, or in other words the neutral medium of humanism that makes possible the scientific study of objects within a single-point perspective system, and the political agreement of subjects within a common system. Historical and social novelists distinctively preoccupy themselves with two fundamental and related problems: the problem of negotiation between individuals and constituencies, and the crucial problem of locating the vantage point from which to view them.

Social order in nineteenth-century narratives, then, is not a reality to be reflected but a problem to be solved. In solving it, novelists rely on the same grammar of perspective that founds history (as described in Chapter Two) and that supports representational politics. That grammar makes available a common denominator, time or space, that anchors the comparative cases from which individual and collective forms emerge.

Pascal's often-quoted phrase applies well to the narrative as to the political project: 'Plurality which does not reduce itself to unity, is confusion. Unity which is not the result of plurality, is tyranny' (Starzinger, 1991: 55). A new plurality of worlds faces the requirement to negotiate on common ground, for better or worse. New questions are raised about what constitutes such a social entity. What kind of an entity is it? What is the basis of membership? Is everyone equal? If not, why not? Who should enjoy legal protection? Are the constituents of society individuals, or groups? Who is a citizen? Group membership – in families, or genders, or classes, or towns, or nations – no longer seems automatic.

Constituencies – not the same thing as classes – figure at all levels in the narrative of incorporation fostered by historical and social novels: working classes in Gaskell's novels, the urban poor in Dickens, the disappearing artisan class and the emerging electorate in George Eliot, the young born into anachronistic gentility in Meredith and Trollope. The negotiations between new constituencies figure conspicuously in mid-century social narrative: between industrial north and agricultural south, between traditional village culture and modern urban life, between life in the country house and life in the growing towns, between social classes, between the sexes, between Parliament and 'the public', between past and present, even between motives within a single individual. At every turn differences present themselves for mediation.

The problem of social class appears both in nineteenth-century social novels, and even more in twentieth-century readings of those novels. Class is such an embattled concept – one might almost call it a taboo subject – that it needs careful attention of the kind recently attempted in several books, most notably Peter Calvert's *The Concept of Class: An Historical Introduction* (1982). It is of interest for this discussion largely as a submerged issue in nineteenth-century novels. The conception that society is an entity first needs to be established, and then various new constituencies require to be considered. Charles Dickens more than any other writer accomplishes both these tasks, and the job is carried on through the century by Gaskell, Eliot, Meredith, Oliphant, Hardy, Gissing, Moore and many hundreds of others. The social novel acts literally as an experimental laboratory for considering the role of new constituent elements in a newly identifiable social entity.

But the issue of social class, or of any constituent groups for that matter, has a problematic presence at best in Victorian novels. Some commentators conclude that a system of takeovers prevented Victorians from ever completing the social analysis upon which the social novelists embark with such vigour and popularity. The ' "gentrification" of the commercial and industrial class', Joel Mokyr writes, 'marks the failure of Victorian Britain (Mokyr, 1985: 19). It has often been noted that the aristocracy and gentry manage to keep their power through the period, in a kind of class bonding (Briggs, 1983: 199), and to assimilate new groups to their exclusive and essentially undemocratic, even feudal agendas. It has even been noted that this translation is accomplished partly *through* novel reading (Blake, 1989: 146–52).

Other commentators, on the other hand, find that between 1840 and 1890 the balance of power shifted towards democracy through collective bargaining of the union movement, though 'it was after 1870, however, that a new working–class culture with a distinct way of life took shape, the product essentially of segregation' (Briggs, 1983: 198–9). Democratic agendas and the possibility of socialism thus are seen to arise in solidarity movements like Chartism, feminism, and the working–class movement that produces the Independent Labour Party started by Keir Hardie in 1893 (Halevy, 1966; Thompson, 1974; Himmelfarb, 1991). But such movements also create new divisions to be negotiated as they produce new constituents for inclusion in the social entity. For novelists like Elizabeth Gaskell or Charles Dickens, who focus on the most obvious casualties of urbanization and industrialization, the goal is inclusion, and precisely not 'assimilation' which in effect erases the differences that constitute a social entity in the first place. This erasure of social difference is precisely the effect Feuerbach attributes to religion.

Social segregation by class receives thundering denunciation by novelists from Dickens to Hardy, as something that runs athwart the very medium of historical narratives. But the other extreme of socialist reduction of class differences does not appear as a solution, except implicitly in the later part of the century where novelists like Gissing and Moore define society in terms of its poorest and most helpless members. Some even claim that the divisive idea of class arises late; some trace it, paradoxically enough, to the work of Scottish and English democrats and their efforts to translate a quite limited French Enlightenment idea of class into an English context where it retains a 'confusion of economic and political overtones' and accumulates in the twentieth century, through Marxism, an eschatological emphasis (Calvert, 1982: 25).

For the present discussion, what deserves notice is the insistent individualism of mid-Victorian novels. It testifies to the presence of a complex struggle between two different definitions of the social entity, and two different systems of obligation. A 'self-policing economic individualism' keeps solidarity among workers at bay (Best, 1971: 268), despite efforts by writers like Elizabeth Gaskell and Charles Dickens. It is often economic conditions that contribute to the lack of political solidarity, especially among women (Cosslett, 1988). In sum, the questions about the definition of corporate social identity broadly inform the development of nineteenth-century social discourse, from musical forms to political theory. Literature has most latitude for the experiment. By comparison with the complex perspective systems of the social, historical novels like Trollope's *The Prime Minister* or Eliot's *Middlemarch*, the insistent individualism even of J. S. Mill's forward looking political thought seems oddly monocular despite his massive contribution to the definition of social constituency.

There was a decidedly conservative undertow in broadly available popular writing, for example in the political philosophy of Walter Bagehot. Something of a minnow compared to Mill, Bagehot expresses in his *The English Constitution* (1867) a fear precisely of these 'new constituencies' (Bagehot, 1928: 276). The 'natural' perfection of the English Constitution, as Bagehot sees it, is as much a question of '*style*' as of law (ibid.: 9, 129, 243); obviously distinctive style is a form of social communication, but it is not what philosophers and activists like John Stuart Mill have in mind when they philosophize about politics. Mill is the major theorist of *Representative Government* (1861), as of political liberty and of the rights of women. But even he remains resistantly individualistic in his vision of political representation. He is scarcely willing to confront issues of corporate representation of the kind presented by new union among workers. Although his *The Subjection of Women* still has currency as an analysis of women's political situation in Britain, and has had immense influence in the women's movement internationally, still Mill does not foresee that women would need to act collectively in order to achieve legal and other rights.

Whereas novelists probe the whole difficult problem of social identity – the way in which individuality by definition is comparative, a product of relation with others and not a 'natural' or God-given identity – Mill insistently regards the social and political constituent as an individual, despite his clear sense that society is a construct and a largely inherited set of conditions. Ideally, he says, everyone participates in sovereign power (Mill, 1975: 187, 197–8), both for their own sakes and also for the sake of society. Participation encourages activity and a process of individuation, in fact individuality *is* development; passivity, on the other hand, only encourages emotions like 'envy' ('that most anti-social and odious of all passions' (ibid.: 96; also 182, 192)). In addition, the polity at large requires to have the benefit of these developed individual talents. But Mill explicitly rejects the idea that society's constituents might be groups.

This idea that social order depends on individual difference finds its most powerful rationale in Mill's classic statement *On Liberty* (1859). 'Individuality is the same thing as development' he writes (ibid.: 79), and his political theory of social liberty rests upon this thought. The aim of government, as of personal life, should be to foster whatever preserves the individual's freedom to differ, and to constrain whatever blocks it. The more voices the better. In this position Mill explicates one of the key dispositions of his culture and its narrative, the disposition that links individual and social identity democratically, that is to say, on the horizontal and in process of serial and collective development, not in the vertical, hierarchical and naturalized mode of traditional English social usage. Individual choice and individual development may or may not produce genius, but they are the source of whatever is valuable. 'The initiation of all wise or noble things, comes and must come from individuals; generally at first from some one individual. The honour and glory of the average man is that he is capable of following that initiative' (ibid.: 80–1).

But specifically corporate activity of the kind engaged in by working men's unions, and later by the suffragettes, Mill calls 'sinister interests', and he regards them as the second greatest danger to representative government – the first and greatest danger being stupid representatives. Even though Mill heeded the new voices of women that, since 1800, had been contesting the political and economic conditions of women (Campbell, 1989), and even though he wrote the single most powerful argument against what he calls *The Subjection of Women*, despite all this Mill did not envision the need for corporate feminism, which he probably would class with 'sinister interests' of the kind that hold out for their own good in conflict with the good of the whole community (Mill, 1975: 237). They foster 'class legislation' (ibid.: 245). While his complex and problematic proposal for proportional representation understandably got nowhere – he favours representation weighted on the side of accomplishment and merit – it reflects the intense nineteenth-century experimentation with definitions of social constituencies, and the awareness of the corporate dimensions of the identities to be 'represented' in Parliament.

Social novelists explore the corporate construction of identity in less insistently individualistic terms than either the conservative Bagehot or the liberal Mill. 'Self' has its entire meaning and value in a social context, in negotiation with other selves and groups of selves; it has dignity socially, not naturally or cosmically, where, as a fallen Christian soul, it confronts moral perfection or material immensity. And the conferring of ontological status is mutual. Society can be an entity, and not merely one class on a natural hierarchy, *only* because of such individual differentiation; otherwise 'society' would simply be equated with particular individuals as it is, Feuerbach claims, in theological religion (see Chapter Two, pp. 109–112). Consensus of the formal sort, that founds historical forms, cannot materialize *without* dissent; dogma does not support history, except as a history of error and a revelation of *a priori* truth. Trollope's treatment of Phineas Finn, MP, or George Eliot's treatment of Gwendolen Harleth, depend entirely on the open-ended possibilities of history. So, similarly, the social entity can only emerge where individuality is something socially constituted. Just as the dissent makes the consensus, the individual makes the difference that produces the condition for mediation; mediation and the consensus arise precisely between constituents whose mutuality is newly conceived in the same breath as their differences. Historical, social narratives show over and over again that formulations pitting Individual against Society are the falsest of expressions.

Mill's discussion of libertarian social order, *On Liberty*, captures as no other document does this relation between individual specialization and corporate identity. Self and Society are born simultaneously in what amounts almost to a Mystery of the historical and social narrative. Mill argues that individual development fosters the greatest good of the greatest number. The encouragement of individual difference fosters the strength of a social entity. Far from disrupting social coherence, individual differences sustain it. By recognizing a difference, in other words, by accepting the validity of different views and practices, society confirms its own definition and widens its options; by foreclosing on difference and emphasizing what is customary, whether in religious, or class, or any other terms, a society forces individuality to fade and thus undermines its own survival.

Mill, however, does not envision decline or chaos any more than he envisions corporate action. *On Liberty* shows in various places how the potentially radical implications of Mill's liberalism are held in check by a lingering reliance on what is 'natural' (in human 'nature' for instance). Mill holds that the social system is the sum total of individual efforts collected over time; it has no 'essential' identity. But he also says that truth will prevail if given enough liberty. Like Adam Smith, who had such influence on nineteenth-century social ideas, Mill trusts to nature for the balance of opposing claims that, he argues, it is the business of a free society to maximize.

On Liberty puts forward as the heart of politics the same principle of differentiation that every historical and social novelist relies upon and that Feuerbach enunciates as the first principle of culture. Both Feuerbach and Trollope could comfortably take responsibility for these lines from Mill, in which he states that:

> the unlikeliness of one person to another is generally the first thing which draws attention of either to the imperfection of his own type, and the superiority of another, or the possibility, by combining the advantages of both, of producing something better than either.... Europe is, in my judgment, wholly indebted to this plurality of paths for its progressive and many-sided development.
>
> (ibid.: 88–9)

These ideas very much resemble Feuerbach's argument (which Mill undoubtedly knew) that culture depends upon qualitative distinction between individuals, and that religion 'extinguishes' this very distinction and thus does not contain 'the principle of culture' (Feuerbach, 1957: 158–60). Mill himself criticizes religion for crushing the very initiative that produces the equality among constituents that makes a social consensus possible in the first place. Catholicism creates class, by creating an élite which can read key texts and a mass which cannot. Protestantism, although on the side of progress because it lends itself to individual choice in religion, does not in its radical forms extend that tolerance beyond religion, as in Calvinism which, Mill says, delights in crushing human initiative and encouraging surrender (Mill 1975: 48–9, 76–7).

What limitations might apply to individual expression remains a question in the liberal politics Mill espouses. Social novelists like Eliot or Trollope certainly present systems capacious enough for a wide range of social behaviour, from the eccentric and the criminal to the morally fine and the socially creative; but accommodating such a range in the social medium proves a matter of infinite delicacy and fine tuning. Mill's idea of the equality of all citizens, combined with an inclusive idea of citizenship, implies that all major social questions would always concern everyone, but historical and social novels show this to be unrealistic, at least in the short term. In the long term, though, this is precisely what historical novels propose: that even the remotest achievements of individuals long dead shape at every moment the condition of the living. Because Mill resisted the idea of social units smaller than the totalized 'society', 'social'-ism became a logical destination for him. Like later liberal economists, he would have found it nonsensical to ask whether there is any stopping place between individualism and collectivism. Nonsensical because they are the same thing. It is the small but aggrandizing constituency that Mill regards as a sinister interest. 'Syndicalism is the enemy' (Robbins, 1939: vii–viii), as one of Mill's twentieth-century heirs has put it.

Yet at the same time Mill considers worst of all the idea that government should control people, in effect substituting itself for religion. He rejects the

> theory of 'social rights', the like of which probably never before found its way into distinct language; being nothing short of this – that it is the absolute social right of every individual, that every other individual shall act in every respect exactly as he ought.... So monstrous a principle is far more dangerous than any single interference with liberty; there is no violation of liberty which it would not justify.
>
> (*On Liberty*, in Mill, 1975: 110)

His corporate entity is an entity-in-process. When he has given up the rationalism of utilitarianism, and asks what system he comes up with to replace it, Mill's answer is 'a no-system' (Mill, 1924: 113): in other words, a set of conditions and a method, rather like science. Or like George Eliot's de-centred narrative networks such as *Felix Holt* and *Middlemarch*, a network of mutually influential but loosely organized arrangements that allows social organization but does not hamper difference. The problem of 'how to accommodate difference without hierarchy' was, in Mill's and George Eliot's time as it still remains in the late twentieth century, the central problem of liberal political organization (Owens, 1983: 62).

The historical novel is by definition social because it always implicitly places individual considerations into a context of social common denominators. But the possible range of formulation is immense. Mrs Gaskell's social world tends to be quite dualistic in its comparisons between different regions, different economic circumstances, and different classes, and the duality always implies a hierarchy of value where one term (north and south, rich and poor) depreciates the other. Dickens favours commanding metaphors like Chancery, or the prison. George Eliot's society is a web, a headless and footless network of relationship where tradition and the individual talent contribute to a gradually shifting social emphasis. Across this considerable range, social and historical novels provide an experimental laboratory for exploring new social options.

The social novel, which shows the symbiosis of individual and social entities, necessarily concerns itself with difference. Difference in custom, wealth, language, tradition, class and experience: these constitute the basis for that mediation, that overriding common denominator of social, historical time; these provide the fractures and fault-lines that make social bridges necessary. By formal fiat the historical convention, with its grammar of perspective, constructs a common world. Whether or not the characters in these novels make a mess of it, as they most often do because they lack sufficient perspective to recognize social mutuality, the very narrative medium asserts the existence of that solidarity. The business of the social novel is to demonstrate to readers, and to the occasional representative character, that these social fissures can and even must be bridged. 'Every difference is form', George Eliot writes (1963: 433), and this was about as far as she wanted to go in characterizing what the social entity might be. Because a plurality of worlds is possible, recognizing the differences between them is the beginning of order.

An important register of the nineteenth–century's problem of corporate identity can be found in the lists of new journals that appear year upon year, each for a different constituency. After the repeal of the newspaper tax in 1854 and the advertising tax in 1855, such publishing developed rapidly. The increase of interest groups, all of them writing to be read, produced a journalistic explosion during the nineteenth century. Well before 1840 the number of journals for different audiences and interest groups had proliferated into the thousands; by the end of Victoria's reign at least 30,000 different serials had come into, and in many cases gone from, the scene; some estimate the actual number (many were short-lived) to have been more like 50,000. There were journals for Methodists, missionaries, fashionable ladies and gentlemen, maidservants, families, zoologists, Catholics, sportspersons, citizens interested in news, the arts, literature, gossip, and so on and on across a range of specialization. These are the 'constituent parts' of a culture (Fulton and Cotee, 1985). Historical and social novelists wrote for this audience, made more aware of itself as an entity by publications such as these.

Newly enfranchised constituencies pressed their new representatives with new demands for better education and working conditions, and new journals gave public voice to the interests of ever-diversifying new constituencies. To some the social scene seems only a site of conflict and hubbub, but to many others it appears an immensely creative potential of collective order. The need to mediate this proliferation of social voices produced an increasingly libertarian politics, based more than ever on a consciousness of constituencies, and less than ever on inherited rank alone. The historical narrative, that is, the narrative perspective system described in Chapter Two, is precisely the medium wanted. This increasingly libertarian ideal of social order, according to George Watson, is 'the' British ideology (1973: 14–15, 19). No divinely sanctioned privilege exerts absolute and unmediatable control in a system constituted in the first place by the differences among its defining constituencies.

Like political parties, these interest groups do not tend to regard themselves primarily as opponents in a fight – though fights there were; they were collaborators in a common project of articulation in which particular beliefs and opinions had to be negotiated through a newly respected 'public' opinion. The country labourers in George Eliot's *Adam Bede*, who learn to read and write in Bartle Massey's night school, are preparing to join a common enterprise and, in so doing, to cross a threshold between one social order of things and another. Their rural way of life, and the faith it inspires in a 'natural' fitness of things that includes inequality in essence and before the law, all this gives way in this novel to a new social order associated with the factory towns lying just over the horizon. In that order, hypothetically, everyone is brought to book by the same laws regardless of their condition.

The voice of 'public' opinion is much, much more than the Voice of Mrs Grundy, or of evangelical righteousness. It is the ineffable voice of social self-awareness, the Nobody narrative function (see Chapter Two), the narrative voice of an emerging social entity. The special, particular narrative awareness that materializes in the narrative language of historical novels, and that broods over the narrative world in Gaskell, late Dickens, Trollope, Meredith or George Eliot, is like the voice of society, speaking to itself.

THE ECONOMIC EXPERIMENT WITH CORPORATE ORDER

The economic construction of corporate order becomes a major factor in nineteenth-century social debate, and in the narratives that explore new social possibility. The full effects of the Industrial Revolution were only beginning to be felt in the 1840s when its supporting economic system began to centralize. The reconstruction of social order associated with such massive changes necessarily 'took' very gradually. Even then, two economies co-existed, one belonging to a traditional agricultural, trade, and artisan economy, the other belonging to fledgling modern technologies for producing things like cotton, iron and paper, and the engineering and railroads to design and transport them. Helped by a lack of government involvement, and by such blows to the agrarian economy as the 1846 Repeal of the protectionist Corn Laws of 1815 and 1828, the smaller and developing industrial segment of the economy 'began to expand and spread at an unprecedented rate, and eventually supplanted the traditional economy altogether' (Mokyr, 1985: 1, 5, 44). Ironically it was the very lack of centralization in Britain that permitted the rapid development of an economy, a main result of which was centralization.

The consolidation of economic power evidenced by the enclosures of the eighteenth century produced incalculable, drastic alteration in the way people lived their lives, thought of their identity, assumed relationship. 'It is almost impossible to imagine the scope and impact of the process of enclosure', writes Robert Heilbroner. 'The market system, with its essential components of land, labor, and capital was thus born in agony – an agony that began in the thirteenth century and had not run its course until well into the nineteenth. Never was a revolution less well understood, less welcomed, less planned' (Heilbroner, 1980: 30–1).

The structure of wealth undergoes correspondingly radical redefinition in the middle of the nineteenth century. Various legislation, like The Bank Charter Act (1844), fostered the growth of central banking, the minting of a common currency, and the decline of local, country banks which had evolved to serve private customers and various industries like textiles and wool, and even to issue their own currencies. Such moves towards centralization and standardization enhanced the even more powerful influence of an expanding railroad system that was transforming the markets and reducing the need for local banks. When joint-stock banking was legalized in 1857, banking rapidly became more independent of the trade and other business pursuits out of which it arose (Pressnell, 1956: 510, 158, 2, 14). After the 1840s the existence of a common currency and a common banking system was an important element in the social self-awareness that explores its options in social novels.

Social novelists register this seismic activity in the material of their art. Trollope especially anatomizes the encounter between tradition and money, and particularly the way an aristocratic social order revises itself out of existence; many of his characters are out of their depth in one capitalist venture or another. Dickens shows the social costs of funding old exclusions with new money, and his suicidal financier, Merdle, is one of many in Victorian fiction. George Eliot treats the new economy as a way of life that, for better or worse, is changing forever the traditional rural society where her novels are largely situated; Mrs Poyser makes butter enough for the family but resists making it for strangers; Silas Marner is the last of a vanishing breed of hand-loom weavers. Colossal financial failures, with attendant suicides, motivate plot in Margaret Oliphant's *Hester* (1853), in Dickens' *Our Mutual Friend* (1864–5), and in several Trollope novels. Railroads stray into the margins of *Middlemarch*; in both Trollope and Dickens the steam engine performs a kind of double duty, as a juggernaut of industrial progress and as an instrument of suicide for failed financiers (*The Way We Live Now, Dombey and Son*). The strikes and riots that figure in Elizabeth Gaskell's *North and South* and Eliot's *Felix Holt* suggest a reading public urgently aware of the need for structural and political reform. The real foundation work, however, lies not in treatment of particular issues, but in rebuilding the corporate system within which those issues can be treated. The massive social and cultural re-adjustment required by industrial society prompts experiment with new forms of corporate order across the cultural range from politics to music. Economic and social versions of corporate social identity compete in nineteenth-century narrative, and the novelists tend to emphasize the limits of the economic system and to show the social destructiveness of those committed exclusively to it.

The idea that society is an economic entity is an almost theological idea. It derives from Adam Smith, whose 1776 treatise on *The Wealth of Nations* provides a massive and continuing influence on conceptions and formations of social order. Because Smith ignored the industrial revolution, his work was already nostalgic and out of date in his own day so far as its particulars were concerned, especially in its anti-corporate emphasis (Heilbroner, 1980: 53; Mokyr, 1985: 13). Economic naturalists like Ricardo and Malthus who followed him had more precise estimates of the actual working of an industrial economy. But Smith provided the most powerful generalization: the idea that society was an entity.

The ensuing difficulty has been that Smith conceives this entity entirely in economic terms. It may be, as Robert Heilbroner argues, that 'after *The Wealth of Nations* men [sic] began to see the world about themselves with new eyes; they saw how the tasks they did fitted into the whole of society, and they saw that society as a whole was proceeding at a majestic pace toward a distant but clearly visible goal' (Heilbroner, 1980: 39, 51). But the 'whole of society' is not quite as holistic as this suggests. Smith's construction of a social entity defined in economic terms, as well as the laissez-faire attitude belonging to it, rests on a fundamentally religious belief in 'nature' that gives a sort of absolution to even the meanest mercantile conceptions. While it is very far from the meanest, Adam Smith's *Inquiry into the Nature and Causes of the Wealth of Nations* depends nevertheless on contradictory agendas that function to this day and that acted like a powerful, if often invisible planetary influence on the developing sociality of nineteenth-century England. Smith's social entity, at once economic and 'natural', simply conflicts at the root with the newly self-conscious social awareness among nineteenth-century constituencies. It is worth taking a look backwards to refresh acquaintance with this economically defined social system that has such continuing power through the nineteenth century.

Smith assumes that his economic system is 'natural' – an assumption that finds expression in ways that are both bizarre and all too familiar. Left to itself, Smith's economic mechanism – that newest and most artificial of constructs – regulates itself 'naturally'. For Smith any attempt to control this 'natural' system by regulation or monopoly (or other syndicalism) only produces evils. It is scarcely possible to comprehend the extensive power of this essentially romantic and religious idea of a natural (in the eighteenth century this meant rational) system which, *left to itself*, will generate social order in a balanced and self-limiting way. Providentialism here translates itself straight into the market economy.

Smith's vocabulary for describing the natural 'balance' of his system is positively Platonic. The 'natural price' seems to be a kind of static form existing transcendent, and apart from the actual market price that only approximates it:

> When the *quantity* brought to market is just sufficient to supply the effectual demand and no more, the market price naturally comes to be either exactly, or as nearly as can be judged of, *the same with* the natural price.
>
> (Smith, 1986: 188; emphasis added)

The market price approximates, but never becomes exactly 'the same with the natural price'. The market price is but a shadowy reflection of an essence: something *representative of* some 'natural' price that belongs to an order of things beyond social agency altogether.

Smith's use of the term 'quantity' becomes almost a coded reference to 'nature'. Although Smith seems to consider 'quality' as part of 'quantity', presumably because qualitative considerations necessarily influence demand and supply, still Smith almost never uses the word 'quality', while the word 'quantity' is ubiquitous. The problem with 'quality' is that it directly raises questions of collective value and intervention, and these are not relevant to the functioning of Smith's mechanism. His emphasis on 'quantity' accounts partly for the congeniality of his theories to the culture of historicism and realism, which quantify in order to produce intelligibility.

When Smith describes the way this economic entity functions, it sounds almost like a Newtonian planetary system:

The *natural price*, therefore, is, as it were, the *central* price, to which the prices of all commodities are continually *gravitating*. ... The whole *quantity* of industry annually employed in order to bring any commodity to market, *naturally* suits itself in this manner to the effectual demand. *It naturally aims* at bringing always that precise *quantity* thither which may be sufficient to supply, and no more than supply, that demand.

(ibid.: 189; emphasis added)

'It' is 'the market', and it operates entirely apart from individual agency or direction, like a force of nature or a planetary system complete with a gravitational centre. It is a system with its own principles that should be observed but not interfered with. The phrase 'Invisible Hand', which appears only once in *The Wealth of Nations*, does justice to the naturalizing of social and economic mechanisms here; Smith puts them beyond human intervention and at the basis of a vision that incorporates social life into cosmic order, however secularized that order may appear to be. It is not hard to see how such a providential notion of economics gets translated into confusedly social terms.

In this vision, the limit of individual 'initiative' is a sort of Darwinian desire to 'truck and barter' that essentially separates 'human' from animal nature (no one ever saw a dog exchange one bone for another (ibid.: 198)). The desire to accumulate is acceptable because it is 'natural'; prodigality and monopoly are evil because they interfere with nature. Of itself, 'the uniform, constant, and uninterrupted effort of every man to better his condition' is a principle of life that can do more than doctors to restore 'health and vigour to the [individual] constitution' (ibid.: 239–41). Enlightened self–interest reigns unproblematically so long as 'nature' is left to take its course. Looking after oneself in this pre-industrial universe is not only an economic necessity, it is a sacred duty. Smith's ideas of consciousness and social identity are very restricted, belonging chiefly to that immediate and relatively short-term consideration comprehended by individual economic self-interest.

The rationale of this economic entity is all too familiar. Competition alone regulates this society which would otherwise have no order beyond individuals grasping for gain at the expense of others; and competition is regulated by a 'natural' self–interest that permits 'the system' itself to regulate supply and demand. The existence of more than one economic structure (according to energy source, for example: Wrigley, 1988) does not alter the holistic quality of economic explanation. The pre-industrial and quasi-Providential quality of this explanatory system has given it

138

tenacity far beyond its explanatory power. From its origin, then, laissez-faire economics maintained the same contradictory blend of cultural and 'natural' explanation that gives interest and impetus to so much social experiment and social narrative in the first half of the nineteenth century. The religious overtones remained especially reassuring in a century of religious crisis; and this is what recommended it to periodical writers who spoke of 'the natural law of supply and demand' (Anon., 1851: 13).

Adam Smith's work, including its paradoxes, had vast influence: not only on Thomas Malthus and economic theorists, but also, and through Malthus, on Darwin, on the Philosophical Radicals born of utilitarianism who did so much to change nineteenth-century legal and political arrangements, and on all laissez-faire economists since. But the subtexts of Smith's treatise are often overlooked. For one thing, his treatise shows that society can be described as a self-regulating, self-sustaining *economic* entity only when the entity and the processes sustaining it are naturalized. His faith in 'natural' arrangements gives a quasi-religious authorization to economic description, but leaves moral and more broadly social questions aside. But what if the social entity is not at all 'natural'? What becomes of the economic mechanism then? These are central questions for novelists like Dickens, Gaskell, Trollope, Oliphant (a Scot) and Gissing, to name a few.

Defined in economic terms only, Smith's social order produces; and what that order produces is wealth. Anything that does not produce wealth (what he calls 'unproductive labour') – for example, service work – does not belong to the social entity except parasitically. Composed of three capital-producing classes – landowners, merchants, and labourers – his 'inclusive' society is a self-regulating mechanism. This, from the point of view of the nineteenth century, is actually an exclusive group depending for regulation upon the excluded: upon invisible hands and feet. Women's production is for the most part simply excluded from the realm of value (Delphy, 1984: 60–2, 71, 140–1, 179), something that continues two centuries later to be justified by the same pre-industrial legend in the form of wage discrimination in the modern workplace, where women's wages are depressed below and kept outside the realm of economic competition by unscrupulous governmental and employer policies (Lundahl and Wadensjö, 1984: 9, 176). In this pre-industrial theory there is no essential need for the kinds of mediate consciousness – social, philosophical, religious – that nineteenth-century narrative makes prominent as it struggles with sudden changes in the magnitude of communities and with the social issues of industrial society.

Smith's developing economic structure comes with an entail of naturalized, even religious apologetics that universalize its claims to explanatory power. Rather than appearing as just another constituent part of a larger social entity, the economic definition of social order appears as being itself the definition of sociality. Economic issues are naturalized at the expense of all others. Despite numerous expressions of social awareness in *The Wealth of Nations*, its social vision remains by definition economic, static, and ahistorical. There is nothing here of culture and motive; nothing of the Benthamite modification of the law of markets by social standards, where the 'working rule' is that everything serves the greatest happiness of the greatest number (Robbins, 1970: 79–83) and where democratic impulse is implicit. There is, in short, nothing here of the social problematic evident in the novels of later Dickens, Gaskell, Trollope, George Eliot and Meredith.

Social novels focus on precisely what Smith leaves out: the relationships and gaps between systems. In historical and social narrative, Society is not primarily a mechanism for growing and harvesting cash. The interstices between capital-producing classes are filled with consciousness, time, history and hope, the mediations of a moral, philosophical, religious human nature that knows and needs a lot more than getting and spending. The economic construction of Society inherited from Smith appears in nineteenth-century novels as *the* primary obstacle to sociality. Dickens' fictional capitalists, Gradgrind (*Hard Times*) and Mr Dombey and Merdle (*Little Dorrit*), victimize others or themselves by their cold-hearted, relentless pursuit of money; Elizabeth Gaskell's John Thornton (*North and South*) survives capitalism, but her Henry Carson (*Mary Barton*) is turned into a monster by it. These similar fictional cases bring into view precisely that part of the human social order that Adam Smith dismisses with a negative definition as 'unproductive labour'. By this he means the servants, the working poor, the women: in short, and as social novelists are fond of pointing out, the entire economic underclass that constitutes the essential support system for Smith's three capital-producing classes.

Social novelists, and this increasingly towards the later part of the century, show that the working classes are anything but 'unproductive' – a fact that became especially evident when they engaged in syndicalist activity, that is, when they organized and went on strike. In order for his theory of production to work, Smith must define the service economy negatively, because to include it, as the more inclusive social and historical nineteenth-century narratives do, simply threatens the basis of his theory that society is an economic entity. The social novel, with its very different construction of the social entity, shows the mutual reliance between the productive and the so-called unproductive classes: shows that the so-called Invisible Hand proves itself to be nothing other than the hand of the poorest class supporting those balances that are taken to be 'natural' by richer groups. As George Eliot put it in *The Mill on the Floss*, the 'light and graceful irony', the claret and carpets of the wealthier classes, require 'nothing less than a wide and arduous national life condensed in unfragrant deafening factories, cramping itself in mines, sweating at furnaces' (1961, IV, iii: 255).

For social novelists the developing monetary structure of obligation is almost always a substitute for a social one. In Trollope the characters motivated by money are destroyers like Lizzie Eustace, her charlatan husband, and the speculator, Ferdinand Lopez. Trollope takes up these issues in *The Prime Minister* (1876): for example, in this conversation between Lopez and his brother-in-law to be, Everett Wharton, an idle son of a wealthy barrister. Lopez is smarter, capable of an amusing turn, but uncommitted; Wharton is committed, sort of, to a life larger than money, so long as no particular effort is involved. Wharton begins:

'Money's a very nice thing.'

'Very nice', said Lopez.

'But the search after it is debasing. If a man could make money for four, or six, or even eight hours a day, and then wash his mind of the pursuit, as a clerk in an office washes the copies and ledgers out of his mind, then –'

'He would never make money in that way, – and keep it.'

'And therefore the whole thing is debasing. A man ceases to care for the great interests of the world, or even to be aware of their existence, when his whole soul is in Spanish bonds. They wanted to make a banker of me, but I found that it would kill me.'

'It would kill me, I think, [says Lopez] if I had to confine myself to Spanish bonds.'

(Trollope, 1983b: ch. 2)

The social lassitude of this conversation is striking. The 'great interests of the world' are imagined only vaguely by the one, and are confined by the other to a financial universe larger than bonds. This delicious passage, especially in context, catches the timbre of character in the tone of the speakers and the fact that, between them, they do not have a single social thought.

Dickens persistently compares the economic and the social systems of obligation. Instead of a flexible, open-sided system of obligation that generates and encourages forgiveness ('forgive us our debts as we forgive our debtors'), the market encourages an enervating, ontologically threatening competition for finite resources. Mr Dombey, whose single-minded pursuit of wealth is implicated in the death of his wife, attempts to explain money to his young son who is also dying of neglect. Sitting with his father, little Paul, nearly five years old, asks about money:

'Papa! what's money?'

The abrupt question had such immediate reference to the subject of Mr. Dombey's thoughts, that Mr. Dombey was quite disconcerted...

Mr. Dombey was in a difficulty. He would have liked to give him some explanation involving the terms circulating-medium, currency, depreciation of currency, paper, bullion, rates of exchange, value of precious metals in the market, and so forth; but looking down at the little chair, and seeing what a long way down it was, he answered: 'Gold, and silver, and copper. Guineas, shillings, half-pence. You know what they are?'

'Oh yes I know what they are', said Paul. 'I don't mean that, Papa. I mean what's money after all?.... I mean, Papa, what can it do?'...

'Money, Paul, can do anything.'...

'Why didn't money save me my Mama?' returned the child. 'It isn't cruel, is it?'

'Cruel!' said Mr. Dombey, settling his neckcloth, and seeming to resent the idea. 'No. A good thing can't be cruel'.

'If it's a good thing, and can do anything', said the little fellow, thoughtfully, as he looked back at the fire, 'I wonder why it didn't save me my Mama'.

(Dickens, 1970: ch. 8)

Money systems are one thing – and they are Mr Dombey's Alpha and Omega. But the social casualties of that system start piling up, right in Mr Dombey's own family. *Dombey and Son*'s eventual plot resolution involves the inhuman capitalist's providential recognition of a moral debt to his wronged daughter, Florence, and, implicitly, to his wronged dead wife and his wronged dead son. The moral standard and the gold standard compete for Mr Dombey's soul, and eventually the moral standard wins. An explicit parallel like this marks the extra margin beyond mere economics required for a social economy; it is the margin of forgiveness, of mercy, of sympathy, of qualitative distinction and limitation – all things that the market system cannot match.

Dickens compares these competing systems of obligation in every novel. It is especially explicit in *Dombey and Son* (1848), in the anomalous

Hard Times (1854), and again in *Great Expectations* (1860–61) where his greater mastery of the grammar of perspective, and his shift away from providential explanation, permit him to avoid simplistic conclusions and to focus on the importance of social justice by exposing its shams. *Great Expectations* unearths a whole calculus of exchange, riddled with betrayal and set in motion by Compeyson, who understands only a calculus of compensation, debt and bribe, and nothing of the 'justice' the novel insistently seeks and fails to find. Compeyson's exposure, the unravelling of information about his secret links with Miss Havisham and Magwitch, is less important in the end than the parallel plot of Pip's betrayals and lapses of commitment. Increasingly Dickens questions whether such moral awakenings are not simply 'too late', like the final discoveries of Esther and Detective Bucket in *Bleak House* (1853), a novel that implicitly likens the detective's effort to sort out truth to the effort of bailing out the universe with a bucket.

Anthony Trollope pays special attention to the insidious ways that the structure of indebtedness slips between moral and monetary terminology. Even in the most apparently private matters these structures of obligation compete. In *The Small House at Allington* (1864) the Dale family 'owe' their daughter's life to Dr Crofts (Trollope, 1991: 425, ch. 38); and Mrs Dale in *The Last Chronicle of Barset* (1867) ruminates in banker's terms on the contrast between the failure of Lily's engagement and the success of Grace Crawley's: 'Could any credit be given to Grace for her success, or any blame attached to Lily for her failure'? (Trollope, 1967: 296–7, ch. 28). The callow fiancé, Crosbie, who jilts Lily in favour of more vulgar but more aristocratic in-laws, begins thus the 'the career of owing' his soul to patronage that becomes a measure of his moral default and a set-up for his eventual well-earned ruin (Trollope, 1991: 438, ch. 40). So completely does Crosbie confuse the 'society' of the upper class with Society in general that (when he reappears in a later novel, deeply in debt and widowed) he courts Lily again because now she has money. Even his worldly friend Pratt finds this too callow (Trollope, 1967: ch. 53).

Debt is another locus where economic and moral, even religious meaning conflict. In the nineteenth century, debt was a crime one went to jail for; in narrative it becomes an omnibus carrier of social cautionary tales. Debt remains an inescapable structure of experience, almost a metaphysic, even when the monetary debt has been paid. In Dickens' *Little Dorrit* (1857), Mr Dorrit emerges from debtors' prison half-way through the novel, but imprisonment has put an end to his capacity to change; he remains a prisoner and a debtor until his death when, presumably, the very calculus of earthly debt and payment will be permanently transcended. Mr Tulliver's debts in *The Mill on The Floss* (1860) precipitate the family's bankruptcy and ensuing psychic losses. Lydgate's debts in *Middlemarch* (1871–2) mark for him the choice between two very different ways of life; by attempting to finesse the moral choice, he ruins his career. Margaret Oliphant's *Hester* (1883) subtly anatomizes a society ruled by banks and their failures. In one of the few positive treatments of debt, Gwendolen Harleth's indebtedness to Daniel Deronda for return of her pawned necklace motivates her painful emergence from being a marketable item to being a socially responsible grown-up.

The competition between social and monetary motives, especially when it comes to debt, produces ironies that continuously delight Trollope. *Framley Parsonage* (1861) is the most thoroughgoing example. By bringing debt on his family and the bailiff into his house, Mark Robarts betrays those who support him. Debt clearly is a symptom of moral default and, like other essentially virtuous Trollopian debtors (Phineas Finn is another), Robarts does not borrow the money himself, but instead offers his signature – literally agrees to 'give his name' (Trollope, 1984: 497, ch. 42) – for a debt incurred by another, less worthy man. Like Finn, Robarts incurs this debt almost carelessly, from a corrosive but vague ambition for advancement (ibid.: 41, ch. 1), and thus throws himself into bad company like Mr Sowerby, one of those who are 'as poor as debt can make a man – but who, nevertheless, enjoy all the luxuries which money can give'.

> Such companions [as Mr. Sowerby] are very dangerous. There is no cholera, no yellow-fever, no small-pox more contagious than debt. If one lives habitually among embarrassed men, one catches it to a certainty. No one had injured the community more fatally than Mr. Sowerby.
>
> (ibid.: 68–9, ch. 4)

Robarts virtuously refuses to save himself by accepting the signature of a wealthier friend in place of his own; this stops what promises to be a continuous loss of personal integrity and social identity. When Robarts's wife teaches him to 'recognize' the debt as his own (ibid.: 496, ch. 42), he begins to regain his opportunity, his place in society, literally his name. Both in Dickens and in Trollope, debt interferes with the emergent possibilities inherent in the historical form.

Trollope identifies the system of political patronage as an especially pernicious and essentially anti-social version of debt. For example, in *Phineas Finn* (1869), the titular hero offends his political patron, Lord Brentford, by courting the woman Brentford has marked out for his own son, Chiltern. In their conversation, Finn acknowledges 'a debt which I can never pay' (Trollope, 1972: 562), signalling the way that patronage operates like a currency, and implicating the entire system of Parliamentary influence that depends upon it. In the case of Lord Brentford, the implicit message is 'I patronize you, so you must do as I like': '...give me your word that you will think no more of Miss Effingham...Say that, Mr. Finn, and I will forgive everything'. Finn, of course, and with Trollope's complete approval, says that Lord Brentford has no right to ask it (ibid.: 562–3). Still, it is Lord Brentford who controls the political opportunity.

Finn's debt entails not only an erasure of personal identity and freedom but also an erasure of the liberty upon which a free society, depends for its very existence. The patrons and other holders of debt that Trollope loves to pillory would all probably approve of Mrs Thatcher's remark that there is 'no such thing' as society. Trollope is careful, however, to acknowledge the ways in which the failure of the social order can generate debt, not just be generated by it. The high-minded poverty of Mr Crawley, the curate at Hogglestock, threatens the very lives of his cold and underfed family. At the same time as he is admired for resisting debt, he is criticized for sacrificing to it those who depend on him (Trollope, 1984: 190, ch. 14); when debt is forced upon him, his willingness to accept it shows an admirable moderation of his excessive pride. It is here in a homely example that the competing structures of social and financial obligation meet.

Trollope reserves the coldest place in hell for the futures speculator, Ferdinand Lopez in *The Prime Minister*, who gambles and loses most of his money, and other people's, in speculation on Kauri Gum and, appropriately, guano. Mrs Parker, the angry wife of Lopez's disappointed business partner, uses the word 'gambling' in this exchange with the aggressively innocent wife of Lopez. Socially astute, Mrs Parker clarifies some of the social costs for the hopelessly uninformed Emily Lopez, who asks (of her own husband):

'Does he gamble?'

'What is it but gambling that he and Mr. Lopez is a-doing together? Of course, ma'am, I don't know you, and you are different from me. I ain't foolish enough not to know all that. My father stood in Smithfield and sold hay, and your father is a gentleman as has been high up in the Courts all his life. But it's your husband is a doing this.'

'Oh, Mrs. Parker!'

'He is then. And if he brings Sexty and my little ones to the workhouse, what'll be the good then of his guano and his gum?'

'Is it not all in the fair way of commerce?'

'I'm sure I don't know about commerce, Mrs. Lopez, because I'm only a woman; but it can't be fair. They goes and buys things that they haven't got the money to pay for, and then waits to see if they'll turn up trumps. Isn't that gambling?'

(Trollope, 1983b: 56)

Mrs Parker has it right so far as Trollope's novel is concerned, and Emily eventually acknowledges this debt by saving Mrs Parker from starvation. Whether or not it is recognized as such, speculation is a social debt, because, as Mrs Parker notices, it is a game of few winners and many losers, and thus it operates by a principle at odds with the sociality envisioned by writers like Trollope.

'There's one or two of them sort of men gets into Parliament, and has houses as big as the Queen's palace, while hundreds of them has their wives and children in the gutter. Who ever hears of them? Nobody.'

(ibid.: 57)

This speech has a certain resonance in the discourse of historical narrative, where 'Nobody' literally materializes as the systemic function that coordinates the grammar of perspective into a single-point system in ways discussed in Chapter Two. In historical, social narrative, it is precisely 'the narrator' function that is the unshakable site for social connection; it is precisely 'Nobody' who hears of and sees those who are invisible to the City speculator. This Nobody – which I have argued is nothing less than the aura, the horizon of possibility, the grammar of consciousness of a particular society in all its material definition – sustains a continuous resistance to the reductive, less complex and varied, and in so many ways illusory, 'market' system. The social narrative in Trollope asserts that social democracy is precisely *neither* a market *nor* a merely abstract 'formal democracy' (cf. Zizek, 1991: 166; 1989).

The caveat against lucre reappears in social novels as a caution to the architects of a new social entity. In novel after novel, the system of 'natural' money encourages a kind of passivity and parasitism at odds with social order. Trollope's shiftless Sowerby in *Framley Parsonage* gets into debt by relying on chance, rather than his own effort ('... he would no longer prey upon his friends.... If only he could get another chance!' (Trollope, 1984: 288)). For people who rely on chance – and they are legion in Victorian novels – passing time literally compounds the problem rather than developing a more positive, more material effort (ibid.: 238). Gamblers are the most destructive characters in Dickens and George Eliot. One of the worst in all nineteenth-century novels is Little Nell's grandfather, in Dickens' early novel *The Old Curiosity Shop*; the old parasite drains life from the small child who relies on him, and who eventually dies from various forms of malnutrition. Gambling in George Eliot makes one person's loss into another person's gain, and thus poisons the mutuality of the emergent social entity. The absorption of gamblers around the casino roulette wheel that opens *Daniel Deronda* substitutes an atmosphere that is 'dull, gas-poisoned' for the clear light of common day; it is a long road for the heroine, Gwendolen Harleth, to the confession that in gambling there is no 'success'; elsewhere in George Eliot's novels the 'gamble' is about marriage or about real and metaphorical gold (*Felix Holt*, *Silas Marner*). What ails these social parasites is the market mentality. They give new meaning to Mill's thought that 'a man is not likely to be a good economist if he is nothing else' (quoted in Robbins, 1935, p. 150). Dickens' Gradgrind in *Hard Times* is only a good economist when he becomes something else.

CRUISING THE BOUNDARIES OF DIFFERENCE: CLASS, PERSONALITY, SYSTEM

The problem for the social novel is thus double: a problem of constituencies; and a problem of the point from which to view them. Point of view in narrative is always a matter of awareness, and in realism it is always awareness *doubled* by the wider historical recollection 'in' which each individual moment takes its place. Deep in the very historical form they explore is a continuing, unresolved problem of oversight. How much distance is enough distance? When is knowledge sufficient to the action or the choice?

The narrative that homogenizes the medium of time in order to make it a common denominator can potentially result in a homogenization of the 'human' problem, and a search for common denominators at the expense of difference. At this extreme we find the featureless creations of socialist realism where all are one, in a strange echo of Feuerbach's theological religion. More moderate instances are 'lesson' novelists, like the capable Harriet Martineau and many less capable ideologues who wrote novels as instruction for new and uneducated readerships about particular social, religious, and even economic issues. Dickens' moral intensity in *Hard Times* may account in part for the peculiarly un-Dickensian, schematic, abstract quality of that novel.

At the other extreme are novels that diversify the perspective system to

147

the point of bringing it into question. The grammar of perspective takes a turn in the later century towards impressionism: narrative where perspective shifts increasingly towards the conditions of perception. All Henry James's novels make this their extraordinary project. His *Portrait of a Lady* (1881), is an early version of the familiar Jamesian pattern in which even, or especially, those with the strongest awareness feel the shock of recognizing the absolute limits of their system of perception, even as they renew their commitment to it. Joseph Conrad makes the problem of 'seeing' primary, and even introduces a personified narrator, 'Marlow', in an attempt to show how the complexity lies in the conditions of seeing, not the condition of things seen. George Moore's narrative perspective remains ineffably in possession of one or another character, even in descriptive passages like this one from *Esther Waters* (1894):

> 'I'm going, mother.'
> 'Well, take care of yourself. Good luck to you.'
> Esther smiled sadly, but the beautiful weather melted on her lips, her lungs swelled with the warm air, and she noticed the sparrow that flew across the cab rank, and saw the black dot pass down a mews and disappear under the eaves. It was a warm day in the middle of April; a mist of green had begun in the branches of the elms of the Green Park; and in Park Lane, in all the balconies and gardens, wherever nature could find roothold, a spray of green met the eye.
>
> (Moore, 1991: 104–5)

This passage does not so much elaborate character or plot as it instead suggests the fragile objectivity of the world: the way physical events stimulate pleasure or hope, and are 'seen' only through them. This narrative style owes something to Moore's own experience as a painter, and to his study of French Impressionist painters (who first exhibited in 1874). Such late-century narratives emphasize two of the long-implicit features of the grammar of perspective: the arbitrariness of the commanding perspective and the changeableness of its conditions.

The contempt Oscar Wilde expressed for Moore's style, to the effect that Moore discovered the sentence and went on in triumph to discover the paragraph, may rest partly on the fact that, more than many other social novelists, George Moore maintains a neutral and inclusive narrative perspective; his narrator neither makes the dramatic juxtapositions of Dickens and Gaskell nor maintains the interpreting opacity found in Eliot or Trollope. Moore's language is most often assignable to nobody in particular, and it makes none of the exclusive discriminations between Us and Them that Wilde's wit requires. In Moore's social medium, the self-reflecting pirouette might seem witty were its contempt for poverty and deprivation not simply odious.

Even toward the end of the nineteenth century, the historical convention does not reach a breaking point, and the world of common denominators remains intact even through the rough seas of Conrad and the exfoliating syntax of James. The best mid-century social novelists train a new readership to avoid the ill-fitting generalities to which utopian realism is liable and, at the other extreme, to avoid getting lost in details which do not produce the emergent social form. Each author tries a different experiment with social time; each specifies in a different way the same grammar of perspective.

In order to pay some attention to the complexities of these formative social experiments, and to avoid writers who slip to one or the other of the extremes just noted, I choose from the vast range of novelists three, all deservedly canonical writers: Charles Dickens, Anthony Trollope, and George Eliot. Each formulates a different kind of perspective for a different kind of social attention: Dickens at the margins of society, Trollope in the middle of conversations, and George Eliot at the intersection of cultural preparation and individual action.

Class differences: seeing things whole in Dickens

Class difference in Dickens disrupts social wholeness. While most social novelists take up their vantage point well within the range of relevancies, Dickens is exceptional. He maintains his vantage point at the margins of social life, from which he can see the social entity as a whole. This tactic accounts in part for the mythic qualities of his realism. About midway through his career, he shifts away from picaresque and episodic narrative strategies to more integrated plots that lock motivation and causality into a commanding structure of social significance. In his later works, Dickens employs unifying figures and converging double plots to represent not just a few particulars, or even the laws that operated in them, but the whole 'identity of things'. Dickens' largely urban world positively teems with eccentric variety. His novels include a total cast of thousands; in *Bleak House* alone there are nearly a hundred separate characters. The fun of reading Dickens comes largely from the crazy vitality of these various centres of energy, literally 'ex-centric' forces, sometimes including animals or furniture or other non-human entities, galvanized and on the loose in an incompletely realized social entity. Silas Wegg's wooden leg has a life of its own (*Our Mutual Friend*); and the carthorse, left to itself, will promiscuously strike up a speaking acquaintance with lamp-posts (*Old Curiosity Shop*). As their names often suggest, many Dickens characters seem more like walking characteristics than complete individuals; they have names that reflect the one aspect that constitutes their particular quality or behaviour, and they identify themselves by repeating that behaviour. Meagles, Merdle and Barnacle (*Little Dorrit*); Miss Flite, Mr Vholes, Krook and Smallweed (*Bleak House*); Quilp, Swiveller, and Miss Sally Brass (*Old Curiosity Shop*); Estella and Havisham (*Great Expectations*): such characters act as their names suggest, with a kind of fruitlessly repetitive behaviour – a dramatic 'signature' – that hints at a lack of organic connection, a stasis or dislocation in the social order of things. The kind of internal personal divisions that plague individuals in George Eliot's novels, in Dickens are parcelled out among two or more characters: as for example with Eugene Wrayburn and his sinister shadow, Bradley Headstone (*Our Mutual Friend*); or with Pip and his multiple doubles, Magwitch, Drummle and Orlick (*Great Expectations*). It is as if the elements of a single healthy entity are scattered, dissociated, left in pieces by unresolved social conflict (Ermarth, 1983: 182–97).

Differences in class and wealth cause these intractable social rifts in the Dickens world. *Bleak House* asserts English social failure as powerfully as any Dickens novel. 'What is the connexion' between the poor boy sweeping the crosswalk and the haughty Lady Dedlock? The answer is, 'mortality'. What joins Jo and Lady Dedlock, by a route circuitous but sure, is smallpox. The fatal contagion is a degenerate expression of the common human connection between the upper classes and the shabby poor whom they try perilously and unsuccessfully to ignore.

Dickens asserts the unity of the social world not only by the grammar of perspective, of which his converging double plots are one feature, but also by other and unifying devices, as mentioned in Chapter One, and particularly the amplified metaphor. All Dickens' later novels feature converging plots as a central structural event. And his double plots in turn owe much to his intimate knowledge of Shakespeare. Theatrical events and the kind of plots where such action develops do not figure in George Eliot or Trollope, who interest themselves in the social forms of a locality and the behaviour of more fully realized (more in-perspective) individuals. Double plots in George Eliot's last novels, *Middlemarch* and *Daniel Deronda*, do not converge as they do in Dickens; they remain tantalizingly parallel to infinity. The hero and heroine each have separate marriage problems and each goes a separate way. But Dickens uses double plotting to reveal *the* 'identity of things'. His plots generate tension and conflict in order that they may be resolved.

For example, the undisclosed legacy that Mrs Clennam, in a twisted sort of revenge, keeps from Amy in *Little Dorrit* turns out to be what links the Dorrit and the Clennam plots. Social healing in *Our Mutual Friend* depends upon establishing friendship between men of different classes, in this case between Eugene Wrayburn, the sauntering gentleman with no vocation, and the unlikely if Shakespearian gentleman in disguise, John Harmon (alias Rokesmith, and The Secretary). A world of social rift, dust and death, is redeemed by male friendship across class barriers (Ermarth, 1983: 197–221). This is the anxious way toward the construction of society as an entity.

In his most experimental treatment of social division, *Bleak House*, Dickens splits the narrative medium into a third-person present-tense account and a first-person historical account. By dissociating what historical narrative normally puts together, the novel disrupts the very medium of common life. The historical narrative belongs to a distressingly repressed and dissociated young woman; the contextual narrative connects nothing with nothing, because the present tense disrupts the neutrality of time and the possibility of development. The mutually informative measurements that social and historical time allows can only be made with the greatest difficulty in this novel. Each sees part of the world of which the other knows nothing, and neither sees the life that links them until it is 'too late'. The two narratives converge only after the death of the aptly named Lady Dedlock. Both the 'natural' reunion of mother and daughter, and the union of disparate social elements, remain unachieved.

Though Dickens' later novels of social breakdown end with at least limited resolution, he limits its expression pretty much to domestic affairs: sometimes, as in *Dombey and Son* (1846–48), the domestic solution is limited to the domestic affairs of one household. But by implication Society is a family, and susceptible to similar reunion. After the early picaresque novels, of which *Martin Chuzzlewit* (1843) may be the last, there is no comprehensive social solution even in sight. There is a disproportion in the narrative between the happiness provided to Esther Summerson, or Florence Dombey, on the one hand and, on the other, the dismal, unjust outcomes provided to the beggars, Jo and Alice, or to poor Miss Tox, the single lady who proves to have more heart than we supposed, and who stays stuck in her lonely 'world' while other worlds go on without her. An alarming 'happy' marriage concludes *Our Mutual Friend* (1864–65) when the lively Bella Wilfer, until then conspicuously independent, literally 'disappears' into her husband's embrace; otherwise in this novel social hope glimmers in the cross-class friendship between two men, but against a pretty dark background. Happy marriage, or friendship, becomes the (patently unsatisfactory) domestic solution to a social problem. The problems of injustice at the Court of Chancery in *Bleak House*, like those posed by the financial 'house' of Dombey, are not resolved; they are merely walled out by a happy family group at the end: a family group that, notably in Florence Dombey's case, turns out to have excellent investments.

The historical narrative works well precisely in such a riven social universe; it positively requires such fractures in order for the characteristic mediation to occur. Dickens persistently conveys the sense of there being common denominators where none seem likely. To take only one example, the ancient beggar woman in *Dombey and Son*, whose daughter has long been lost to her, solicits money in passing from another, wealthier crone accompanying Edith Dombey. As they pass on, the beggar thinks prophetically: "You're a handsome woman", muttered her shadow, looking after her; "but good looks won't save us. And you're a proud woman; but pride won't save us. We had need to know each other when we meet again!" (Dickens, 1970: 665, ch. 40). The suggestion lingers that she thinks of meeting on the other side of the grave, where all are one and wealth means nothing, and there is also the suggestion of solidarity between women on this side of the grave. The counting-house culture of *Dombey and Son* has separated the beggar from her lost daughter, and has turned mothers and daughters against each other. Will Edith sell Florence in the marriage stakes as she herself has been sold? These doubled pairs of women are a rich instance of the kind of mutual reference across difference that Dickens' doubles provide. Like the 'two houses' of the estranged Carker brothers, located on opposite sides of London, these doubles suggest common denominators where they might least be expected. As Dickens' relentlessly converging plots demonstrate, the social entity includes both, and the 'exclusiveness' of the upper classes testifies to their destructive social unfitness.

Dickens' amplified metaphors direct attention beyond individual people to the 'identity of things' that, in Dickens, one sees only from the margins of social life. These are something more intensive than the metaphors that work their way into any good narrative language, as webs and mirrors work their way into *Middlemarch*, or debt and coalition work their way into *The Prime Minister*. In Dickens they become almost properties of nature. To take only one example here, the ocean in *Dombey and Son* operates as a unifying figure. 'What the waves are always saying' to Little Paul, who can't understand it, is that life is terminal; like the sea, the social realm has its 'scaly monster of the deep' (Mr Carker, ibid.: 477, ch. 27); Mr

Perch at the office swims in the mysteries of the deep (ibid.: 237, ch. 13); Mrs MacStinger attempts to trap Captain Cuttle in an ocean of soap suds (ibid.: 405, ch. 22); in his marriage Mr Dombey tries to silence distant thunder with the 'rolling of his sea of pride' (ibid.: 649, ch. 40); Walter Gay is 'lost' at sea and then rescued from it; and the 'voices of the waves are always whispering to Florence, in their ceaseless murmuring, of love – of life, eternal and illimitable, not bounded by the confines of this world, or by the end of time, but ranging still, beyond the sea, beyond the sky, to the invisible country far away' (ibid.: 908, ch. 57). While Mr Dombey sits confined by his narrow horizon, the sea corrects him with a wider margin or rim of human possibility. The sea takes away Little Paul, while the child of Florence and Walter is 'born at sea' (ibid.: ch. 59). The Shakespearean figure here evokes the human unity, the human entity, as something larger than the narrow social exclusions of Mr Dombey's class and money.

Such figures can undermine the grammar of perspective to the extent that they establish universal or 'natural' truths beyond any grammar. They belong to an effort to see the social entity whole, if not steadily. They can undermine the middle distance of realism by suggesting that the moral universe extends beyond the social. These are the drawbacks of taking up a narrative perspective at the margins of life. A certain apocalyptic undertone in Dickens seems to undermine the provisional and inclusive consciousness that, by careful historical relays, brings everyone together into a common system of awareness. This perspective, constituted by the continuous slide between varied series of viewpoints, is an abstraction that emerges uneasily from the very narrow or unrepresented minds of Dickens' characters. But Dickens' holistic approach may nevertheless be the reason for his great and enduring popularity. He makes it possible to imagine the social entity by standing just outside it, albeit on a very narrow ledge. That narrow margin outside sociality suggests that there is a standing point and a fulcrum outside the social entity where the abstraction, Society, dissolves in familiar moral truths. The difficulty in Dickens of maintaining the middle distance of realism and history testifies to the state of social breakdown; and it also gestures towards the limits of the historical narrative technique.

Personal differences: Trollope and life in nuance

Personal, not class, differences occupy Trollope. His people belong mainly to the educated middle classes, with occasional brilliant representatives from the upper aristocracy or the depths of the stock exchange. He is less interested in plot climaxes and resolutions – in seeing Society whole – than in the communication, or lack of it, between persons and in the indirect but powerful influence of those unheroic, private moments in public life. His plots meander undramatically, sometimes intersecting but rarely converging in the way Dickens' plots do, and sometimes extending through several novels, like the six 'Barchester' novels or the six 'Palliser' novels. But if his plots meander, his texts do not; in fact they have a tautness, even a surface tension, that shows how little social and realist narrative require gesture in order to produce events. The drama in Trollope lies not in events of physical performance, like Dickens, but in events of language.

Trollope is interested in the achieved results of long habit, and especially in the *sound* of those results in the tones of conversation. His range of social interest is not as inclusive as Dickens' or George Eliot's but, within his chosen limits, his range seems almost infinite. He can capture as no one else the nuance that kills, the telling throwaway, the differentiated reasons (restraint, cowardice) for leaving things unsaid. He focuses with increasing felicity on the nuance of conversation, for example the speech that indirectly conveys numerous stories, capturing various strands in one historical moment.

This brief description (in *The Duke's Children*) of an after-dinner scene, for example, contains several amusing ironies about a particular company and their mix of gender, age, class and political allegiance:

> When the ladies were gone the politics became more serious. 'That unfortunate quarrel is to go on the same as ever, I suppose', said the Duke, addressing himself to the two young men who had seats in the House of Commons. They were both on the Conservative side in politics. The three peers present were all Liberals.
>
> (Trollope, 1983: 281)

As this and other of the 'Palliser' novels make abundantly clear, 'the ladies' are often the ones with most political sense, so the formulation – obviously one close to the minds of the gentlemen present – that politics becomes 'more serious' with their departure is undercut by the entire drift of the novel. This small pleasure of the doubled narrative perspective is succeeded by other similar ones having to do with the ironies of relationship between social class and political allegiance. Trollope's straight-faced though staccato comment, that the peers are all Liberals and the young men all Conservatives, has zephyrous ironies in it. These ironies – almost continuous in Trollope – maintain the reader's link with the Nobody narrator and the vision that always exceeds that of anyone present – two MPs and three peers, for example.

Another instance of Trollope's unspoken realm of awareness, hovering just outside speech, appears in this passage from *Phineas Finn* describing the Duke of Omnium, who contributes to his country by maintaining a certain deportment:

> He was tall and moved without a stoop; and though he moved slowly, he had learned to seem so to do because it was the proper kind of movement for one so high up in the world as himself. And perhaps his tailor did something for him. He had not been long under Madame Max Goesler's eyes before she perceived that his tailor had done a good deal for him.
>
> (Trollope, 1972: 543, ch. 57)

As usual Trollope exploits the doubled perspective of historical (realist) narration to produce a pleasurable set of ironies. Again the accumulated weight of such episodes tells in the emphasis of the passage. The Duke's power is exerted in a public world that knows very little of his tailor's accomplishment; and his successor as Duke, the earnest and committed Plantagenet Palliser, shows by contrast how much hollowness can be covered by the manners of a certain social class. Besides being a delightful undercutting of the Duke, this description also gives us a sense of the inimitable Madame Max. It is one of the private observations that reveals both her power of awareness – her power to be Nobody – and also her ability to manage it and so to be very much somebody.

Such moments are never single; they contain a swing of consciousness between one site and another in an internal world accessible mainly through conversation, and not through plot 'actions' more grandly conceived. In such passages, as in all good historical novels, the author represents not a particular situation so much as the grammar of a situation, and shows that social life is all about that grammar, and not about simpler causalities. It is no accident, then, that Trollope's material is circumscribed: confined to a world rather far from the poverty and want that appear in novels by Dickens and Gaskell.

To a large extent such passages constitute the 'action' of a Trollope novel; in them he explores the subtle differences that influence the development of character. And in Trollope, character is everything. Where the action in Dickens moves from various different localities and groups towards a centred social entity, the action in Trollope moves from such tropisms of daily life to the centre of one character after another. The social 'centre' must take care of itself, although with Parliament Trollope comes close to it. The act of attention Trollope requires of readers is complex, because every statement is saturated with the atmosphere of a particular character. In one of Madame Max's first conversations with Phineas Finn, the level of repartee and intelligence between them reveals that, despite their very different lives, they are made for each other (ibid.: 411, ch. 41). But how do such people get together? It takes several novels to answer this question.

Another example of such 'action' appears in the constellation of perspectives surrounding a political comment by Lady Mabel Grex in *The Duke's Children* (1879–80). The Radical party, the most successful group of reformers early in the century, is described by Lady Mabel as 'a party so utterly snobbish and down in the world' that 'everybody that is worth anything is leaving them' (Trollope, 1983: 72). To evaluate this comment, and the position of the Radicals, one must catch the tone of Lady Mabel's comment and the reflex of her character, as well as the history of the Radicals. Lady Mabel is an intelligent aristocrat, if always a bit sharp, but there is also an edge of irresponsibility or even hysteria in her conduct which often seems self-destructive, even careless of her own real interests, including the main objective that she articulates in rather coarse terms (she must marry money to live in the style to which she has been accustomed). Catching the tone of her conversation is a bit like Frith catching the collective moment at Paddington Station (see pp. 107–108, in Chapter Two): catching in a single frame the variety of tiny conscious, semiconscious and subconscious tides and undertows that constitute personal moments, all underway simultaneously and criss-crossing each other.

When Trollope comes to Parliament he comes to the heart of his commitments. He himself ran for Parliament (and failed to be elected) as the Member for Beverley. He regarded politics as primarily the means by which he could improve 'the condition of his fellows': anyone who undertook politics for any other reason he denounced as 'a political intriguer, a charlatan, and a conjurer, – as one who thinks that, by a certain amount of wary wire-pulling, he may raise himself in the estimation of the world' (Trollope, 1993: 269). Whether or not this commitment to politics is, as he puts it, 'highfaluten', it certainly gives occasion for some of his most brilliant portraits of the way individuals negotiate their differences. An example is the following, still-timely description (in *Phineas Redux* (1873–74)) of Conservatives disgruntled with their Prime Minister. The immediate issue is profound enough: nothing less than a bill brought by the Conservative Prime Minister to separate church and state in England. Party members don't like it, but are bound by party to support it and their Prime Minister:

And there had for a while been almost a determination through the party to deny their leader and disclaim the bill. But a feeling of duty to the party had prevailed, and this had not been done. It had not been done; but the not doing of it was a sore burden on the half-broken shoulders of many a man who sat gloomily on the benches behind Mr. Daubeny.

(Trollope, 1983a: 245)

We can foresee that this mixed, eddying feeling in the group certainly will influence future and as yet unspecified results, even though it has not effectively expressed itself on the present issue.

Trollope is brilliant at dramatizing these powerful but nuanced gestures. His long plot sequences suggest through an accumulation of such moments the ways in which personal choice influences public life, and in which public life pressures personal choice. Both emerge together in a social context that is always in incremental motion, always shifting slightly. Standard plot 'events' like marriage are elided in favour of the contextual interests. A reader hoping for a marriage at the end of one novel finds, at the beginning of another, that it has already taken place between books and now opens new horizons and implications. The promising Scottish MP of one novel loses his mind in another; the penniless politician of one novel, who seems so likely to become a creature of events, eventually proves a man of character; the unpromising arranged marriage proves strong and resilient. In the story of his interesting outsider, the Irish MP Phineas Finn, Trollope shows ability and luck feeding each other undecidably. Trollope's emergent individuals are perhaps the most opaque and changeable in Victorian fiction, each clearly marked by class and other determinations, and yet each capable of surprises.

Over the course of a long career (his output includes forty-five finished novels), Trollope's social focus gradually shifts from the country to London. The 'Barchester' novels deal with rural communities and domestic issues; and the 'Palliser' novels (named after Trollope's liberal aristocrat, Plantagenet Palliser) deal with politics and with Parliament during the period of reform. Even in the last Barchester novels, *The Small House at Allington* (1864) and *Last Chronicle of Barset* (1867), the centre of social focus shifts towards London and away from the rural house or parsonage. In each one, the lack of social resolution in the rural and largely courtship-centred plot (Lily Dale does not marry her Crosbie, and lives unhappily ever after), is balanced by the unexpected success of Johnny Eames, the young man from the country, who loses Lily Dale to a less worthy competitor but who has the sterling character that enables him to develop literally from one world into another, from the rural and agricultural scene of traditional power to the London offices administering a new society.

The Palliser novels, which anatomize Parliament and parliamentarians during the era of Reform, are all linked by a central cast of characters who appear in most of them with different degrees of importance. Plantagenet Palliser, the liberal aristocrat who works tirelessly for an egalitarian system that will marginalize his kind (though he momentarily lapses into ducal snobbery when he moves from public to private affairs like his own daughter's marriage); his wife, Glencora, the original, intelligent Duchess; her friend, Marie Goesler; the rising Irish politician, Phineas Finn; Laura Standish and her fox-hunting and socially violent brother, Lord Chiltern: these characters appear and reappear, each time part of a different social, political and personal experiment by Trollope. The foreground of one novel becomes the background of another as Trollope's social world keeps showing its apparently inexhaustible variety.

In a late novel, *The Prime Minister* (1876), Trollope introduces a metaphor for the balanced social relationship, the metaphor of coalition. Coalition becomes a metaphor for the kind of temporary contract that binds together willing parties towards a particular end, and that forces them – whether they like it or not – to confront the necessity either to work together or to break apart and break down. Trollope's hero in *The Prime Minister*, Plantagenet Palliser, is a new sort of statesman: an aristocrat and a liberal, dedicated to egalitarian reform but living in a social situation of extreme privilege. His creed is getting the job done, and he reflects little on what others think (Trollope, 1983b: 105). Despite this inauspicious personal tendency, and against his inclination, he presides as Prime Minister over the first government in England to be run by a coalition. The cloakroom tensions and private personalities are wonderfully drawn out in this association that remains tenuously intact, coherent but always contested. The coalition endures as a successful experiment in the politics of the greatest good of the greatest number, in defiance of what Mill calls 'sinister interests'.

This metaphor of coalition also plays out on a private scale in the Prime Minister's arranged marriage to the immortal Glencora. Palliser's triumph, especially given his well-bred peculiarity, is that he manages to preside, at home as at the ministry, over a coalition of relative equals. He and his wife are equally powerful individuals, each with money and tradition of their own, and, like any coalition, continuously troubled by imbalances in power and capability. He likes to talk about cork shoes and decimal coinage, and he runs the country; she likes to talk about politics, and she runs households. Still the coalition represented in their marriage works. It is also permanent, whereas the coalition in the cabinet is shorter-lived. But in both public and private cases of coalition, Trollope features a new kind of association across differences of temperament and viewpoint.

Such marriages are rare in Trollope, and practically non-existent in the rest of nineteenth-century narrative. That particular negotiation of personal difference seems more problematic than most. In the project to mediate social difference in the interest of social unity, narrative comes up against obstacles in the home; in the newly unifying social system, home is where the fault line lies.

Systemic differences: George Eliot and the world as language

The social entity in George Eliot has neither the centred unity of Dickens nor the middle-class solidity of Trollope. Instead, her world is a web of relationships, a network of crossing and re-crossing pathways that has immense mutual resonance across space and across centuries, and nothing like a 'heart' or a centre, not even in London. George Eliot's society is composed of sub-systems, and she occupies readers at precisely those interfaces between systems, those liminal phases of social order where different systems of belief and value overlap and must negotiate their relation. Her historical narrative is a perspective system made up of perspective systems. The social problem she raises is how to negotiate the systemic differences that inform each choice, each apparently individual gesture or unique event.

George Eliot did much to prepare us for our current interest in language as a model for all economies of belief and value. Her novels focus on those moments when one economy or discourse or system meets another, and on the way in which such cultural languages make the world habitable at the same time as they limit our horizon. She shows that to know a language is to inhabit a world, and that society is less an entity than it is an indefinitely marked composite of infinitely varied discourses, or cultural languages. For example, when Gwendolen Harleth in *Daniel Deronda* (1876) accepts the proposal of marriage from Henleigh Grand-court, she imagines mainly the difference his wealth would make to her world; her acceptance seems to 'entail so little'. But Grandcourt's wealth does not exist in her world, it exists in his; acceptance of the one entails acceptance of the other. She must speak or keep silent as he wishes; she must dress to suit him. She must learn the hard way the vast difference between her small vision and the 'hard, unaccommodating Actual' with which she has to deal. Actuality is composed not of rocks and stones and trees, but of other people's systems of belief and value, other people's languages and cultural imperatives. When Gwendolen recognizes the existence of this multiplicity, she begins to grow up.

As a translator, as a traveller, as an outsider in the 'normal' society of her time, George Eliot understands more than most the multiplicity of systems within a social network, and the evils of focusing on only one. Her English society is a network of interpretive systems, all overlapping and irrationally mixed: unified much as Mill's society is unified, by the fact of difference, except that in Mill's case the differences are as between individuals while in George Eliot differences are largely systemic. In *The Mill on the Floss* (1860), Mr and Mrs Tulliver's traditional system is one in which curses are written in the front page of the family Bible and in which locked-away bonnets and linens function as household gods; the alternate system in the same novel concerns commerce and lawcourts and banking, and it interferes with the 'eternal fitness of things' in rural St. Oggs, bringing in another solar system just as if a second Reformation were at hand. Survival depends on the ability to negotiate between systems; and the fact that so many of the main characters in the novel die (Mr Tulliver and both his children) testifies to the difficulty of this negotiation. Similarly in *Daniel Deronda* (1876), the well-to-do Arrowpoints keep to a traditional system not far from that of rural farmers, except that, in the Arrowpoints' case, observing tradition involves keeping their property in white, Anglo-Saxon hands. In the same novel, however, and in the margins of the Arrowpoints' lives, a Jewish culture exists that turns out to have considerable implications for the Arrowpoints and their kind. Where myopic characters think their social system is the only system, the novel invariably proves otherwise.

Every narrative moment in George Eliot, as in Trollope, belongs to an entire capillary system of awareness; but Eliot goes well beyond Trollope and most of her contemporaries in the multiplicity and complexity of the traditions that inform individual transactions. A small instance is this little commentary from *Middlemarch* on the subject of the pernicious French influence on English tradition. Lydgate has taken his newfangled ideas about germs and other medical matters from suspect French sources:

'Lydgate has lots of ideas, quite new, about ventilation and diet, that sort of thing', resumed Mr. Brooke, after he had handed out Lady Chettam, and had returned to be civil to a group of Middlemarchers.

'Hang it, do you think that is quite sound? – upsetting the old treatment, which has made Englishmen what they are?' said Mr. Standish.

(Eliot, 1956: 68, ch. 10)

Here George Eliot delightfully multiplies and balances the perspectives that include both the forward-looking doctor and the backward community. As he is throughout the novel, here Lydgate is 'known merely as a cluster of signs for his neighbour's false suppositions'. And a system of false suppositions can be as efficacious as a system of accurate ones, as Mr Brooke proves when he transfigures Lydgate's (supposed) ideas into his own particular way of putting things. Thus transfigured (which is to say, misunderstood), Lydgate's ideas receive firm opposition from Mr Standish, whose own interest itself requires a certain deconstruction.

Throughout such passages there is also that extra edge belonging to the Nobody narrative voice, that margin of wider perspective that implicates much that remains inexplicit in the speeches. In this passage, that margin includes more than just other moments of individual awareness: the development of early nineteenth-century science, especially medical science; the emerging professions; an international context for English parochialism to look small in. The pleasure of such narrative moments has to do with the complexity of the viewpoint and the clarity concerning differences between viewpoints, and between much larger systems of value that those viewpoints specify and, in some cases, alter. Such shifting constellations of viewpoint gather, and dissolve around one centre of interest and attention after another. The series of such moments constitutes George Eliot's narrative sequence; the sum of their expressions constitutes whatever can be identified as a unified society. But its borders are permeable and uncertain, always open to new constructions of old forms and to innovations yet unimagined.

This emphasis on the differences between systems means that, in George Eliot, the question of social 'unity' is always a fairly local matter of adjustment across boundaries. Mr Standish may never understand Lydgate, but he may learn to respect his abilities. This in itself constitutes a moment of social connection of the kind Eliot's Nobody narrator always maintains. Even to view these differences requires a vantage from which to view them. That vantage belongs to a power of mediation, that Nobody of narrative, so much in evidence in George Eliot's novels: a sort of invisible community composed of the implicit links between one mind and another, one moment and another, one pathway and another.

Compared with other Victorian novels, the narrative medium in

George Eliot confronts readers with a requirement to consider discursive complexity that may feel like mountainous travel. The characteristic difficulty lies in the reversibility of all but the most carefully formulated conclusions. For example, egoism is clearly wrong in Dickens, and even Trollope, and generally it is punished. Such an absolute, however, is hard to maintain in George Eliot. No sooner do you conclude something definitive about her novels than you confront a counterbalancing consideration, a qualifying remark, a perpetual 'on the other hand'. Perhaps the archetype of such moments is that one in Chapter 29 of *Middlemarch*, when the narrator says 'One morning, some weeks after her arrival at Lowick, Dorothea – but why always Dorothea? Was her point of view the only possible one with regard to this marriage?' The narrative then gives us the counterbalancing viewpoint. There is never a single way of looking at things in George Eliot. 'Hang it', as Mr. Standish would say, there is always that 'on the other hand' that makes general conclusions difficult. Not impossible, but difficult.

The subject of egoism presents a useful locus, and especially its treatment in the pier-glass description:

> Your pier-glass or extensive surface of polished steel made to be rubbed by a housemaid, will be minutely and multitudinously scratched in all directions; but place now against it a lighted candle as a centre of illumination, and lo! the scratches will seem to arrange themselves in a fine series of concentric circles round that little sun. It is demonstrable that the scratches are going everywhere impartially, and it is only your candle which produces the flattering illusion of concentric arrangement, its light falling with an exclusive optical selection. These things are a parable. The scratches are events, and the candle is the egoism of any person now absent – of Miss Vincy, for example.
>
> (ibid.: 195, ch. 27)

This passage has often been taken as an irony at the expense of egoism. Certainly there are many examples in George Eliot's novels of egoism working its destructiveness besides that of Miss Vincy: Arthur Donnithorne, Tito Melema, Edward Casaubon, Henleigh Grandcourt. The destructiveness of these egoists might seem rather unproblematically to recommend altruism. If thinking of oneself is worst, then thinking of others must be best. It seems an obvious conclusion, and has often been stated.

But the sociality, which is nothing more nor less than a medium, no sooner allows for this than another voice whispers, 'on the other hand'

That little twist at the end of the passage just cited – the catty remark about someone who is absent – might sound the warning that all is not quite as it seems here. The curious thing about this pier-glass metaphor is its double message about egoism. On the one hand there are several obvious examples of egoism in *Middlemarch* to which this passage might apply – Casaubon, Raffles, Bulstrode, and of course poor Miss Vincy. Clearly egoism can't be a good thing. On the other hand, Dorothea Brooke presents an important exception. Following the Nobody narrator, the reader's awareness is spirited away from conclusion and towards some further qualifying knowledge.

Dorothea, for example, is always thinking of others; she considers Sir James from Celia's point of view. She *likes* giving up things as her 'carnally minded' sister complains (ibid.: 35). In fact Dorothea is far too good at the selflessness business, and it gets her into trouble. She is so badly inexperienced at acting on, or even knowing, her own personal feelings that she very nearly leaves her chance for happiness pointlessly in the dust. She is the altruist whose example recommends egoism. 'We should distrust a man who sets up shop purely for the good of the community', George Eliot wrote in an essay (Pinney, 1963: 156). Altruism in George Eliot turns out to have little to do with selflessness or lack of ego; instead, it has to do with balancing the conflicting claims between ego and community. Pure egoism may be destructive on the one hand; but, 'on the other hand', a developed ego is necessary to independent and adult life. Dorothea's example simply stands in the way of what might have been an easy generalization about the pier-glass. The metaphor asserts the powerfully narcissistic potential of ego, but it also asserts the *importance* of ego as a condition of light and order.

This complex outcome of narrative sequence keeps forcing readers to the middle distance from which the relevant comparisons become evident. This is the continuum of awareness that constitutes 'society' in George Eliot. Society is not buildings and ball gowns, nor tonalities of conversation, nor class definitions; it is the whole potential of human mental life enacted, incarnated in this or that particular moment. There is very little of moral hierarchy or of any secure dualistic distinction in her novels. She pushes readers beyond the duality between egoism and altruism, for example, and beyond the implicit hierarchies that underlie any such formulation (one term of a dualism is always privileged over the other). Her narratives engage us in a different kind of problematic, where the important questions are matters of scope and emphasis, and not at all of deciding which side wins in a dualistic opposition between better and worse. This commitment in George Eliot's work is one reason why she favours metaphors of webs or networks: because they are headless and footless systems of relationship without a common centre.

This 'on the other hand' returns us once again to language because, with each such shift of viewpoint, George Eliot invokes a difference, and a difference that depends on deep structures. In her novels, a 'valid claim' is never solely an individual matter; it is always cultural and systemic. Rosamond Vincy in *Middlemarch* is not just an individual young woman, she is the flower of Mrs Lemon's school; it is no good complaining of narcissistic performances that are put on at the request of the community and with their entire approval. Where was Rosamond to learn otherwise? She meets *her* first 'on the other hand' from Will Ladislaw, who is not interested in female flowers. Her husband, Lydgate, also has inclinations and practices formed by systems much larger than he is. Science has fostered his intellectual independence; his carelessness is gender-specific. George Eliot's interest in conflicting valid claims prompted her 1856 essay on 'The Antigone and Its Moral' (ibid.: 261–5), where the moral is that both Antigone's religion and Creon's politics have claims of equal validity; conflict between them can be a conflict to the death, but there is no 'right way', as some of George Eliot's more simple-minded characters think; one must simply 'dare to be wrong' (ibid.: 265). This sounds almost like existentialist advice, like Camus' 'I rebel, therefore we exist' in *The Rebel* (Camus, 1956: 19). It is not far from that social vision, nor is it very far from Mill's idea in *On Liberty* that even the extreme expression or the failed experiment usefully expand the possible definition of sociality.

Whatever the event, a conflict of claims or a meeting of strangers, in George Eliot the event always rests upon something larger and more grammatical. It is precisely because of their grammatical properties that actions and events are intelligible or perhaps even possible at all. George Eliot's genius appears in the way she makes visible this difficult, complex fact that each individual action specifies anew some traditional arrangement, some systemic order, modifying in some minuscule way a broadly interconnected balance of things. It is precisely thus that unheroic acts become powerful: in their specification of a grammar of belief and value.

The effort to understand a strange book, the refusal to burn a will, the silence about injustice that breeds guilt and violence: these moments are never merely individual or single; they carry the traces of systemic organization. The religious tradition that brings Thomas à Kempis to Maggie Tulliver combines fatally with the tribal narrowness that makes her heed him. Mary Garth's family life gives her a set of principles, a grammar of independence, that prepare her to refuse Featherstone's request to burn his will. Gwendolen Harleth grows up in a culture and a family riddled with misogynistic prejudice and obsequiousness before money and rank; these are powerful preparations for her fatal choices. Society is thus constituted not only of determinate events but also by the potential that its discursive variety, its cultural grammars, can allow. These grammars can be uncoordinated or even conflicting. What unites everything is only the fact that they belong 'in' the same historical sequence, and thus to a common medium and, in some way, to a common world.

Because the conflict of valid claims is never an individual matter, always a discursive one having to do with a cultural grammar, the conflict can *not* be settled easily, or perhaps at all. The conflicts between systems, between languages, between discursive formations in George Eliot admit of no absolute distinction between right and wrong. What solution is easy or 'right' to the conflict in *Adam Bede* between feudalism and modernity; to the conflict in *The Mill on the Floss* between clan law and more modern rules; to the conflict in *Daniel Deronda* between national and ethnic cultures? What is right for one is wrong for another, what invigorates a strong mind may derange a weak one. There is always that dratted 'on the other hand'. Even Rosamond Vincy has her excellent reasons. Even Rosamond Vincy has her chance to differ from herself.

Her grasp of the fundamental differences between languages accounts in large measure for George Eliot's happy grasp of systemic limitation. Knowing even two languages teaches as nothing else can do the limits of all systems. To learn a second language is to discover a second system for formulating everything. The gain in perspective is powerful. Even if one rarely uses it, a second or third language always presents a limit and an alternative to any way of formulating or perceiving. One's native language is no longer *the* language, but instead only *a* language among others: one way, and only one way, of mapping the world and managing practical affairs. As a thoroughly modern philologist, George Eliot knew that language determines possible perception. Her 'on the other hand' belongs to this deep knowledge.

The cruxes of all George Eliot's novels have to do with moments when such grammatically separate worlds intersect. These intersections constitute society; there is no other location and no final definition. In *Adam Bede* (1859), for example, the fist-fight between the carpenter and the squire brings two systems into conflict: one where men are equals and one where they are not. The last-minute pardon for Hetty is brought by Arthur Donnithorne, who thus re-enacts an old gesture of privilege, but he does so under constraint of a new world where law, not privilege, prevails. In Renaissance Florence, various worlds collide (*Romola* (1863));

in the reactionary religious teaching of Savonarola and in the garden of humanist scholars we find writ large certain cultural differences that are also writ small in the confrontation between Romola and Tito. In *Middlemarch* (1871–2) Dorothea's world and that of the Vincys revolve side-by-side, encountering each other occasionally but remaining pointedly separate. When Lydgate leaves Miss Vincy in the lane to go and attend Casaubon, or when Dorothea goes to Rosamond about Lydgate's disgrace, the encounters involve two different ways of constructing the world, not just two individuals. The meeting of Dorothea and Rosamond is informed not only by the sympathy that Dorothea attempts, more successfully in their second meeting than their first, but also by the powerful disparity between these two women's conditions of intelligibility, the difference in their grammars of experience. And those differences are nothing to the differences between the planetary systems of her next novel, that brilliant, massive, and completely unified epic, *Daniel Deronda* (1876).

These social moments are the growing points of George Eliot novels: the moments of opportunity for individuals and plot, as one system of intelligibility encounters another. Such moments almost always redirect character and plot. A most striking example is that of Gwendolen Harleth, when she realizes that the man she has had mentally wrapped and delivered to be her husband is not only devoted to someone else, but also is a Jew and a Zionist to boot, as well as the English aristocrat she thought she desired. Suddenly an entire order of things, a grammar of belief and value that 'had lain aloof in newspapers and other neglected reading', enters her life 'like an earthquake' and dislodges her for the first time 'from her supremacy in her own world': reduced in her own mind 'to a mere speck' (Eliot, 1967: 875–6, ch. 69). When Deronda tries to reassure her that their 'minds may get nearer' it could seem a little lame, except for the fact that it has the authority of George Eliot's whole narrative style behind it: the authority of that invisible community, constituted as Nobody and including all individuals but congruent with none. The invisible bridge Deronda mentions is the thing that really counts in realism because it is the potential of the future – the more-than-this that makes, not for righteousness, but for experiment, adventure, generosity, even play.

The problem of the plurality of worlds, as it was called by seventeenth-century cosmologists, has been present in English traditions since the Reformation. Certainly it was the religious dimension of the problem that most exercised George Eliot and her contemporaries. As George Eliot's work shows so well, no 'faith' can be absolute because every system is finite: it is really faith in a particular way of doing things, a particular system of belief and value as distinct from other equally valid ones. The question often raised in the nineteenth century was, if you change your belief once, why not a hundred times? And then where does true belief lie? In *Middlemarch*, a cantankerous old Mrs Farebrother takes up this contention with Lydgate of an evening. Besides seeming to echo the debates of the Oxford movement, she also states the case of the feudal traditionalist seeking the replication with exactitude of long established patterns. She certainly regards changing one's viewpoint as the next thing to disease:

> I shall never show that disrespect to my parents, to give up what they taught me. Any one may see what comes of turning. If you change once, why not twenty times?

Lydgate suggests that 'a man might see good arguments for changing once, and not see them for changing again', to which the old lady retorts that such shifting only leaves you liable to argument.

> If you go upon arguments they are never wanting, when a man has no constancy of mind. My father never changed, and he preached plain moral sermons without arguments, and was a good man – few better. When you get me a good man made out of arguments, I will get you a good dinner with reading you the cookery book. That's my opinion, and I think anybody's stomach will bear me out.

Her metaphor changes the subject, as Farebrother observes, but his mother is having none of *that*. ' "My mother is like Old George the Third", says the Vicar, "she objects to metaphysics" ' (Eliot, 1956: 126). Fortunately, and like many another in George Eliot, Mrs Farebrother is better than her opinions. In any case, George Eliot allows her readers no such security. Around Mrs Farebrother's rock wash the heavy tides of Middlemarch's narrative language. They entirely put the lie to such protected constancy. Argument is precisely the human condition. Perpetual contest, anchored by the grammars of commitment passed down by centuries: these are the elements of social order. This constant shifting of perspective to which George Eliot subjects her readers maintains the narrative medium of time and consciousness, the life of Nobody who is everyone inclusively. This highly achieved narrative medium provides an outside to every inside, a margin to every system. It is a trial for those who, like old Mrs Farebrother, have determined never to change; but it is a welcome opportunity for those interested in the emergent form of a social entity.

4

DILEMMAS OF DIFFERENCE

The fundamental resettlements of Victorian narrative – its detachment from natural explanation, its exploration of historical conventions, and its struggle to conceive society as an autonomous, inclusive, humanly constructed entity – all this necessarily produces a rethinking of the problem of difference. If there is nothing 'natural' about social distinctions, then what is their justification? The questioning of the 'natural' applies across the range of cultural distinctions, from nationality, to race and to gender difference. What is 'the' difference between the British and the French, between Europeans and Asians, between men and women?

The very questions appear odd to anyone who views sociality as a complex, laminated, open-ended, non-natural, non-essential field of action and reflex. Such a view is implicit in the twentieth century in the work of poststructuralists who, following Ferdinand de Saussure, emphasize the systemic and constructed nature of all values, however 'natural' they may seem. Luis Buñuel and René Magritte, Alain Robbe-Grillet and Marguerite Duras, Vladimir Nabokov and Julio Cortázar, Hélène Cixous, Jacques Derrida and Michel Foucault have put into twentieth-century artistic and philosophical terms an insight already grasped in the nineteenth century: that *all* values are contextual and systemic, especially those we take most for granted, and that every such value has only differential definition in the sense that it can be understood only systemically, not 'naturally' or in itself as it really is.

Although the range of emphasis changes from the nineteenth to the twentieth century, the perception remains much the same. George Eliot explains in *Middlemarch* how 'a man may be puffed and belauded, envied, ridiculed, counted upon as a tool and fallen in love with, or at least selected as a future husband, and yet remain virtually unknown – known merely as a cluster of signs for his neighbours' false suppositions' (Eliot, 1956: 105, ch. 15). The historical convention, exploited fully, treats a world where difference multiplies without *a priori* rationalization. The rationalizations are supplied by the various systematic intentions, in Lydgate's case the intentions of his neighbours to celebrate, depreciate, use or marry him. The radical change between the nineteenth and twentieth centuries comes with the dissolution of the common denominators of time and space, the media of modernity that guarantee every system belongs to the same world. But in terms of the social universe this dissolution is by no means firmly established even in the late twentieth century.

In the social universe of the historical novel, the qualitative distinctions once appropriate to a cosmic hierarchy give way to the quantitative distinctions of common, infinite, neutral space and time. In the historical novel form, the production of meaning always has to do with amounts of time, or amounts of evidence; or numbers of viewpoints; it is always cumulative and provisional. Each novelist exploits historical conventions differently, but the more fully a novelist exploits those conventions, the more fully we see that any human result is open to intervention, and that it could have been otherwise. By virtue of its medium, then, historical narrative renegotiates within a common horizon hierarchical differences that have lost their naturalized status. Differences based on class, gender, ethnicity or nationality all submit to the new horizon and new inclusiveness of history. John Stuart Mill luminously argues this point with regard to gender in the opening sections of his essay on *The Subjection of Women.*

But while historical novels, moving between different individuals and groups, implicitly acknowledge the plurality of possible positions, these silent inscriptions of historical form often are defied by the social material on view in such novels. The *form* may work to sustain for readers the Nobody narrator, the neutrality of social time, and thus the inescapability of acting in ways that are mutually relevant, but at the level of plot and character the narrative continually presents division and failure. Especially endemic in social novels is what might be called the Two World Problem. Whereas the historical medium insists on the mutuality between different classes or different moments, a habit of making dualist distinctions seems endemic in the social life presented. In the case of gender distinctions particularly, the division is so extreme that it threatens the very existence of the common medium, historical time.

DIFFERENCE AS DUALITY: CLUB, CLASS, CLAN

Dualisms are really masked hierarchies of value that act to *sublimate difference* by implicitly depreciating or even erasing the second term. For example, in the opposition between Good and Bad – whether it is art, or persons, or food – the second, depreciated term is often little more than a negative definition, that is, often merely a container for whatever is Not-Good – in art, persons, or food. One term tends to slide under the other in any dualism, whatever the oppositional differences may be (light and dark, white and black, rich and poor, fact and fiction, male and female, British and French, European and Asian, north and south). The slippage towards duality and hierarchy ultimately forecloses on the choice which is a pre-eminent value of historical conventions (in history it could always have been otherwise), and instead simply enthrones a prejudice. My good art may not be yours, but if I pronounce mine Good, then yours if it differs is by definition less than Good, even Bad. This conflict between the medium and the moral accounts for a considerable amount of the interest and suspense in social novels.

The dualistic habit of thinking goes back through Christian cosmology to the Greeks, and has been preserved in English education by the double emphasis on both traditions. Nothing could be farther from the historian's pluralizing than the dualistic, or oppositional, treatment of difference. Dualism depends on a prior structure and not on cumulative evidence; its terms are fundamentally and by definition naturalized; and its results could not have been otherwise. The struggle between good and evil – the struggle between Clarissa and Lovelace, for example – is a struggle that cannot be deflected by chance interventions. The dualist structure of difference precludes mediation and negotiation because the differences at stake are qualitative and absolute (Ermarth, 1983: 3–16; 1992: 162–70). Many a mid-century social novel plays on the effort to translate the quantitative terms of historical narrative back into the qualitative terms of (always an implicitly 'natural') hierarchy. Dickens and Trollope especially ridicule the social climbing of mere financiers (Merdle in *Our Mutual Friend*, Lopez in *The Prime Minister* and Melmotte in *The Way We Live Now*), who attempt to buy standing in the (old style) 'social' hierarchy by purchasing a title; it is an attempt literally to translate quantity into quality.

Dualistic thinking, being essentially hierarchical, remains inimical to historical assumptions. Late in the century writers like Joseph Conrad took pleasure in showing the paradoxes in such dualist oppositions. White over black in Conrad's Africa has a way of suggesting a reversal in which anything is preferable to the white lie. But in historical narratives, where differences appear in a headless and footless chain of continuously negotiable relationship, such oppositional dualisms become a focal part of the social criticism.

Throughout the nineteenth century, and probably well beyond, dualistic habits continue to tilt the historical narrative away from its most radical potential, and towards hierarchy however implicit. To take only one example, Disraeli makes much in *Sybil: or, The Two Nations* (1845) of the distinction between rich and poor. England is 'two nations':

> between whom there is no intercourse and no sympathy; who are as ignorant of each other's habits, thoughts, and feelings, as if they were dwellers in different zones, or inhabitant of different planets; who are formed by a different breeding, are fed by a different food, and ordered by different manners, and are not governed by the same laws... THE RICH AND THE POOR.
>
> (Disraeli, 1950: 67)

Is this not commendable morality? Certainly it is often found in nineteenth-century novels from Dickens onward. In the case of *Sybil*, the historical novel format inevitably problematizes the possibility of making such oppositional distinction in the first place. Rich and poor belong to the same world, so the medium's message goes. But at the same time, the very dualistic nature of the distinction between Rich and Poor, however well motivated, divides the world in two so that one must be assimilated into the other (implicitly the poor should become richer; does this mean that the rich should become poorer?). The dualistic formulation enables thought to mediate the difference, but it actually precludes the kind of pluralism that would problematize poverty, and thus suggest ways to correct it.

Without the historical format, however, similar distinctions between haves and have-nots can as easily be used to justify the preservation of class difference rather than its eradication. In 1898, for example, and on the brink of the twentieth century, W. H. Mallock published an argument which uses historical narrative to peddle a distinctly ahistorical line. In *Aristocracy and Evolution: A Study of the Rights, the Origins, and the Social Functions of the Wealthier Classes* Mallock uses the naturalized distinction between the 'exceptional' and the 'average' man to justify a whole world of social-class opposition. He argues, like a minister of Truth, that happiness comes from accepting inequality.

> The education proper for the rich is not a type but an exception. These false theories [e.g. of a universal right to education] rest on the false belief that equal education could ever produce equal social conditions.... Only the efficiently exceptional can rise out of their own class.... The Average Man should be taught to aim at embellishing his position, not at escaping it.
>
> (Mallock, 1898: vii–xxxiii)

This passage from a late-century text almost exactly echoes one in Dickens' *Dombey in Son* half a century earlier, where the morally corrupt Mr Dombey disapproves of 'what is called by persons of levelling sentiments, general education'. He approves of schools to the extent that the 'inferior classes should continue to be taught to know their position' (Dickens, 1970: 117, ch. 5). Like Mallock's exceptional (i.e. 'wealthy') classes, such people precisely do *not* see themselves as belonging to the same species as those who carry their water and produce their steel. Different laws apply to what are in effect different species. It is interesting that even Darwinian evolutionary values, which could have quite different application and which depend upon historical conventions, here are used to justify social arrangements that are essentially feudal and literally pre-historical. If there were not Two Englands, the profiteers of social hierarchy would have to invent them.

Compared with Disraeli's, Mallock's, and Mr Dombey's oppositional class vision, the anthropological narrative of Henry Mayhew's *London Labour and the London Poor* (1851) records the language, commentary and self-description of 'those disestablished citizens whom Her Majesty's census-taker chose totally to ignore' (Mayhew, 1968: I, v). Thirty thousand of these were costermongers (they sold fish, vegetables, fruit), a category of person that does not appear at all in the census of 1841, even though they 'appear to constitute nearly three-fourths of the entire number of individuals obtaining a subsistence in the streets of London' (ibid.: 3–4). The inclusive gesture of this narration is in keeping with the historical format in which it appears, and not in conflict with its format like the passage from Mallock. Unlike Mallock, Mayhew emphasizes similarity between the poor and others, and even the superiority of the poor on some points. Costermongers, for example,

> never steal from one another, and never wink at any one stealing from a neighbouring stall. . . . Property worth 10,000 £ belonging to costers is daily left exposed in the streets or at the markets, almost entirely unwatched, the policeman or market-keeper only passing at intervals. And yet thefts are rarely heard of, and when heard of are not attributable to costermongers, but to regular thieves. . . .
>
> I myself have often given a sovereign to professed thieves to get 'changed', and never knew one to make off with the money. Depend upon it, if we would really improve, we must begin by elevating instead of degrading.

(ibid.: 26–32)

Mayhew's purpose is didactic, but his drift is historical, both in format and intention. His project, like Dickens', is to mediate between these different classes: 'My earnest hope is that the book may serve to give the rich a more intimate knowledge of the sufferings, and the frequent heroism under those sufferings, of the poor' and to spur ameliorative action (ibid.: Preface, p. xv).

He explains various apparently eccentric features of street people in ways that generalize them: the origin of street language as a protective code, useful in circumstances where the law victimizes rather than protects them; their victimization by usurers who get away with rates of up to 20 per cent per week; their exclusion from so-called 'free' trade; and the causes that led them to be street folk in the first place (not infrequently they have been discharged by an employer when they became ill (ibid.: II, 466). Mayhew's narrative works to bridge the differences between classes, emphasizing the similarity in both human and economic terms.

> However unsatisfactory it may be to the aristocratic pride of the wealthy commercial classes, it cannot be denied that a very important element of the trade of this vast capital . . . is in the hands of the Street-Folk. This simple enunciation might appear a mere platitude were it not that the street-sellers are a *proscribed class*. They are driven from stations to which long possession might have been thought to give them a quasi legal right; driven from them at the capricious desire of the shopkeepers. . . . They are bandied about at the will of a police-officer. They must 'move on' and not obstruct a thoroughfare which may be crammed and blocked with the carriages of the wealthy until to cross the road on foot is a danger. . . . Now these are surely anomalies which it is high time, in these free-trade days, should cease. *The endeavour to obtain an honest and independent livelihood should subject no man to fine or imprisonment;* nor should the poor hawker – the neediest perhaps of all tradesmen – be required to pay £4 a year for the liberty to carry on his business when the wealthy shopkeeper can do so 'scot-free'.
>
> (ibid.: II: 3)

This 'wealthy shopkeeper' does not belong to a world divided dualistically but, on the contrary, to a world of mutual relevance and dependency. The historical and humanist language remains consistent with the text's formal inclusiveness, and does not lapse back into invidious oppositions. Mayhew precisely does *not* resort to that commonplace dualism between RICH and POOR that translates a quantitative and variable distinction into a qualitative and absolute one.

If dualistic (i.e. hierarchical) class-distinctions between rich and poor were really only about money, they would remain quantitative distinctions and thus at least potentially un-hierarchical and wholly historical. But in these nineteenth-century English texts the distinction between two nations remains a hierarchical and qualitative distinction, and thus a moral issue couched in terms belonging to an older tradition than the historical. In such analyses, the local terms are less important than the hierarchical dualism that contains them; that is what primarily informs awareness. Rich and poor, better and worse, gentry and merchant, public and private, male and female, inside and outside, north and south, country and city: the divisive habit floats from context to context. The dualism remains, even though occupancies change.

Such social division between Them and Us is like a floating dice game: always the same game despite a difference in location. It is an Us-*versus*-Them game, and not the I-and-Thou game that the historical novelists, the theorists and philosophers of democratic politics, and a generation of existential theologians (beginning with Strauss and Feuerbach) would have it. Rich parvenu *versus* titled aristocrat, poor labourer *versus* middle class, working class *versus* professional class (as if professionals don't work and workers have no profession): depending on the dualism, both the rich parvenu and the poor labourer alike may eventually end up on the depreciated side of a social dualism, but they may never discover their solidarity because there are so many sliding scales.

Nineteenth-century historical narrative does not always exploit fully the levelling implications of its infinite horizon and common world. Chapters Two and Three showed how differences between individuals and groups can support the mutually informative measurements that unify the social unity; how ethnic difference, gender difference, national difference and even class difference can be a site for negotiating linkage, and thus for treating difference without resorting to hierarchy. It is not the difference that makes for hierarchy, but a *blurring* of precisely those differences deriving from practical function that makes the opportunity for divisive dualisms: for the Manichean alignment of what, to the eye of history, appears much more complex and interdependent.

This sublimation of difference – this erasure of the actual variability of the world in favour of *a priori* value judgements – is a frequent target of social novelists, who pursue it in its many guises. One particularly interesting variety of this Them-and-Us game, and a familiar plot motivator in novels by Trollope and George Eliot, is gossip. Social novelists, those interested in the maintenance of a common and egalitarian world, treat gossip as a form of tribalism, a way of constructing history without regard to veracity, a substitute for the inclusive Nobody narrative with one whose coordinates cannot be known. Gossip, because it is full of mistakes, often cruel ones, is a great plot motivator. Trollope's *Barchester Towers*, to take one example only, makes gossip into a major obstacle to social renewal. Gossip in Barchester, without much regard to accuracy, uses partial information for the larger purpose of generalizing and disseminating pre-existing norms. 'Gossip', we recall, was once the name for the person who acted at baptisms as a stand-in for God. This God-function is undiminished in Barchester gossip, where it literally stands in for history. It is a Barchester law that an eligible widow must be in want of a cleric to marry; unfortunately for Eleanor Bold, town gossip gets the wrong cleric. The potentially serious consequences of the gossip emerge once the danger is over, and after Eleanor Bold has made the marriage so important to the community's future. The local 'story' concerning her affections and allegiances alienates her from her social group and even from her own father in ways that, in a less comic novel, could have tragic consequences. Gossip here preserves the group from confusion, doubt, even choice, but at the cost of truth and even vitality.

Gossip is a form of narrative which requires only one point of view. It is in every way inimical to the open pluralities of historical narrative. Gossip from Barchester to Middlemarch involves private conversation that relies on unverified information; after all, verification might require taking a different point of view. These conversations – ballooning into a kind of social chorus – cause immense public and social damage in novels that, like all historical novels, are dedicated to the preservation of a candid world. Such social functions as gossip may have (Spacks, 1985) pale into insignificance in Victorian novels by comparison with the secrecy it encourages and the damage it thus does to the maintenance of a shared world. Gossip prevents particular differences of viewpoint or belief from performing their creative and essential social function as sites for mediation (see Chapter Two, 'Mediate Power, pp. 86–100).

Tribal exclusiveness, like gossip which may be a form of it, also has a detrimental effect on the maintenance of the common media essential to egalitarian social agendas. Among all the symptoms of dualist and hierarchical unregeneracy in social novels, the chief symptom is tribal allegiance. The ethics of the tribe, whether in the club, the class or the clan, depend upon the 'spirit of communal exclusiveness – the resistance to indiscriminate establishment of strangers' that typifies the peasant mentality whether it dresses in rough cloth or in dinner jackets (Pinney, 1963: 282). Peasant mentality is not restricted to rural villages, as social novelists like George Eliot, George Meredith and Anthony Trollope are fond of showing. The hopelessly ignorant and narrow aristocrat and the arriviste who imitates him or her both exemplify a peasant tribal mentality fully as much as a rural farmer might do. George Eliot and Dickens have little patience with aristocratic peasants; Elizabeth Gaskell, George Meredith, and Anthony Trollope take more interest in anatomizing them.

A most thorough critique of clan behaviour in a rural setting can be found in George Eliot's early work, *Scenes of Clerical Life, Adam Bede,* and *The Mill on the Floss.* The latter contains her funniest portraits of rural clan behaviour in the families of the Tullivers, Pullets and Gleggs, all united by marriage through the inimitable Dodson sisters. The Dodson ways are the only ways. Dodsons have only one view of things, the 'right' one (for which the historical novelist reads the 'traditional' one); there is no other. Mrs Glegg (*née* Dodson) may have two windows in her house, and thus two points of view from which to consider the failings of her neighbours; but as she sees the same thing from both, the double perspective yields no perspective *system* but only the parochial reiteration of sameness. The Dodsons' habitual 'faithfulness to admitted rules' results in two dangerous and even potentially fatal habits (Ermarth, 1974a: 587–601): one, an utter inability to question themselves; and the other, a compulsive persistence in questioning everyone else.

But in a world with only one point of view on every question, the only possible questions are small ones having to do with eating preserves and keeping plate polished.

> A female Dodson, when in 'strange houses', always ate dry bread with her tea, and declined any sort of preserves, having no confidence in the butter, and thinking that the preserves had probably begun to ferment from want of due sugar and boiling. There were some Dodsons less like the family than others – that was admitted; but in so far as they were 'kin', they were of necessity better than those who were 'no kin'.
>
> (Eliot, 1961: I, vi, 40)

> A Dodson would not be taxed with the omission of anything that was becoming, or that belonged to that eternal fitness of things which was plainly indicated in the practice of the most substantial parishioners, and in the family traditions – such as, obedience to parents, faithfulness to kindred, industry, rigid honesty, thrift, the thorough scouring of wooden and copper utensils, the hoarding of coins likely to disappear from the currency, the production of first-rate commodities for the market, and the general preference for whatever was home-made.
>
> (ibid.: IV, ii, 240)

The strengths of such parochialism appear clearly in George Eliot's treatment, and are perhaps given added interest by virtue of being on the brink of extinction. The amusement about the fidelity of Mrs Tulliver (*née* Dodson) to her 'household gods' arises in part from the sense that her culture and its gods are imperiled by historical change.

At the same time, Eliot demonstrates the deeply antisocial tendency of this parochialism, despite its strengths and charms. As in all George Eliot's English country stories, a more inclusive civilization is always visible in the margins of the rural social order. *Adam Bede* (1859) records the lingering end of a rural, feudally organized social culture governed by customs, not laws. Mrs Poyser makes her butter, as she and her forebears always have, for the sake of her family and neighbors. She has no interest in making more butter, only better butter: and no butter for strangers. The young man of the manor, Arthur Donnithorne, avails himself of the ancient squire's privilege over milkmaids, even though he would be appalled to recognize it in that light. Adam Bede, at least initially, has the yeoman's passivity with regard to social arrangements. The industrial world visible in the margins presses in upon this colourful and naturalized order of things, bringing the milkmaid to judgement in a law court and the whole sunlit world of 'natural' society to the point of collapse. Even the novel's metaphoric language changes from richly colourful impressions of a timeless traditional order to something darker, and perhaps more adequate to a difficult modern world.

When 'small tribes are united into larger communities', Darwin writes in the *Descent of Man* (1871), we have 'advances in civilisation' (Darwin, 1979: 100). Maybe so, but the uniting is not a matter of mere aggregation; it involves a negotiation between different viewpoints that the peasant mentality finds difficult or impossible, and that requires of it to leap from a world of received truth to a world of provisional position. In *The Mill on the Floss* (1860) the rural community of St. Oggs gives way to the town centre where 'clan' values of uniformity and unquestioned truth clash with other, different (if equally unquestioned) truths about banking and law. Mr Tulliver's inability to adjust to the presence of this 'antagonism of valid claims' (Pinney, 1963: 264) prompts disaster by his insistence on pursuing his essentially tribal code of revenge in modern courts of law.

But farmers are not the only peasants. A particular scandal in *The Mill on the Floss* is the mentality of the Oxford man, the Revd Stelling, whose teaching comes so 'naturally' to him that he sets about it 'with that uniformity of method and independence of circumstances, which distinguish the actions of animals understood to be under the immediate teaching of nature'. Mr Stelling has the same tribal mentality as Trollope's 'indubitably right' Archdeacon Grantley. He tutors Tom Tulliver accordingly – 'in the only right way – indeed, he knew no other: he had not wasted his time in the acquirement of anything abnormal' (Eliot, 1961: I, iii; II, i). In this tendency the Revd Stelling behaves exactly like the members of the rural clans to whom he feels himself superior. The Oxford man and the Midlands farm wife alike equate their ways with the 'eternal fitness of things'. And these narrow minds are relatively benign compared with the aristocrat in Eliot's last novel, *Daniel Deronda* (1876), who regards his will as law, and goes on crowding and crushing anyone who differs from him with an easy, sauntering, insouciant conviction that his way must be the only way. The content of a peasant's tribal mentality may change, but the method remains the same.

The spirit of communal exclusiveness, therefore, by no means confines itself to rural settings or even to the lower and middle classes. Trollope's best novels deal with the culture of the privileged classes, where his portraits are subtle and damning. Lord Brentford, the patron of young MPs like Phineas Finn, brooks no opposition on any matter he chooses to consider, whether or not his judgement is appropriate. You agree with Lord Brentford, 'or else'. The narrowness and violence of Trollope's fox-hunting Lord Chiltern might be amusing and, because he marries the fabulous Violet Effingham, even forgivable, were it not for the fact that all his splendid potential is spent on supporting the hunt, a singularly noisome expression of unearned class privilege which even the *aficionado* Trollope eventually abandoned. Plantagenet Palliser, the man who manages coalition politics, stands as a lonely exception in a genteel crowd with tribal instincts, and not only in Trollope but in nineteenth-century English novels.

Trollope makes sure his readers particularly detest the vulgar ease with which members of the wealthiest class use the system for their own private interests, confusing what is social with what is theirs: conflating, that is, a modern idea of society with a feudal one. Men's clubs appear in his novels as a locus of political difficulty: critical to the functioning of Parliament on the one hand, and on the other hand, segregated by class and gender to the extent of producing yet another tribal entity. 'I envy you men your clubs more than I do the House', says Lady Laura in *Phineas Finn* (Trollope, 1972: 98). Trollope's treatment of politics makes clear what considerable strain exists between on the one hand men's clubs, and on the other the House, a political system that theoretically operates on principles entirely at odds with those of the tribe. The Palliser novels especially (*Can You Forgive Her?* (1864), *Phineas Finn* (1869), *The Eustace Diamonds* (1873), *Phineas Redux* (1873–4), *The Prime Minister* (1876) and *The*

Duke's Children (1879–80)) anatomize the irreducible conflicts between these two systems, the tribal and the almost-constitutional. When the House is knotted together by men's private clubs, and its work is carried on in those clubs, the chief instrument of democracy is held hostage. Trollope's faith in Parliament fades, but not his faith in the libertarian political experiment which the House represented and which he presents as the Great Adventure.

The whole dreary system of primogeniture, with its devastating effects on the personal growth of its supposed beneficiaries, especially plagues Trollope's young people in the Palliser novels. Lady Mabel Grex in *The Duke's Children* dies by inches, like Lady Laura Standish before her, as a hostage to its brutalities. A rare example of independence from this culture occurs in the same novel in the young Lord Silverbridge. He demonstrates his capacity to mature when he braves the (ultimately inconsequential) upper-class version of the spirit of communal exclusiveness and marries an American, the independent Isabel Boncassen – relative of Henry James's own American Isabel in *The Portrait of a Lady* (1881), and cousin to many an American heroine in English history.

Like the more rural clan, the London club contains occasional subversives. Trollope's most extended political portrait is that of the appealing Plantagenet Palliser, eventually Duke of Omnium. Here is the aristocrat who sees the point of democracy, and who even works to ensure that it takes precedence over the system that confers upon him his own privileges. Palliser in Parliament, like Maggie Tulliver in St. Oggs, can 'dare to be wrong' – dare to offend the received opinion and 'correct' views, dare to confront a tribal culture with historical change. Palliser is willing to be the citizen of the candid world: someone with a horizon wide enough to permit something like a social vision. Characters like this are rare in the social novel; they approach the broad vision represented by the Nobody narrator and implicit in the differences between systems always centre stage in Trollope and George Eliot. In so doing, they emerge from and mark the limits of the tribal culture, with its certainties, its single explanations, its refusal to respect or even to recognize what differs.

Tribal culture thus eradicates, as a point of honour, the very differences that constitute the basis of order and form in the humanist, historical and social grammar of perspective. It is what Feuerbach would call a culture of 'egoism' – essentially 'monotheistic' in consistency and narrowness. Tribal culture aligns the entire human universe into Us and Them, and simply treats the one who differs as a creature belonging to a different species, probably an inferior one. There is 'kin' and (with the logic of a medieval theologian) 'not-kin': a negative difference that enshrines one way, one group, one and only one 'right'. To appear problematic, difference must belong to a world of common denominators and must eschew such cultural egoism. But to the tribal mentality, difference is only a matter of better and worse.

Such a culture, as J. S. Mill notes in *The Subjection of Women*, provides an entirely unsound basis for democracy.

> In the less advanced states of society, people hardly recognize any relation with their equals. To be an equal is to be an enemy. Society, from its highest place to its lowest, is one long chain, or rather ladder, where every individual is either above or below his nearest neighbour, and wherever he does not command he must obey. Existing moralities, accordingly, are mainly fitted to a relation of command and obedience.
>
> (Mill, 1975: 477)

'To be an equal is to be an enemy': a mantra for a tribal culture implacably opposed to multiplied viewpoints and emergent form. In historical and social novels, the hierarchical chain of subjection has no place. In historical and social novels, the whole point of the narrative convention is that different viewpoints emerge: that is how such narrative explores the potential of the inclusive social entity. Nothing could be farther from the clannish exclusiveness of tribal mentality.

The struggle between hierarchy and horizon, like the struggle between dogma and hypothesis, appears incarnate in social novels as the Nobody narrator carries attention from one story to another, one class to another, in perpetual violation of tribal distinctions and parochial settlements. The coach-riding narrator at the beginning of George Eliot's fourth novel, *Felix Holt* (1866), stands for all these Nobody systems, as the narrative rolls past the timeless static order of 'the shepherd' who views such mobility as pointless. ' "Gover'ment" ... whatever it might be, was no business of his ... : his solar system was the parish; the master's temper and the casualties of lambing-time were his region of storms'. The very form of historical novels gives value to mobility rather than to stasis, and shifts attention from one singular 'solar system' to another. In historical and social novels there is no centre but a temporary one, and this eloquent fact of the form belies at every moment the stasis and the holism of traditional and tribal culture.

Class distinction may be implicit in tribal culture, but the very notion of class in its post-Marxist construction has very little to do with the tribal groupings of a feudal culture. Class is a social term, implying a social entity that remains entirely foreign to the naturalized and hierarchical distinctions of tribal culture. It remains unclear how the changing social distinctions of the nineteenth century compare with the ones functional in the twentieth. Is class consciousness merely tribal mentality writ large? Is it an unassimilated tribal mentality, forced by modern technological and political conditions into a kind of semblance of social unity? Is class only a figment of Marxist imaginations (Calvert, 1982; Furbank, 1985; Blake, 1989)? In any case, these days it is an uneasy subject, even, as T. H. Pear suggests, 'taboo'. But then, as he reflects, paraphrasing a French sociologist, 'there has been little field-work among the English upper classes' (Pear, 1941–42: 343–4). Such fieldwork is precisely what Trollope and Meredith so brilliantly provide in their many witty treatments of the gentry and the aristocracy. But treatments of class as such, rather than this or that particular class, require a particular breadth of horizon and experience available to few novelists. Dickens more than most writers characteristically shifts from one class to another across the whole social spectrum, but his agenda is more didactic and less like fieldwork than that of either Trollope or Meredith.

As with other forms of difference, class difference is not in itself necessarily a basis for hierarchy, but it is always a basis for segregations of the kind that threaten to dissolve the social entity. It is, rather, Pear argues, precisely class *unconsciousness* that makes possible and preserves the parochial, tribal mentality discussed here. In the early twentieth century, for example, Pear finds that *still*, half-way through the twentieth century, a divided English society pays the price for its habitual hierarchical habit: the price of persistent segregation between competence and power. 'Public life is administered by people who, quite literally, know next to nothing at first hand about the life of the public, are not even conscious of their own ignorance, and tacitly assume that they are typical English men and women. This is not class consciousness, but class *unconsciousness*' (ibid.: 351–3).

This segregation of competence from power Pear traces directly to an educational system that is geared to the production of ladies and gentlemen, something that almost all Victorian novels consider whether in historical or in providential terms. Training ladies and gentlemen, as distinct, say, from citizens, means training 'people who *are* rather than people who *do*'. A gentleman, for example, is interested in nothing in a professional way; he knows nothing about political economy and less about foreign governments; he prefers sport to learning; he is inattentive to technology; he 'is passionately devoted to excessive secrecy in finance and method of production', and to nepotism in appointment, 'discounting ability and relying upon a mystic entity called "character"'; he lacks imagination; his social loyalties are narrow (ibid.: 359). Though its terms are somewhat different, this twentieth-century view amplifies one found throughout Victorian fiction. The narrow, trivializing education of women – even narrower and more trivilalizing than the 'good' classical one Edward Casaubon got at University – is a subject taken up by everyone. For Charlotte Brontë, Thackeray, George Eliot, Meredith and Trollope, it is a locus of discussion about The Woman Question, as the nineteenth century rather oddly called it.

Like class, nationalism plays a role in the developing idea of a social entity. Even as late as the early nineteenth century English nationalism remained socially segregated; it was scarcely 'national' in the sense we would understand it today, as marking an inclusive social entity however problematic. In fact, Linda Colley argues, the English state had never supported the usual engines of national awareness like the explosion of newspapers and journals and presses, and like foreign wars (the Seven Years War, the American colonial war, the Napoleonic wars). In fact, the state took a curiously peripheral role in the development of a nationalist feeling that might introduce either a meritocracy, or a secular state that would compete for power with the Church. Any mobilization on a national scale, including military mobilization, would threaten en-trenched privilege. 'Not surprisingly, then, the only outlet for popular nationalism which the British government felt able safely and consistently to encourage during the French Revolutionary and Napoleonic wars was the cult of the monarchy'. Various groups appealed to nationalist feeling, but for sectarian, class agendas; similarly 'the people' became associated with various political bodies, but not with an all-inclusive body politic (Colley, 1986: 107–10). It was precisely the definition of that inclusive social entity that was at stake in social and historical narratives.

The potential for using foreign countries as excuses for a kind of negative self-definition is evident in the margins of mid-century novels, and becomes more evident as, towards the end of the century, the Empire appears in writing by Kipling and Conrad. For most of the century, however, foreigners play a marginal and cautionary role in novels. Dickens' Rigaud, Trollope's Signora Neroni and Madame Max Goesler, or George Eliot's Herr Klesmer, all appear in the margins of novels set in England. Dickens' *Tale of Two Cities* or George Eliot's *Daniel Deronda*, both novels that compare English culture with another, are exceptional. Foreigners are at best sources of unsettling energy; foreign sites might have exotic and occasional value, but nobody would want to live there. When Trollope wants to send his poor heroine, Lady Laura, to hell, he sends her to live in Dresden; and Charlotte Brontë chooses Brussels as the worldly city of her pilgrim's progress in *Villette*. To Mr Podsnap, Dickens' comic reduction of national chauvinism, the problem of nationalism is simple: everything British is Providential. But if national feeling can in the main be expressed only negatively, it is not surprising, given the still uncertain sense of what exactly constituted social identity.

Almost any social differentiation – class, race, nationality, gender – can act as a basis for dualist alignment of difference. Like race, gender is an issue peculiarly suited to the application of dualistic segregation. The physical differences between men and women, like those between races, offer an easy prop to the traditional or tribal mind unwilling to seek further for its distinctions: especially the mind trained to dualist habits. But where class, national and even racial differences vary with conditions, sexual difference has the dubious distinction of being at least somatically universal. In nineteenth-century England, racial segregation was publicly debated, but the issue was treated as an import, from America or the Empire. Gender issues, on the other hand, were omnipresent.

HOME IS WHERE THE FAULT-LINE IS

At some fatally auspicious moment between 1500 and 1700, and in the pursuit of an exciting new vision of a unified world, Western culture invested in a dualistic separation between public and private. In other words, at more or less the same cultural moment (post-Renaissance but pre-Enlightenment), two things happened: time and space were reconstructed as the neutral media of modernity; and these neutral media – 'in' which activity and causality and agency operate – became public property. Neutral time and space, the media of realism and history, became the common denominators of collective life; they testify to a humanist faith so profound and inspiring that it took in and recovered virtually everything in a human horizon rather than in a divine order of things: in a horizon that was single, public, infinite, and common to all.

All, that is, except those who inhabit the Other Side of the dualistic distinction between public and private. The realm of alterity called 'private' (in time or space) is defined by contrast to, even in opposition to, the 'public'; the private world is finite and contained and everything in it is finite, from opportunity, to wealth, to life itself. Of course, 'the public' theoretically derives entirely from this private realm; but in fact it operates on entirely different principles, 'in' effectively different space and time. This double standard has fatal consequences for those confined to domesticity. This discursive 'move' to divide public and private, part of the humanist and historical cultural reformation in seventeenth-century

England, belongs to a different argument, but a brief speculation here is in order. The distinction produces narrative that confines those threats of ending and of finitude to a finite 'private' realm of consideration; there, limited success is possible, but failure is also relatively limited. Only the larger 'public' realm is shareable and, more importantly, infinite (in its humanist construction, not in its feudal usage). In other words, what is not shareable is Private and remains incidental and marginal to whatever is Public. This dualist separation coincides with a constriction of the extended family, and the birth of the nuclear kind so familiar to twentieth-century social and gender ideology (Davidoff and Hall, 1987: 85). The 'private' unit thus attenuated becomes a site of unusual contest through the nineteenth century, and through the novel. One critic goes so far as to say 'that the emancipation of women and the emancipation of the English novel advanced together' (Cunningham, 1978: 3): a comment that suggests the extent to which cultural advancement depends upon the erasure of gender segregation.

Gender hierarchy is a form of tribal or class privilege that reinstates, at the heart of a society seeking new democratic measures, a fatal inequality.

> All the selfish propensities, the self-worship, the unjust self-preference, which exist among mankind, have their source and root in, and derive their principal nourishment from, the present constitution of the relation between men and women. Think what it is to a boy, to grow up to manhood in the belief that without any merit or any exertion of his own, though he may be the most frivolous and empty or the most ignorant and stolid of mankind, by the mere fact of being born a male is by right the superior of all and every one of an entire half of the human race.
>
> (Mill, 1975: 522–3)

To give the subjection of women a 'natural' justification is, Mill says, to lay claim by form to an arbitrary privilege. This practice has evil effects for its victims, which include everyone. It has the effect on the holders of that so-called privilege of making them socially shallow and stupid, trained as they are to consider only their limited conception of self–interest.

The condition of women in the nineteenth century is a litmus test of the idea that society is a self-sustaining and inclusive entity, and consequently their condition rivets public attention. The so-called Woman Question continually focuses attention on the problem of constituting the social entity. When well over half of the English population, regardless of their social or economic status, live in legal and economic slavery, it simply is not possible to sustain the liberal idea of society as an entity. In literature and journals, in political forums, and eventually on the streets, women and men in the newly industrialized Atlantic countries protested the social consequences of the subjection of women.

The problem was that what the liberal conventions of history and humanism promised in theory, they did not yield in practice, because the archaic social hierarchy remained founded on the marginalization of half the population. Over and over again in nineteenth-century novels, fictional women act out the conflict, often a fatal conflict, between their ideological preparation for inclusion in the social project, and their actual experience. Nearly worshipped, on the one hand, as care-givers and supports of social morality, and subjected, on the other hand, to a condition of legal and economic helplessness without access to education or public recognition, women endured a grotesquely conflicted set of expectations. The Woman Question heightens more than any other single issue the problematic functioning of the floating dualistic habit of definition.

These dilemmas of women can be seen as markers or codes for other dilemmas of difference caused by culturally marginal groups like servants, slaves, and colonized people generally. The question was, how such marginals could be assimilated in the social order that historical narrative unfolds, or whether they could be assimilated at all. In this way The Woman Question tests the very conditions of survival for the grammar of perspective that underwrites history. Humanist conventions, and pre-eminently the historical convention that produces individuality *as* a social differentia, make 'the individual' and all its claims to freedom and agency dependent upon a 'human' definition that is inclusive and rational. But women, as most social novelists and a few social commentators showed, found those conventions to be merely segregationist and, in Lyotard's useful phrase, 'terrorist' (Lyotard, 1984: 63–5): false fantasies of inclusion designed to cripple their powers and suppress their voices.

The social entity that historical narrative makes conceivable depends for its very existence on the cumulative relationships between individuals. Unequal relationships cripple the whole social entity, not for moral reasons (though those do apply) but for much more formal reasons. The very existence of neutral time and space depends upon the total inclusiveness of the perspective system that produces these media in the first place. The social standard implied by such perspective systems, and by the very existence of these media of modernity, positively requires by definition the inclusion of competing, contesting elements. Camus' 'I rebel, therefore we exist', cited in Chapter Three, sums up the sense of the liberal mid-century, so clear in Mill's writing, that being part of the contest is essential. Being 'protected' from it is a little like being 'protected' by the Mafia: it amounts to being denied choice. In his essay on *The Subjection of Women* (it treats more fully and more systematically some of the points Mary Wollstonecraft introduced in her ground-breaking *Vindication of the Rights of Women* (1792)), Mill explains to a nineteenth-century audience that gender inequality is the single most pervasive obstacle to the construction of society as an entity. It is a monopoly that institutionalizes inequality. For Mill, the ultimate 'sinister interest' is male chauvinism: the monopoly based on physical characteristics and maintained by violence either to the minds or the bodies of half the world.

The entire education of young Victorian girls is likely to be informed by the idea, enunciated in many novels and tracts, that normal women have no desires. Young girls were taught a trick damaging not only to them: to have desires not for themselves but always 'for' others. And when they grow up and inevitably fall ill from this repressive regimen, they can seek help from doctors who employ the same prejudices that informed their twisted education in the first place. Dr William Acton assured the public that women 'aren't much troubled by sexual feeling of any kind'; that, as Florence Nightingale angrily paraphrased it, 'women have no passion' (Nightingale, 1991: 200 ff.). Here is one of Acton's cases; one can only wonder that his conclusion was treated as 'scientific':

> In _____, 185–, a barrister, about thirty years of age, came to me on account of sexual debility. . . . His wife assured me that she felt no sexual passions whatever; that if she was capable of them they were dormant. Her passion for her husband was of a Platonic kind, and far from wishing to stimulate his frigid feelings, she doubted whether it would be right or not. She loved him as he was, and would not desire him to be otherwise except for the hope of having a family.
>
> I believe this lady is a perfect ideal of an English wife and mother, kind, considerate, self-sacrificing, and sensible, so pure-hearted as to be utterly ignorant of and averse to any sensual indulgence, but so unselfishly attached to the man she loves, as to be willing to give up her own wishes and feelings for his sake.
>
> (William Acton, *Functions and Disorder of the Reproductive Organs*, London, 1857; quoted in Helsinger *et al.*, 1983, II: 61–2)

Nancy Cott and others have argued that the legend of female lack of passion 'liberated' women from the danger of being constructed as sex-objects (Cott, 1977: 219–36; Helsinger *et al.*, 1983, II: 74, 218–19). But that is a small boon in an otherwise appalling situation where this construction of womanhood has little or nothing to do with women's actual sexuality in the first place. Acton's description of an ideal wife testifies in full to what women were up against. The standard of 'purity' is casually applied, as always in opposition to what is 'sensual', and this familiar dualism shifts women towards the end of purity; a sensual life for her plainly would be mere 'indulgence'. The contradiction in the last sentence remains unnoted: presumably the wife who gives up desire because she has no desire, must have some desires after all. In the end, it is difficult for a late-twentieth-century reader to accept such justification of sexual suppression, and Acton's bizarre prejudicial account suggests the physical extremity in which many women found themselves. Finally, we note how easily the supposed absence of sexual desire translates into the supposed absence of any other 'wishes'. One cannot help thinking of Dorothea Brooke in *Middlemarch*, married to a withered elder with whom the idea of sexual union is unthinkable. It gives still more horror to her quiet assertion to her more enlightened doctor, 'I have no longings.'

While Acton's view was not the only view of women's sexuality, it seems fair to call it an orthodoxy with considerable currency; his book went through six editions in Britain and four in America, as well as many abridgments and translations over 43 years. Such views as Dr Acton's are not rare or eccentric in a culture where men and women are segregated early in life and 'treated' as adults by medical men (the century was well on before women could both qualify and practise as doctors) who have no idea of, and take no responsibility for, the close limitations of their own judgements. In the pronouncements of Dr Edward H. Clarke, for example, Harvard physician and Acton's counterpart in America, prejudice filters unnoted from one area of social discourse to another and turns up in the language with which he explains the workings of the female anatomy. For Dr Clarke, whose terms read like a fantastic blend of Adam Smith and Darwin, the internal organs of women are engaged in a constant competition for limited resources. 'The brain cannot take more than its share without injury to other organs', particularly in women's reproductive organs [men's apparently do not compete or the competition is not worth mentioning]; women's brains compete with their reproductive organs so that too much blood to one means too little for the other. A woman who thinks is liable to damage her ovaries. Think of the danger to the production of heirs! Women must choose between babies and thought. Here, in a peculiar physiological-cum-moral expression, we find an economy of competition similar to the one more familiar in monetary terms. Such stories are amusing only when one forgets the millions of girls and women whose lives were twisted by such ideas and by such men. This 'willingness to let [so-called] science serve ideology' results in 'terrible suffering for both sexes' (Edward Clarke, *Sex in Education or, a Fair Chance for Girls*, Boston, 1873; quoted in Helsinger *et al.*, 1983, II: 75). It is also a stunning example of the immature and ungenerous belief that one person's gain must be another person's loss: an attitude that reinforces women's separation from the life of affairs, intellect and worldly commerce.

The fashionable physician, S. Weir Mitchell, must not go unmentioned. He is the man who invented a 'rest cure' for women that consisted of 'force-feeding, total bed rest, and complete submission to his will' (Helsinger *et al.*, 1983, II: 73). The feminist Charlotte Perkins Gilman was briefly one of his victims. Virginia Woolf was another victim, and it is not at all clear that Mitchell didn't immensely aggravate her private miseries, causing rather than curing the psychic trauma of someone who was sexually abused by her male relatives when she was young. Certainly Woolf's character Clarissa Dalloway, who endures 'the cure', feels it to be an assault; so does the narrator-heroine of Gilman's powerful novella, *The Yellow Wallpaper*. The view of normal female 'health' perpetrated by unobservant doctors like Mitchell, Acton and Clarke spread widely well past the end of the nineteenth century, and it led to 'remedies' as barbarous as foot-binding. If plain repression failed to suppress a woman's sexuality, for example, actual physiological correction could be achieved surgically. 'Respectable' doctors recommended such surgical modification of women's bodies as a proper way to 'restore' women to 'normal' life (Helsinger *et al.*, 1983, II: 73).

There were also true scientists, and presumably true husbands as well, who found such prejudices unacceptable, and tried to dispel rather than codify them. Dr George Drysdale, a Scottish physician, argued that a complete sex life was essential to a woman's health (George Drysdale, *Elements of Social Science* (1860), quoted in Helsinger *et al.*, 1983, II: 67–9.) Thomas Huxley and Mrs E. B. Duffey argued, in the latter case directly with Dr Acton, that it was a woman's mode of life, not her 'nature', that produced physiological illness. William Thompson likewise complained of the entire regimen: it encourages a husband to regard his wife as an 'involuntary breeding machine and household slave' who 'is not permitted even to wish for any gratification for herself. She must have no desires' (Thompson, 1970; quoted in Helsinger *et al.*, 1983 I: 29). As early as 1825, and well before Victoria's reign, Thompson enunciates the critique later taken up by Mill in, among other places, *On Liberty*: 'Exaggerated self-abnegation' of the kind fostered in domestic contexts works against individuality and freedom, and eventually erupts into conflict (Mill, 1975: 476). Such self-abnegation is a version of the religious self-abnegation Feuerbach deplores (referred to in Chapter Two) as being hostile to the principle of culture.

In narrative treatments of marriage and family, signs of hopelessly conflicted agendas appear most strikingly. On the one hand, the family is regarded as a refuge for certain values: for moral and social responsibility, for individual development, and for personal freedom. Such values are increasingly out of place in a global marketplace informed by the naturalized economic thinking of Adam Smith, yet they are values central to English ethical and religious traditions. Such values, obviously, must be privatized. This liminal threshold between public and private life is not something new in the nineteenth century; it was invented in the Renaissance (Ermarth, 1983: 47–9). But Victorian novels endlessly negotiate this threshold in their experiments with social conditions. The dualistic divide between the public and the private realms consigns certain values to each: in particular, moral values to 'the home' and to the care of women who 'naturally' and, unlike men (so the fantasy goes), operate for the good of others.

In this arrangement 'the home' operates as a refuge from the marketplace. At the same time, however, the domestic unit also operates *as* a market for improving its fortunes by selling its marriageable children for money or status. Thomas Hardy's *The Mayor of Casterbridge* (1886) begins with the sale of a wife in a kind of grim parody that literalizes the metaphor. As William Thompson's *Inquiry into the Principles of the Distribution of Wealth* (1824) points out, and as Barbara Bodichon (1859) later agreed, men essentially buy women as they buy everything else in a capitalist economy, and marriage is simply another form of sale. The private refuge – 'home' – provides a liminal space, a kind of bracket, for containing unresolved conflicts between these two incompatible social definitions. The conflicts between social and feudal arrangements, between moral and economic values, turn up as domestic problems in social and historical narratives. Dickens sums up this schizoid situation in *Great Expectations* in his portrait of Mr Wemmick, who spends his day as a hard taskmaster in an office, and his evenings as a gentle man in his home which is literally a castle-and-moat in miniature.

George Gissing treats uncompromisingly the peculiar symbiosis between the idealization of women and their degradation. *The Odd Women* (1893) begins precisely with the misogynist behaviour of the fond father, Dr Madden, soon to die leaving absolutely no financial provision for his three daughters. Dr Madden believes in the home as refuge. 'The home must be guarded against sordid cares ... women, old or young, should never have to think about money' (Gissing, 1911: 2). After several hundred pages of grinding poverty, alcoholism, and death for his daughters, this callow paternalism seems most sordid of all. And its social consequences come home in a chilling way at the end of the novel. After a career of entire ineptitude in the one case and, in the other, a history of secret addiction, the two surviving Madden spinsters propose to improve their prospects by passing their wisdom along: they will open 'a school for young children' (ibid.: ch. 31). Gissing's irony here is bitter, and his terms are consistently economic. Gender segregation continues for economic reasons. The prevailing system, with its pieties about home as refuge, actually makes no room either for the helpless females envisioned by misogyny or for the considerable talents of a woman like Rhoda Nunn, one of the few Victorian women prepared to pay the price of independence. 'The home' instead produces moral and emotional cripples like Mr Widdowson, who lives on his investments and who, Gissing takes care to note, occupies his leisure by reading Adam Smith.

The practices of keeping property out of the hands of daughters, and of training them for marriage as their only profession, meant that, like the bank robber, Willie Sutton, daughters had to go where the money was, but, quite unlike him, they had to go of necessity and regardless of their inclination. This, as Barbara Bodichon and others pointed out, is tantamount to prostitution. Not to *have* goods in the general economic system, but instead to *be* the goods on a marriage market, reduces the life of middle-class women very close to prostitution. In 1856, Bodichon, 'the most important unstudied figure of mid-century English feminism' (Helsinger *et al.*, 1983: 147–8), writes scathingly of the system that produces this effect:

> Idiots and imbeciles must be fed all their lives; but rational beings ask nothing from their parents save the means of gaining their own livelihood. Fathers have no right to cast the burden of the support of their daughters on other men. It lowers the dignity of women; and tends to prostitution, whether legal or in the streets.

In a social scheme founded on prostitution, legal or not, adult social relations are all but impossible, and consequently so is a democratic society. All the analyses still current at the turn of the twenty-first century were available in the mid-nineteenth century in the essays of Mary Wollstonecraft, Harriet Taylor, J. S. Mill, William Thompson and others.

What might well be called the 'home function' in Victorian novels has little to do with the individualistic terms in which it is often presented. What function is served by the fantasy of home as refuge? Mill makes a case in *The Subjection of Women* for the view that it provides a space where every 'clodhopper' and 'nobleman' alike can express his will to power. Assimilation of women's entire lives into economic bargains at the cost of their own inclinations is a condition that Mill associates with a rule of force, not law: which makes the home into a jail. Mill explicitly associates the domestic situation with slavery. People are not aware, he wrote, 'how very recent' the rule of law is. 'Less than forty years ago, Englishmen might still by law hold human beings in bondage as saleable property'. While such power has been regulated everywhere else, it still remains true of the power of men over women, and is 'common to the whole male sex . . . it comes home to the person and hearth of every male head of a family, and of every one who looks forward to being so. The clodhopper exercises, or is to exercise, his share of the power equally with the highest nobleman' (Mill, 1975: 438). Mill's colleague, Thompson, argues in the same vein that men have brutalized themselves with habits of exclusion and competition which arise from the distribution of wealth, and contrasts this system unfavourably with a more cooperative economy where women have access to intellectual culture, political participation and economic security in their own right. When men cannot buy their wives, Thompson writes, they must learn to please if they want to be loved (Helsinger *et al.*, 1983, I: 37). Given the economics of marriage, very few Victorian heroines can hope to be pleased instead of bought.

The ironies of this ripple endlessly through historical and social narratives. Trollope increasingly looks at the ironies of a domestic situation that provides the political world with second-raters ready to vote in a block on command and that simultaneously confines political creatures like Lady Laura and Glencora Palliser to a world of inaction. While Trollope's interest in Parliament never faded, his hopes for it did. His interesting experiment, Phineas Finn, the Irish outsider, makes it into the circle of power only to find that, in reality, Parliament is engaged in the business of cutting down big stakes into small ones and then spending them on things unrelated to the good of the social entity as a whole. Trollope makes painfully clear that this political outcome belongs to the twisted set of arrangements that segregate women from the world of affairs and, at the same time, treat them as commodities on a marriage market.

George Meredith makes a career of elaborating the implications of this position. The deranged marriages in *The Ordeal of Richard Feverel* (1859) seem fated by the class system that paralyzes healthy young wills and produces horror; the happy marriage in *Beauchamp's Career* (1875–76), arrived at after endless struggle, lasts only briefly; in *Diana of the Crossways*

(1885) the heroine escapes from a terrible marriage into a limbo, from which in turn she nearly escapes into a brilliant liason but instead, crossed by fate and her own weaknesses, ends up married to someone who has worshipped her steadily from afar. And of course *The Egoist* (1879) traces the career of the young girl who narrowly escapes becoming sacrificed in marriage to the dreadful Sir Willoughby Patterne, a portrait of the utterly rayless, still, egoistic male chauvinist so uncompromising that it made Meredith's friends wince. He anatomizes the debilitated results of the lordly 'patterne' (Williams, 1983: 53–79), and of the kind of female doormat shaped to his requirements. Meredith is the novelist who makes the equality of the sexes his centre of focus, and who shows the social consequences of gender inequality at home.

Meredith explicitly associates advances in civilization – advances beyond tribal culture – not only with the incremental growth in size of communities, but with the increase of equality between the sexes. His *An Essay on Comedy* (1877) develops the idea that the common medium of civilized life, what he calls the Comic Spirit, that resembles the Nobody narrator discussed in Chapter Two, must be egalitarian regarding the sexes. The power of the Comic Spirit depends on gender equality – plain cultural fairness – not because it is right in some absolute moral code, but because without equality, social power is sadly crippled and lopped. To be truly civilized a people must be capable of a kind of cultural aura, or discursive power, that arises from the presence of intellectual interest and equality between the sexes. The cultural capacity for comic perception appears, he says, only where there is intellectual exercise, and where men and women are equal.

> A society of cultivated men and women is required, wherein ideas are current, and the perceptions quick, that [the Comic Spirit] may be supplied with matter and an audience. The semi-barbarism of giddy communities, and feverish emotional periods, repel him; and also a state of marked social inequality between the sexes.
>
> (Meredith, 1956: 53; see also 42, 3.)

Like the Nobody narrator of history, Meredith's Comic Spirit is a medium constituted specifically by the joining together of what a sex-segregated society puts asunder. This mediating medium in social and historical narrative copes endlessly with the contradictions implicit in narratives where the format implies that the world is one, and the social evidence keeps dividing the world in two.

The subtleties of gender segregation occupy a key place in Trollope's novels, especially in his later ones. He renders opaque and visible the glass walls that keep even the most privileged women trapped in the realm of domesticity. Violet Effingham, in *Phineas Finn*, is a strong young aristocrat who dreams of freedom, but who soon perceives the hidden constraints that arise from an entire order of things, a cultural 'law' quite separate from statutes and just as prohibitive.

> In former days she had had a dream that she might escape [from her chaperon-aunt, Lady Baldock], and live alone if she chose to be alone; that she might be independent in her life, as a man is independent, if she chose to live after that fashion; that she might take her own fortune in her own hand, as the law certainly allowed her to do, and act with it as she might please. But latterly she had learned to understand that all this was not possible for her. Though one law allowed it, another law disallowed it, and the latter law was at least as powerful as the former.
>
> (Trollope, 1972: 685)

Violet has her own fortune and she has no parents to interfere with her. She has a legal and economic independence that few women enjoy, the very 'independence' that Gwendolen Harleth in Eliot's *Daniel Deronda* thinks would allow her to do as she likes. But the 'law' that allows an unmarried Violet to keep her fortune conflicts with the powerful law of her social order that says a single young woman in possession of a fortune must be in want of a husband. Otherwise, with whom would she live? Who would visit? How would she travel? How would she perform her social duty as mother and caregiver? Provisions for equality that are merely legal, even when they materialize, can be turned or twisted into very different results, depending upon the cultural disposition of those laws (MacKinnon, 1989). And in Violet's time, those laws had not yet even been written.

The personal costs to women of being confined to domestic caring were never hard to see. As early as 1825 William Thompson, 'the forgotten man of the women's movement' (Helsinger *et al.*, 1983, I: 21), argues in his *Appeal of One Half of the Human Race* that marriage puts an end to all a woman's civil rights. In collaboration with Anna Wheeler, and later with John Stuart Mill and Harriet Taylor, Thompson contributed an uncompromising analysis of the political and economic inequality endured by women, and of the psychological and social effects of such inequity.

> From hours and days of interesting conversation they are excluded: to silence or retirement they are driven, while the males are flowing

with interest, enjoying the emotions of curiosity, judgment, anticipation. . . . The more women are isolated and stultified with their
children, with their fire and food-preparing processes, the more it is
necessary, though the more difficult it becomes, that they should
receive illumination and comprehensiveness of mind from without,
in order to counterbalance this unfavorable tendency of their
situation.

(ibid.: 29–34)

Thompson anticipates Mill with the argument that such exclusion from
intellectual exercise and knowledge is men's way of crippling women so as
to create helpless objects for their contempt.

A quarter-century later, Florence Nightingale echoes these still current
ideas in an essay that she circulated privately around 1850 but did not
publish, despite urging from J. S. Mill. In 'Cassandra' she argues that
women have intellect, passion and morality, 'and a place in society where
no one of the three can be exercised' (Nightingale, 1991: 205). Instead,
'they sink to living from breakfast till dinner, from dinner till tea, with a
little worsted work, and to looking forward to nothing but bed'. Confined
to the ambit of their own family, they have no time for themselves, and no
way to develop and exercise adult faculties. 'The family', she concludes, 'is
too narrow a field for the development of an immortal spirit, be that spirit
male or female. . . . Women dream of a great sphere of steady, not sketchy
benevolence, of moral activity, for which they would be trained and fitted'
(ibid.: 216). But their dreams have no possibility of realization.

Dreaming always, never accomplishing; thus women live – too
much ashamed of their dreams, which they think 'romantic', to tell
them where they will be laughed at, even if not considered
wrong. . . .

In the last century it was not so. In the succeeding one let us hope
that it will no longer be so.

But now she is like the Archangel Michael as he stands upon St.
Angelo at Rome. She has immense provision of wings, which seem
as if they would bear her over earth and heaven; but when she tries
to use them, she is petrified into stone, her feet are grown into the
earth, chained to the bronze pedestal.

(ibid.: 205, 216, 218, 228)

She might be describing Violet Effingham's dreams of freedom in
Trollope's *Phineas Finn* (1869), or Maggie Tulliver's in George Eliot's
The Mill on the Floss (1860), or Eustacia Vye's in Hardy's *The Return of the*

Native (1878). Even if statutory laws permitted women their freedom – and often they did not – cultural laws continued to confine them to a domestic realm separated from the world of affairs by much more than simply legislative fiat.

Cultural law overrides legislation, as Violet Effingham sees, so legislation alone remains insufficient to effect reform. Even when women could finally train as doctors (the London School of Medicine for Women was established in 1874), the women who actually qualified were prevented from practising in England by the Medical Act of 1858. The Act was finally repealed in 1877, but as Florence Nightingale knew, the right to practise and the opportunity to do so were still two quite different things (Dennis and Skilton, 1987: 177). As more and more young girls grow up and find themselves confined to a domestic realm, a growing population of disappointed dreamers feel the irony of contradiction between what they want to do as adult human beings, and what they are allowed to do as domestic carers. 'It is vain to look for the elevation of woman so long as she is degraded in marriage', wrote the American feminist Elizabeth Cady Stanton in 1853 to her colleague, Susan B. Anthony (Helsinger *et al.*, 1983, II: 29).

So long as marriage is woman's only alternative it is a fatality for her, not a choice. She is damned if she doesn't marry, and damned if she does. Two novelists in particular, Trollope and George Eliot, uncompromisingly mark the degree to which women are trained to collaborate in their own defeat. Lady Laura Standish, later Lady Laura Kennedy, wants to have it both ways, with a place in the system and a life of her own. She says (in Trollope's *Phineas Finn*) attractively independent things: 'I envy you men your clubs more than I do the House; – though I feel that a woman's life is only half a life, as she cannot have a seat in Parliament' (Trollope, 1972: 98). But Lady Laura also wants to retain the advantages (if not the name) of a parasite:

> Lady Laura's father was in the Cabinet, to Lady Laura's infinite delight. It was her ambition to be brought as near to political action as was possible for a woman without surrendering any of the privileges of feminine inaction. That women should even wish to have votes at parliamentary elections was to her abominable, and the cause of the Rights of Women generally was odious to her.
>
> (ibid.: 127)

Trollope shows how Lady Laura's whole situation breeds this way of thinking, how she accepts it passively, and how it leads her straight to impasse. Mr Kennedy turns out to be exactly the despot Mill describes in

The Subjection of Women. Laura's husband thinks harmony in marriage comes with a wife's submission. The inclusive grammar of perspective that incorporates this view belies it continually, as a matter of form. Trollope shows with a minimum of comment and a maximum of ironic contrast the contradiction such 'private' arrangements provide in a 'public' world defined in these Palliser novels, especially by the consensual political institutions in which Mr Kennedy himself plays a prominent part.

> 'It will be better that you should consent to adopt my opinion.'
> 'You have the law on your side.'
> 'I am not speaking of the law.... I am speaking simply of convenience, and of that which you must feel to be right. If I wish that your intercourse with any person should be of such or such a nature, it must be best that you should comply with my wishes.... As far as I can understand the position of a man and wife in this country, there is no other way in which life can be made harmonious.'
> 'Life will not run in harmonies'.
> · ...He told himself that a wife's obedience was one of those rights which he could not abandon without injury to his self-esteem.
> (ibid.: 487–8)

Mr Kennedy's mental habits directly precede, and are implicated in, his eventual clinical – not just cultural – madness. The fact that he dies mad is at least partly attributable to his intense concern with his self-esteem, and his inability to establish it except at someone else's expense. For her part, however, and as Trollope's novel also insists, Lady Laura collaborates in a defeat that her entire education has prepared her for; to perform 'well' in the terms her society allows her is to accept a form of social death. The very system that holds out opportunity to her through marriage, forecloses it through marriage. Mr Kennedy will not be content until she is intellectually and emotionally extinct and, like George Eliot's similar heroine, Gwendolen Harleth in *Daniel Deronda*, she is saved from the worst of the 'pinching, crushing' influence (Eliot, 1967: 477, ch. 35) not by her own effort but by the accident of her husband's early death.

One false move destroys a young woman's life, and yet it is a move she is everywhere encouraged to make. Violet Effingham, Lady Laura's friend, takes the point, although in the end she doesn't use it either. Marriage is essential and, at the same time, destructive for women.

> 'What can a woman be if she remains single? The curse is to be a woman at all.'

'I have always felt so proud of the privileges of my sex', said Violet.

'I have never found them', said the other; 'never'.

... 'I shall knock under to Mr. Mill [says Violet], and go in for women's rights, and look forward to stand for some female borough. Matrimony never seemed to me to be very charming, and upon my word it does not become more alluring by what I find at Loughlinter'.

(Trollope, 1972: 489–91)

Kennedy's distinction between law and convenience resembles the two 'laws' that Violet Effingham discovers. A man asserts one, a woman must know two. A man preserves his tribal allegiances entirely negatively, upon the basis of suppressing women. The consequent suppression of knowledge of multiple possibilities, the clinging only to one, simply prevents men from growing up, as both Trollope and George Eliot tirelessly demonstrate. Mabel Grex and J. S. Mill complain of the same thing. A man has only one centre, himself, and a woman has more than one, and no power to unite them. Neither case provides a secure basis for a social order that must be sustained not by magic but entirely by human effort.

The conspicuous casualties are overwhelmingly female, but not wholly female. A similar casualty appears in the case of Osborne Hamley, in Elizabeth Gaskell's *Wives and Daughters* (1864–66), who seems almost a refugee from George Meredith's novels in his crabbed, distorted, disappointing heir's relationship with his father. The heir of the Hamleys, who pride themselves on the age of their line and condescend to the upstart titles in the neighbourhood who only 'came in' at the time of Queen Anne, Osborne marries democratically and secretly, and the strain eventually kills him. In a plot similar to Meredith's *The Ordeal of Richard Feverel* (1859), the hero marries 'beneath' him – in this case to a French *bonne*, rather than a local farmer's daughter – and keeps the marriage secret too long for one of the partners to survive. Young men are also warped and in rare cases destroyed by the English system of gender segregation. But by far the most common case in narrative is the one Meredith presents in the death of the young wife.

Naturalizing cultural distinctions remains the crux of gender inequality: so J. S. Mill claims in his essays, *On Liberty* and *The Subjection of Women*. Arguments for equality have nothing to do with 'nature' but, instead, with power and hegemony. The most significant distinction for Mill, so far as a free society is concerned, lies between one individual and another. Society depends for its solidity upon the difference that each unique contributor

197

makes; in these differences, and these differences alone, can be found the common denominators of social life. Attempting to mark half the population as somehow apart from 'public' affairs, means that no denominator – no norm or standard or measure – can be common, and consequently no modern social entity can exist. While Mill certainly appreciates the biological differences between men and women, he consistently asks about the social use to which such distinctions are put. Sigmund Freud articulates the position opposite to Mill's – that gender distinctions are primarily 'natural'. Freud was an early translator of Mill's essay *On Liberty,* and he wrote in 1885 to his fiancée that Mill had overlooked the 'fact' that 'human beings consist of men and women and that this distinction is the most significant one that exists' (Mill, 1975: xxv). Freud's hilarious definition of women (found elsewhere in his writing) as second-class human beings who attempt through processes of reproduction to restore their 'lack' of a penis – as if men had nothing at all to do with reproduction – entirely mystifies the actual political and economic functions of gender distinction. Women's confinement to domestic occupation and private space is justified by 'nature'. The contrast between Mill's egalitarian, social and political discourse, and Freud's mythologizing one, clarifies the stakes of social organization: either society is a common, or Margaret Thatcher was right and there is no such thing as society, but only a perpetual, 'natural', even cosmic family romance: a hierarchical struggle for precedence writ large.

The terrible consequences of the contradictory messages to women – associating them with natural processes but shrouding the political and social components of those processes – stand revealed in *Adam Bede*. When the very young, pretty, self-centred Hetty Sorrel is seduced and made pregnant by the equally self-centred squire, Arthur Donnithorne, her society is inclined to bury the entire string of consequences – her lost wandering in search of him all alone with her 'natural' processes, her ignorance of the world, the death of her baby. All these George Eliot drops out of the narrative entirely as being invisible to her social group (she has ensured, however, that her readers are well aware of what such seduction scenes would produce). As one of Hetty's best friends says when the sad news all comes out, 'it cannot be!' What 'can' be is the 'public' side, and only the public side of these events: her eventual exposure, her trial, her transportation, and her death. With these, and with her, disappears the bloom of an entire community and an entire way of life. The idle pleasures of milord have terrible costs, but the fault lies squarely with the social acceptance of a gendered distinction between social realms: between his and her space, his and her time, his and her moral standards, his and her responsibilities. It is a mystery how women, with no education in worldly affairs and no experience in the exercise of public power, could be expected to train the next generation of social leaders; it is a mystery how moral values, thus segregated, could have any healthy existence, much less influence in public life. In any case, the domestic realm remains a site of intractable contradictions tearing in opposite directions at the female people who get stuck there.

RUNNING COSTS OF THE MARRIAGE MARKET

The centrality of marriage in Victorian social novels is striking; even more striking is the fact that we rarely see the progress of one. Portraits of any actual marriage, even unsuccessful ones, are rare: ominously rare, given the fact that marriage putatively provides the key linkage between public and private. Almost always it is a marriage-in-the-making that generates plot suspense. Over the sequel a veil is drawn. With a few exceptions like Trollope's Pallisers and George Eliot's Garths, marriage is either something that has already been interrupted by death or, given the crucifixion it is to the participants, probably should be. This is not surprising given the contradictions inherent in the insistence on the patriarchal, hierarchical organization of domesticity quite in opposition to the increasingly democratic and horizontal organization of public life. Women themselves become the break-point between the one system and the other, with predictable consequences for their health and longevity.

Mothers are an especially endangered species in Victorian historical and social novels. Though they are necessary to produce the young people whose courtships carry plots, living mothers are hard to find. Most of the orphans are girls, which suggests a certain lack of tradition in women's lives, even if they accepted their confinement to the so-called 'private' sphere. Dickens' Florence Dombey, Lizzie Hexam, Esther Summerson, Amy Dorrit, Agnes Wickfield, and Estella have lost their mothers. Gaskell's Mary Barton loses her mother in the first chapter, and Molly Gibson loses to death first her biological mother and then her mother substitute, Mrs Hamley. In Trollope, marriageable women like Eleanor Bold, Emily Wharton and Lady Laura Standish lost their mothers long ago, and no more is said of them; Mary Palliser's mother, Glencora, a considerable figure in prior novels, dies in Chapter One of the novel in which her daughter Mary's story becomes interesting; Adelaide Palliser's mother died when she was an infant; and Violet Effingham is an orphan. In Meredith's novels, heroines like Lucy Feverel and Clara Middleton have no mothers (Lucy is an orphan, and her marriageability depends upon the fact that she is a 'lieutenant's daughter'). In George Eliot's novels, Hetty Sorrel is an orphan; Romola has no mother, only a father; Esther Lyon's mother died when she was an infant; Tertius Lydgate, Dorothea and Celia Brooke are orphans cared for by uncles; and motherless Mirah Lapidoth must flee from her other parent who is a destructive gambler. George Gissing's Madden sisters must depend on their incompetent father because their mother is long dead. In all the novels by the Brontë sisters, women struggle along orphaned: Anne's Agnes Grey and Helen Huntington, both Emily's Catherines, Charlotte's Jane Eyre and Lucy Snowe. Compared to this legion of parentless girls, orphaned boys are found much less often; mainly for instance among Dickens' lost children (Little Nell, but also Jo and Pip).

Where a married woman manages to remain alive, she does not live well. Helen Huntington's marriage makes the English country house look like something from Transylvania; Dickens' marriages, like those of the Smallweeds and the Wilfers, are either caricatures of warfare or a sad mismatch between a male human being and a female joke; Margaret Hale's mother in Gaskell's *North and South* is another such and should be a caution to Margaret's suitors; Richard Feverel's strange union, like Meredith's trying marriages generally, is a commuter marriage where no one travels; George Eliot's Transomes and Grandcourts show chillingly the costs to women of the marriage market. While it is true that the motherless are sometimes also fatherless; that the pre-eminence of orphans in Victorian novels testifies to a shift away from defining identity in terms of parentage and inheritance towards defining it in terms of experience and accumulated knowledge and other capital; still fathers and father figures abound by comparison with mothers and mother figures. Even this partial list suggests a certain havoc on the home front.

Considering the risks, it is a wonder that people *permitted* their daughters to marry at all. But then, their daughters were not the issue in the social ceremonies of domesticity. The depreciation of motherhood coincided, according to J. A. and Olive Banks (1954), with an increased interest in women as economic ornaments, well-dressed party givers who reflect well on their husband's economic status. Increasing wealth was thus an important causal factor in the declining birthrate of the time. In the shift towards a consumer economy, conspicuous consumption was increasingly the order of the day. Motherhood plays a limited role in that.

This economic function of women almost never appears in mid-century novels, which are still bent on codifying and experimenting with a relatively new narrative formation. Gissing, however, fully confronts the socio-economic conditions of the Woman Question: their lack of occupation either outside or even inside the home, except as ornament and consumer. The Madden sisters and Rhoda Nunn do not make soap and butter, nor do they manage the making of soap and butter; such things could be made cheaper elsewhere. Their vocation as wives increasingly is gone, even in these limited material ways. In any case, given the fact that novels present marriageable young ladies on the market in their thousands, it is an odd silence that ensues after their stories have led to marriage. The trail of life for women often seems to end there.

Besides the many dead mothers already mentioned, there are all the moribund or damaged women whose losses haunt a whole society. The number of female ghosts, or ghostly women, in Victorian novels testifies to the broadly debilitating presence of the lethal double bind for women. Trollope's Lady Mabel Grex is one: so is Lady Laura Standish, the political animal, who instead of having a political occupation manages from the margins as an eligible heiress, and dies by inches after marrying badly by marrying 'well'. Richard Feverel's unseen mother haunts the margins of his life, a felt absence until she is smuggled in, veiled, to her son's rooms, only then to be smuggled out again and relegated to the penumbral regions where her husband's long denial has cast her. This marital derangement, the novel implies, absolutely conditions Richard's own. The sound of a halting step in the 'Ghost's Walk' at Chesney Wold (*Bleak House*) calls up the precedent of a former Lady Dedlock, lamed by her husband because of a secret life: a portentous precedent for the Lady Dedlock of the novel, who is also haunted by her own suppressed life, its early love and an illegitimate child, and her denial of both to marry a title. She is destined to be a ghost, and her secret literally hounds her to her grave. Miss Havisham in *Great Expectations* stops the clock when she is jilted, and rots on, neither alive nor dead, training her protégée, Estella, to be an instrument for revenge on men. Estella thus grows up, like Lady Dedlock, living in the shadow of another woman's losses. Florence Dombey is a ghost in her father's house and irrelevant to his business; so far as he is concerned, a girl is merely 'a bad Boy – nothing more' (Dickens, 1970: ch. 1); ' "girls", said Mr. Dombey, "have nothing to do with Dombey and Son" ' (ibid.: ch. 10). The degree to which Florence buys this role appears in her marriage: ' "And you, dear Florence?" says her husband, "are you nothing?" he returned. "No, nothing, Walter. Nothing but your wife . . . I am nothing any more, that is not you" ' (ibid.: 885, ch. 56). Dickens may seem to disapprove of this, but he does go on to say in the narration, 'the woman's heart of Florence, with its undivided treasure, can be yielded only once, and under slight or change, can only droop and die' (ibid.: 902, ch. 57). Many potential constituents in the prevailing consensus, who rebel against such constructions of their fate, end up as ghosts in the margins of the social order.

As goods in a marriage market, individual women were disposed of one at a time. The question of their getting together in associations to effect changes in their condition or the conditions of others does not appear in the social novels of mid-century and is not imagined even by J. S. Mill, always the individualist and foe of 'sinister interests'. In America the prominence of women in the sheer physical enterprise of settling the frontier may have presented a more recent memory of equality than in Britain. In any case, it was the American feminist, Charlotte Perkins Gilman, who saw the nineteenth century as the time that saw a 'world-wide stir and getting-together of women' in which the growth of women's associations was the most important single feature. The growth of clubs or informal groups of all descriptions had the effect of bringing women together for quasi-professional purposes. From improving the lot of working classes to getting votes for women, these organizations allowed women to work together in a public sphere and thus to create a space in the public world where the woman, isolated in domesticity, could imagine alternative occupation. There were even international councils which periodically brought together women, from various nations and religions.

In many of those women's groups, feminism was not the agenda – the very term 'feminism' came in later in the nineteenth century – but the very act of working together brought women out of domestic isolation, gave them a mutual awareness, and liberated them temporarily from what Gilman calls 'the domestic altar' and from the sacred law of 'to-every-man-his-own-cook' (Gilman, 1975: 321–2). Gilman put her finger on the central problem when she proposed making housekeeping into a paid profession, like any other. It was the glory of the nineteenth century that women began to cooperate together. 'Fancy the juvenile ignorance', she comments well into the twentieth century, 'that scorns an age in which half the world woke up!' (ibid.: 257). Gilman perceives the economic basis of this awakening, particularly as regards housekeeping. It was not just time to change their social habits, but their economic ones as well. Her *Women and Economics* (1898 (Gilman, 1966)) is an early, and a still lonely, attempt to address in material terms the material limitations of women's domestic lives. Her solution lies in women's associations – the dreaded syndicalism. If individual women like Violet Effingham could do nothing to reform their situation, perhaps women working together could.

In English fiction, however, one is hard pressed to find such alliances among women. Gissing's sketch of a women's cooperative venture, the one managed by Rhoda Nunn, is a late-century construct. But sisterly solidarity requires a clear view of material circumstances, the very circumstances that are mystified by the mythology of home as refuge from economic affairs. From the beginning of the period, novelistic relationships between women give a whole new meaning to the phrase 'market competition'. Thackeray, who has an unerring eye for it, delights in unmasking this competition, though he does not seem to suppose that there is any alternative. In *Vanity Fair*, Becky Sharp, who is all rebellion, uses this market competition among women deliberately to inspire competitive envy, and she succeeds to perfection, especially in Paris and London (Thackeray, 1963: 339, 361, 364, 499). Her idea of triumph is to quash Mrs O'Dowd (ibid.: 273) and Amelia (ibid.: 273, 278), or someone even grander then they, and she doesn't care what women think because she assumes they will follow men's interest in her (ibid.: 443). If women can band together about anything, this novel shows, it is against another woman. After dinner in Lord Steyne's drawing room the women's behaviour to Becky (ibid.: 474) makes even Lady Steyne take pity on the 'friendless little woman'. Mild Lady Jane Sheepshanks maintains a steadfast and entirely unsympathizing disapproval of Becky. As Mrs Bullock (*née* Osborne) rises in the world, she has increasingly faint relations with her sister Jane Osborne, spinster: 'what does it mean when a lady says that she regards Jane as a sister?' (ibid.: 416).

When women do cooperate in Thackeray it is often, as it is in *Pendennis*, for the sake of a man or boy, and it is limited to domestic care. Pen's mother and the faithful Laura give him money for law school, they wait and wait and wait for him to visit or propose, and they nobly refuse any but the honourable and genuine offer in return. For his part, Pen tends to get into 'a great deal of misfortune' over many years from his 'idol-worship' of women (he admires 'purity' and sacrifice (Thackeray, 1871b: 290, 15). 'Noble' women like these, Thackeray shows, collude entirely in the infantilization of such young men. The only time that Pen 'actually thought about somebody but himself', in particular how 'constant and tender' and unselfish his mother and Laura have been, is on the night that he discovers his 'pure' actress is actually somebody else's mistress (ibid.: 150). Laura accepts that 'it seemed natural, somehow, that he should be self-willed and should have his own way' (ibid.: 275). It is, Thackeray says, the way things are:

> It is an old and received truism – love is an hour with us: it is all night and all day with a woman. Damon has [taxes], sermons, parades, tailors' bills, parliamentary duties, and the deuce knows what to think of; Delia has to think about Damon – Damon is the

oak (or the post), and stands up, and Delia is the ivy or the honeysuckle whose arms twine about him. Is it not so Delia? Is it not your nature to creep about his feet and kiss them, to twine round his trunk and hang there; and Damon's to stand like a British man with his hands in his breeches pocket, while the pretty fond parasite clings round him?

(ibid.: 207–8)

This allows for an answer of 'No, indeed!' But the rhetorical question does imply that, though this is objectionable, it is the nature of things. He for the world, she for the world in him. Everyman and Everywoman find their universal antecedents in Damon and Delia, and all parties seem to collude in keeping this particular plot alive. Thackeray portrays a thoroughly misogynistic society and implies that a universal correction in moral attitude is required to cure it. In this context nobody has much collective imagination, especially not women.

There are momentary expressions of solidarity among women scattered through novels, especially in the role of plot engines. In *The Egoist* Mrs Mountstuart Jenkinson gives Meredith's motherless Clara some timely support in her bid to reject Willoughby Patterne. In characters like Margaret Hale in *North and South*, Elizabeth Gaskell focuses uncompromisingly on moral issues of industrial poverty, but in ways somehow detached from political and economic action; Margaret Hale ends up almost by accident managing a large amount of capital, while the capitalist loses his and ends up as her employee. Gaskell's women establish friendship across differences in wealth or class but the motivation is often religious and middle-class charity, not a solidarity tough enough actually to alter the economic or political situation.

No women's alliances threaten the balance of patriarchal power in Dickens, although Edith Dombey does act as a mother to protect Florence from Carker. The beggar women grieving for a dead baby in *Bleak House*, like other poor and helpless females, work together for mutual support in a local situation, but their extreme poverty precludes other agendas. 'I thought it very touching', Esther says, 'to see these two women, coarse and shabby and beaten, so united; to see what they could be to one another; to see how they felt for one another...' (Dickens, 1956: 83). Of course Esther's perspective is coloured by her general uncertainty about her identity and even by her sexual fear. Her strange, strained relationship with her cousin Ada is more like another version of romantic love than like solidarity against the economic structure that supports such love: 'When my darling came, I thought – and I think now – that I never had seen such a dear face as my beautiful pet's' (ibid.: 321). The situation is no better even in the novels of Charlotte Brontë who, like most of her peers, musters only temporary solidarity among women. Jane Eyre's eyrie, or place of rest, is a hearth managed by women who are equals – and considerable attention is paid to the legal and financial terms of their equality – but that sisterhood proves to be only a halfway house towards the ultimate goal which is marriage with Rochester.

Temporary solidarity in George Eliot's novels often provides important plot redirection, although these moments where women reach across what divides them are ephemeral, though creative. They do not exactly qualify as friendship (Cosslett, 1988). Dinah Morris and Hetty Sorrel manage between them and over immense obstacles one of the few socially creative encounters in *Adam Bede*, when Hetty confesses in prison; Romola helps the girl, barely more than a child, whom her husband keeps on the side. Dorothea and Rosamond share similar moments in *Middlemarch*, as do Mirah and Gwendolen in *Daniel Deronda*. Like Hardy's Tess with her circle of female friends, Romola with Tessa, and Maggie with Lucy, Esther Lyon and Mrs Transome refuse to compete with each other for favoured-slave status. Such moments are ephemeral but powerful in George Eliot's vast, reciprocally moving social network. It is not that Eliot under-estimated the power of women's friendship or was incapable of it herself (this is manifestly contradicted by her biography), but she does insist on doing full narrative justice to the isolation of women and to the obstacles their training carefully provides against their forming strong female ties.

Eliot's most outright statement about the importance of women's solidarity appears at the end of her last novel, *Daniel Deronda*, where Gwendolen, her illusions of superiority dashed and her imagination finally grounded in a vast, 'unaccommodating Actual', returns to her mother who allowed the callow man of the family to encourage Gwendolen's disastrous marriage. Gwendolen is back where her troubles started, and she and her mother have an opportunity to begin again. That's where the woman's issue rests in this novel, in the failed but mending relation between mother and daughter: especially important given the decimation of mothers in the Victorian social novel. But these moments of contact are generally occasional causes of redirection and thus of incremental difference in the vast sum of things. To overcome her isolation and to begin again, Gwendolen must start with her relation to her mother, the woman who allowed her to accept the nearly fatal terms of the marriage market and who did not encourage her to develop a will and identity of her own. The rest, George Eliot suggests, awaits the outcome of the renegotiated relation between Gwendolen and her mother. With such

women's friendships, as with Margaret Hale's relation to the impoverished Lizzie in *North and South*, the question arises as to what can be the
relation among slaves? A bonding in the effort to survive provides
intimacy, but does it develop the solidarity required to make material
changes? The conflict between individualist and collectivist approaches to
power breaks apart even the Pankhursts, who did so much to get British
women the vote, and who brought women together across class and
economic barriers to accomplish it. In the end, Mrs Pankhurst and
Christabel opted for personal influence and national power at the top,
and Sylvia Pankhurst opted for socialist solidarity.

It is virtually impossible to think of nineteenth-century social novels
where women manage to live independently by supporting themselves.
One of the most interesting examples is surely George Gissing's late-
century portrait of Rhoda Nunn in *The Odd Women* (1893). It is a brilliantly
uncompromising view of what it takes, and what it costs, and what it is
worth for a woman to consider living on her own in a society where she is
trained to consider herself as others consider her, mainly as 'goods' in a
marriage market. Gissing, like Gaskell, and to some extent like Kingsley
and Dickens, opens to readers an urban and industrial world where
people have to work for a living; but Gissing does not have the religious
agenda that always to some extent governs the plots of those other writers.
Rhoda Nunn's predecessors appear in Anne and Charlotte Brontë's
novels; they have to work as governesses and they endure much, but they
do it in a rural culture that would have been recognizable a hundred or
two hundred years before them, and in a religious framework (discussed in
Chapter One). Rhoda works in town and in a material universe quite
changed from the one assumed by the Brontës. Her great originality lies in
her being able to survive the temptation to marry another of those
attractive, deeply insecure men in search of absolute power.

Rhoda's example sets in relief for the other 'odd' women the problem,
which is precisely how to avoid selling themselves, whether in marriage or
on the street. In *The Odd Women* only Rhoda survives. Monica Madden, in
flight from a grinding and impoverished life as a factory worker, marries
the unbalanced Mr Widdowson who wants her in order to be able to
exercise total power at least somewhere in his life; she finds life with him
worse than life as a factory worker. Eventually he drives her into the arms
of another man, who deserts her to a fate of ostracism and a pauper's
death. Another factory worker, Miss Eade, has a similar fate; she moves
from factory to fickle lover to prostitution, straying in and out of the novel
bearing her hopelessly torn and mouldy ideal of the true love that will
return to rescue her. The key to their distress may be the industrial system

(Gallagher, 1985), but the key to their salvation, as Rhoda Nunn attempts to show, is in their solidarity as women. But these two victims of under-developed patriarchs never grasp the equality that they share. The 'goods' never get together, as Luce Irigaray puts it in an essay precisely about women's association, 'When the Goods Get Together' (1985).

When their very bread and shelter depends upon their ability to compete with each other in the marriage market, women have a hard time in Victorian novels establishing firm and lasting alliances. When women are commodities their relation as 'goods' puts them into a system of value that has nothing to do with their actual weaknesses or strengths, their actual prospects and options. Women frequently resist, even deny the marriage market in Victorian novels, but they rarely escape from it. They are bound to a system of competition where 'success' is not so much to achieve something in particular, as to reduce the 'value' of others in the marriage market and to elevate their own. It is their own sad version of the 'predatory seizure' that passes for 'competition' in other arenas (the terms are Thorstein Veblen's from his *Theory of the Leisured Class* (1894), which claims that late nineteenth-century capitalism dresses up as 'competition' what is really only 'predatory seizure'. (see Heilbroner, 1980: 229). Even J. S. Mill, women's friend, discounts the possibility that they will ever organize. He thinks it is not impossible or undesirable, simply unlikely: 'the whole force of education' works against it (Mill, 1975: 443–4). In Victorian fiction there is a certain amount of evidence that they won't.

The parallels between the domestic politics in novels and national politics are everywhere implicit in these narratives, explicit in Trollope, and directly formulated by J.S. Mill in *The Subjection of Women*. In various national struggles for political emancipation, 'everybody knows how often its champions are bought off by bribes, or daunted by terrors. In the case of women, each individual of the subject-class is in a chronic state of bribery and intimidation combined'. The arrangement of domestic privacy gives men the means to prevent uprisings because women, unlike other slaves, have 'no means of combining against' them (ibid.: 437–9). Thus the 'consensus' that establishes a common world, the formal agreements that sustain neutral time and space, actually applies only to men. It functions for women as a 'terrorist apparatus' to keep them down and keep them silent. Jean-François Lyotard explains why:

> By terror I mean the efficiency gained by eliminating, or threaten-ing to eliminate, a player from the *language game* one shares with him [sic]. He is silenced or consents, not because he has been refuted, but because his ability to participate has been threatened (there are

many ways to prevent someone from playing). The decision makers' arrogance, which *in principle* has no equivalent in the sciences, consists in the exercise of terror. It says: 'Adapt your aspirations to our ends – or else'.

(Lyotard, 1984: 63–4; emphasis added)

Mill, writing in mid-century, observes that political repression, at home and in public, succeeds in part through preventing association among women, yet he does not seem to foresee that such association is precisely what it will take to change the conditions he deplores. At the end of the period, Gissing's Rhoda Nunn (*The Odd Women* (1893)) is only just beginning the long, strange, eventually bloody journey that women collectively began to take towards emancipation from the statutory and the cultural laws that reserve for them a separate world of 'their own'.

The costs to men of this deep social division sustained by gender segregation seem less spectacular than the costs to women; but, as Mill argues, men sustain equivalent damage in terms of personal and political function. The arbitrary power granted to men by virtue of physiology alone simply renders them incapable of self-determination and encouraged to narcissism: 'Think what it is to a boy... [believing that] by the mere fact of being born a male [he] is by right the superior of all and every one of an entire half of the human race' (Mill, 1975: 522–3; see this chapter, p. 184). In such circumstances social justice is impossible. This ancient but far from 'natural' relation between the sexes threatens the very establishment of a free society. The gender hierarchy that fosters domestic 'tyranny' is entirely incompatible with the liberal view of society gaining strength in mid-century. Whoever defines himself negatively, as a superior – to women, to blacks, to whites, to foreigners, or to any other subject group – that person may be a master, and a lamentably petty one at that, but never a constituent of the democratic society envisioned by Mill and codified so broadly after the Enlightenment.

In short, the home-as-market is a feudal holdout that belies in practice the 'silly panegyrics' (ibid.: 519) about woman's moral superiority, and 'natural' qualities preserve a space for the avoidance of the laws that everywhere else govern a modern society. In such an environment, moral training 'will never be adapted' to the actual world because, where social laws and justice are suspended, no regard for the law and for justice can be fostered. A man who is the legal and economic master to those nearest and dearest to him is a man whose only idea of freedom is, as it was in the Middle Ages, a sense of the freedoms that extend from his own importance: 'an intense feeling of the dignity and importance of his own

personality' that depends upon the subjection of that same sense in others
(ibid.: 479–80). The domestic household participates in an economic
structure of slavery and, according to the mythological dimensions of
laissez-faire, a 'natural' one at that.

Individualism is an important instrument in preserving this patriarchal
status quo. Sarah Grand's bestseller of the 1890s, *The Heavenly Twins*, shows
the self-aware young Evadne, potentially a feminist, blaming individual
women for not improving themselves (Grand, 1992: 18); and Evadne
herself goes on to replay the same old story: habitual 'love and respect' for
a father who depreciates her abilities from the first (ibid.: 12); marriage to
a miscreant; and early death. At one point Evadne copies out a passage
from Mrs Gaskell's *Ruth*, but fails to take it to heart personally, to the effect
that cultural laws shackle all but the most resolute individuals: 'daily life
into which people are born and into which they are absorbed before they
are aware, forms chains which only one in a hundred has moral strength
enough to despise, and to break when the right time comes' (ibid.: 133).
Despite her advanced views and awareness, however, Evadne dies of a
bad marriage like other young married women in this novel, and like so
many other Victorian heroines.

Sarah Grand lays at religion's door responsibility for the defections
that continue to produce the same, same old stories of marriage and
defeat. The Angel in the House is a conception sponsored not only by
misogynists like Coventry Patmore, but one *also sponsored by women*: women
like the young and lively Edith, another one in *The Heavenly Twins* who, like
Evadne, also dies of a bad marriage. Where twentieth-century women are
induced to go to heroic lengths (and expense) to meet a physical ideal
disseminated by clothing manufacturers and fashion magazines, these
Victorian women are induced to go to heroic lengths to keep their minds
'pure'. Like their mothers, these women cleave to an ideal of behaviour
that they take to be individual and moral but that, as the following passage
shows, colludes in and subtly reinforces the brutalities of a religion and a
culture with deep patriarchal agendas. This passage is worth quoting at
length for the way it reaches to the subtleties of this collusion.

Mrs. Orton Beg, her mother, and all the gentle mannered, pure-
minded women among whom she [Edith] had grown up, thought
less of this world, even as they knew it, than of the next as they
imagined it to be; and they received and treasured with perfect faith
every legend, hint, and shadow of a communication which they
believed to have come to them from thence. They neglected the
good they might have done here in order to enjoy their bright and

tranquil dreams of the hereafter. Their spiritual food was faith and hope. They kept their tempers even and unruffled by never allowing themselves to think or know, so far as it is possible with average intelligence not to do either in this world, anything that is evil of anybody. They prided themselves on only believing all that is good of their fellow-creatures; this was their idea of Christian charity. Thus they always believed the best about everybody, not on evidence but upon principle; and then they acted as if their attitude had made their acquaintances all they desired them to be. They seemed to think that by ignoring the existence of sin, by refusing to obtain any knowledge of it, they somehow helped to check it; and they could not have conceived that their attitude made it safe to sin, so that, when they refused to know and to resist, they were actually countenancing evil and encouraging it. The kind of Christian charity from which they suffered was a vice in itself. To keep their own minds pure was the great object of their lives, which really meant to save themselves from the horror and pain of knowing.

(ibid.: 155–6)

This 'virtue' Sarah Grand declares to be merely social and political incompetence and denial: collusion in forging their own manacles; collusion in defaulting on social and political responsibility; collusion in the agendas that profit from their habitual not-living-in-the-world; not to mention collusion in sexual self-denial. This novel appeared in print in the last decade of the nineteenth century, when women had recently and finally combined forces to begin changing their legal situation. In that enterprise they had to confront cultural laws operating in the most intimate corners of their lives and underwritten by a conception of religion somewhat like that variety of pastel poppycock which George Eliot so vigorously denounces in painting (*Adam Bede* (Eliot, 1968): ch. 16).

WOMEN AND TIME

The implicit segregation of space and time into His and Hers, public and private, supposedly creates a realm of private value continuous with and nourishing to the public realm. But political and literary narratives show that actual conditions do not fulfil this fantasy. Various forms of exclusion, including the 'terrorist apparatus' mentioned earlier – the universal application of values proper only to a limited group – underwrite the gender segregation that divides the very media of a putatively common world. Distribution of space and time into separate and unequal systems dislocates that world. The gendering of space and time destroys the crucial neutrality of those all-important media of modernity. The social novel makes manifestly clear that a segregated society is a feudal, not a modern one. Gender segregation, an increasingly explicit problem in Victorian novels, threatens the emerging democratic social narrative at the root of form itself.

One of the most telling treatments of the circularities created by gender segregation is Margaret Oliphant's *Hester* (1883). As a Scottish novelist, the prolific Oliphant technically does not figure in this history of the English novel, although the distinction is hard to maintain given the international context in which art has always been made and consumed, and especially in the nineteenth century when the prevailing literary form had its chief precedent in the internationally known art of Walter Scott. *Hester* makes a fitting introduction to this discussion of double standards and democracy. *Hester* is a tough book about women because it shows, still more extensively than *Daniel Deronda* does, how even the most heroic effort undertaken by an isolated individual woman only returns her, and succeeding generations, to the same story, and the same fate, time and time again. Its circularity is, in a way, the denial of history. Cut off from the inclusive neutrality of history, the fruitless circles of women's time produce no change, but only replication.

Oliphant's novel establishes at the beginning a competition between a young girl, Hester, and her family's benefactor, Miss Caroline. Hester's father, unbeknown to Hester, has long since betrayed Miss Caroline's trust in him as bank manager and has absconded with all the bank's funds. By using her own funds, Miss Caroline, acting as one of the family who owns the bank and the only one with the grit to do anything, has saved the bank and the family honour. She does it by working hard for decades – by devoting her life to it in fact – and she has been successful. Hester's father left her ditzy mother entirely unprovided for – one understands the unwillingness anyone would feel to sharing life with a woman who has had the full 'protected' treatment, and has achieved perfect silliness and helplessness. So Hester and her mother come to live in the village as Miss Caroline's pensioners.

There are several of Miss Caroline's pensioners about, in fact, and Oliphant brilliantly shows the complex realities of charity: the real benefit to a family who would otherwise have no resources, especially to Hester's mother who is unfit for much of anything; the entail in envy and resentment in the recipients of charity, especially when it is produced by the blinkered perception of Hester's mother who remains wilfully ignorant of her indebtedness to Miss Caroline; the hardening or numbing influence on Caroline herself, who sees the envy and resentment and laughs it off, becoming herself a kind of outsider, a Nobody figure in the community that she sustains. As Hester grows up from a proud child uneasy with her dependence to a proud young woman still uneasy, her implicit hostility towards Miss Caroline grows. Hester sees herself as Miss Caroline's opponent.

The crux comes when the next generation's shiftless male, this time the one Caroline has 'adopted' as her heir and who has courted and won Hester, also gets tired of being a charity case and of dancing attendance, and permits himself to abscond with bank funds, repeating the crime Hester's father committed against the community and his own family, and about which Hester still remains in the dark. He asks Hester to flee with him and the money.

Hester refuses, and in the end she and Caroline work together to try, once again, to save the bank. This time however, the effort fails. Caroline has to give up everything she has worked for, including even her home, and certainly her support of the pensioners who have till then been less-than-grateful recipients of charity. Hester and Caroline are forced into mutual association, if not sisterhood, by the common disaster. On the eve of Caroline's move from her home – in effect an eviction – to become in effect herself a pensioner, Caroline and Hester, old and young, sit together and Caroline dies in her chair, leaving Hester, just as Caroline was at the beginning, alone, and responsible for a failed bank. Each generation is betrayed by a male who cannot cope with generosity. Hester is left, where Caroline began. The prognosis is not good. Another generation; but the same, same old story for the woman, who ends up strong, betrayed, and alone.

When they denounce gender segregation, critics like Florence Nightingale and John Stuart Mill focus on precisely the deep social disfunction that Oliphant's novel exposes, though Oliphant allows both generations of women to have some public exercise, even though it is through the default of others. Nightingale and Mill are interested in the educational preparation of social conditions, and in the occupations that develop or thwart human faculties. Gender segregation means, pre–eminently, that men's and women's faculties develop differently. While men function heroically in public time, women, as Florence Nightingale puts it, 'do *everything* at odd times'; their domestic situation requires them always to be serving the wishes of others, never concentrating on pursuits of their own. 'If a man were to follow up his profession or occupation at odd times, how would he do it? Would he become skilful in that profession?' (Nightingale, 1991: 218). Nightingale circulated the essay, 'Cassandra', from which this extract is taken, privately around 1850, but resisted Mill's urging to publish it (Nightingale, 1991). Mill himself then developed this thought two decades later in his essay on *The Subjection of Women*, and went on to observe that, even 'if a man has not a profession to exempt him from such demands, still, if he has a pursuit, he offends nobody by devoting his time to it; occupation is received as a valid excuse for his not answering to every casual demand which may be made on him'. Women's occupations, however, can always be interrupted by

> what are termed the calls of society.... She must always be at the beck and call of somebody, generally of everybody. If she has a study or a pursuit, she must snatch any short interval which accidentally occurs to be employed in it. A celebrated woman, in a work which I hope will some day be published [Mill speaks here of Nightingale's 'Cassandra'], remarks truly that everything a woman does is done at odd times.
>
> (Mill, 1975: 516)

Domestic life simply prevents women from developing the focus and the 'constant exercise' of skills that men require to succeed in their more public and professional occupations.

The ordinary jocular misogynist, a still-recognizable type, sees no reason why women cannot progress of their own volition. E. P. Hood, writing about the same time as Nightingale and Mill, has this to say about women's opportunities:

> If men have ... risen, unaided, and in the face of the greatest difficulties ... there is nothing to prevent women doing the same.... There are regular courses of scientific lectures given by persons of eminence for any ladies.... I believe, however, that the demand for them is not greater than the supply.... [In fact] dressing and dancing present much greater attractions to most than Greek or Mathematics.
>
> (E. P. Hood, *The Age and its Architects*; quoted in Dennis and Skilton, 1987)

Of course, and as Thompson, Taylor, Mill, Nightingale and others including the social novelists repeatedly point out, no man rises 'unaided': he rises by benefit of having his housework done by others. No one can be expected to train themselves in Greek and Mathematics at 'odd times' and in between domestic tasks of the kind that Adam Smith dismisses as 'unproductive labour'. How productive would housework seem to the masters of industry, if the houseworkers all went on strike? Women's lack

of interest in fame, and the rarity of women artists or philosophers of the
first rank, are not at all the results of 'inherent' qualities, Mill argues, but
'only the natural result of their circumstances' (Mill, 1975: 516–17).
Women's lack of public occupation, in other words, arises from their sheer
lack of opportunity. The system ensures that lack.

But Mill goes on to notice the particular faculties that this so-called
unproductive labour requires: qualities that are essential to public life but
are yet excluded from public exercise by the system of gender segregation.

> The capacity of passing promptly from one subject of consideration
> to another, without letting the active spring of the intellect run down
> between the two, is a power far more valuable [than the power to
> focus without interruption]; and this power women pre-eminently
> possess, by virtue of the very mobility of which they are accused.
> They perhaps have it by nature; but they certainly have it by
> training and education; for nearly the whole of the occupations of
> women consist in the management of small but multitudinous
> details, on each of which the mind cannot dwell even for a minute,
> but must pass on to other things, and if anything requires longer
> thought, must steal time at odd moments for thinking of it. The
> capacity indeed which women show for doing their thinking in
> circumstances and at times which almost any man would make an
> excuse to himself for not attempting it, has often been noticed: and a
> woman's mind, though it may be occupied only with small things,
> can hardly ever permit itself to be vacant, as a man's so often is when
> not engaged in what he chooses to consider the business of his life.
> The business of a woman's ordinary life is things in general, and can
> as little cease to go on as the world to go round.
>
> (ibid.: 502–3)

The mobility of faculties, the power to keep more than one objective in
view, the ability to shift between different occupations without losing
traction: these are powers that are trained in domestic circumstances but
foreclosed for men and for the public arena by the system of gender
segregation.

What powers do men develop, on the other hand, when they are freed
from household and social duties? They learn to absorb with their whole
minds 'one set of ideas and occupations' in order to reach the highest
point of a particular path. It is worth noting that the 'gentleman's'
education of the nineteenth century focuses on a culture, especially that
of fifth–century Athens, that operated a form of gender segregation so
radical as to qualify as slavery, and that regarded the highest achievement

to be just such thoroughgoing, focused, heroic expression. The socialized ability to focus – to have only one centre, as Trollope's Mabel Grex puts it, and that centre himself – has World Historical Value, but scarcely any social value. Mill continues his critique on this point:

> What is gained in special development by this concentration, is lost in the capacity of the mind for the other purposes of life; and even in abstract thought, it is my decided opinion that the mind does more by frequently returning to a difficult problem, than by sticking to it without interruption.
>
> (ibid.)

Writing to an extremely gender-segregated audience, Mill goes so far as to reverse the dualism that depreciates 'women's' work. He privileges the mental habits of mobility and changeability above those required for focusing without interruption on a single problem. Because men are trained to focus on a particular business, when they are not so occupied they often allow their minds to be quite vacant.

The abilities that Mill here associates with women are abilities that would make them the better historians, better democrats, better citizens of the historical and realist discourse with its ethic of mobility and its emphasis on emergent form. Every historical and social novel of the nineteenth century privileges precisely the abilities to digress, to multiply tasks, to be always engaged but always moving from one site of interest to another. From Dickens' Mr Dombey to Gissing's Mr Widdowson, the inflexible man is a death-dealer. Dickens still finds it plausible to imagine a conversion; Gissing, however, does not.

When each sex develops only half the powers required for full human life and for full social life, neither men nor women have the powers to sustain a common weal. A democratic society requires both capacities: the ability to digress from a single purpose, and the ability to focus completely on one. Alone, the directed ('man's') achievement is narrow, and the digressive ('woman's') achievement is diffuse. A system that segregates these powers cripples not only individual women and men, it cripples the entire social enterprise. Mill's point is almost exactly the one made a century later by Julia Kristeva when she argues that the renewal of social code depends upon the power to undertake both the one identity and the other. 'It is impossible to treat real problems of signification seriously' without dealing both with the logical and productive function of language and social discourse, and also with the digressive and 'undecidable' function that 'univocal, rational, scientific discourse tends to hide' with 'considerable consequences for its subject'

(Kristeva, 1980: 130–5). Trollope's Pallisers exactly reproduce this uncreative dissociation of powers. The ambitious Glencora must influence public affairs indirectly, while her socially inept husband, Plantagenet, is a Prime Minister who flounders for lack of the little social gifts that 'belong' to women.

From Mill's context to Kristeva's the strong implication remains that, in a segregated system, the single-minded pursuit of ends without looking to left or right results in unrealistic, impractical solutions. Where men are incapable of considering 'things in general' and where they insist on rule, even the getting and spending may suffer. Correspondingly, a vision of things, in general, where it is confined to a world of 'small things', has but limited public application. When Elizabeth Gaskell's widower Mr Gibson, heretofore the single parent to his adolescent daughter, Molly, marries in order to provide her with a mother, the stage is set for Molly's first sustained battle with triviality and needlework.

The historical and social novel shows above all that powers of consciousness literally constitute the common denominators that make emergent forms, and especially the social entity, realizable. Divided spaces, divided times, mean divided powers. If the social entity is to function, it must function for all in common, and all individual powers must have common exercise. Mill unfortunately sees no way out of the division of labour that he finds so objectionable in its segregation of mental powers. He even says that, 'for the present', housework should remain in women's hands because they do it best, thus undermining his entire argument; yet it is precisely those tasks that absorb women's time and energies in the ways he describes so well.

For a healthy social system, it is not enough for women to gain legal rights and come up to men's standards of performance; what is wanted is the joint exercise of both the focused and the general vision. The habit of segregating personal from social life, private from public, his from hers, is a habit that prevents the very union of faculties upon which liberty depends. Mill explicitly invokes and rejects the Darwinan metaphor of survival as a war, and opts instead for the non-natural, cultivated virtue of social equality; 'the true virtue of human beings is fitness to live together as equals' (Mill, 1975: 477–9). The ability to digress, to multiply tasks, to maintain different roles without lapsing into chaos, may disarm a public world conceived for the short-term result and the narrow competition; but such a public world is itself disabled by lack of the abilities it excludes. Mill's clear message is that both are required for social health, which means that the system that segregates them has to change.

Henry James depreciates both gender specializations. Like Meredith, he suggests that civility entails equality.

> It is impossible to discuss and condemn the follies of 'modern woman' apart from those of modern men.... We are all of us extravagant, superficial, and luxurious together. It is a 'sign of the times'.... [Women] reflect with great clearness the state of the heart and imagination of men. When they represent an ugly picture, therefore, we think it the part of wisdom for men to cast a glance at their own internal economy. If there is any truth in the volume before us [he is reviewing *Modern Women and What is Said of Them*], they have a vast deal to answer for.
>
> (Henry James, 'Modern Woman' (James, 1868);
> cited in Helsinger *et al.*, 1983, I: 120–3)

The situation in England, James goes on to say, is especially dark because the marriage snare is ridden by class-anxiety. James is reviewing, for *The Nation* (1868), a controversial and anonymously published collection of essays by Eliza Lynn Linton and J. R. Green, especially an essay by Linton attacking the 'Girl of the Period' (soon known as GOP): too uninhibited and unfeminine for Linton, too little like an angel and not a good marriage bargain. This objectionable kind of woman appears in Trollope, as in James, as an American 'girl' (women apparently can be 'girls' long past childhood, unlike men, who are rarely 'boys' past the age of twenty). Articles rejecting the type *as* American were plentiful, and instances of a perpetual anti-Americanism in England. Henry James, before his transplantation, finds in favour of American readers of this particular essay on the GOP, and chimes in with Taylor's, Mill's, Trollope's, and so many novelists' critique of segregationally crippled mid-Victorian society.

> The American reader will be struck by the remoteness and strangeness of the writer's tone and allusions. He will see that the society which makes these papers even hypothetically – hyperbolically – possible is quite another society from that of New York and Boston. American life, whatever may be said of it, is still a far simpler process than the domestic system of England. We never read a good English novel ... without drawing a long breath of relief at the thought of all that we are spared, and without thanking fortune that we are not part and parcel of that dark, dense British social fabric.
>
> (ibid.)

That dark, dense British social fabric gets particular illumination from

Trollope because he focuses on the ruling classes, not the groups disabled by them. By treating brutality and violence and products of poverty and ignorance, novelists like Charles Dickens, Elizabeth Gaskell, Thomas Hardy, George Gissing and George Moore all tend to suggest that more money and education would improve things. Trollope puts the lie to that supposition in his thorough and ironic experiments at the very top of the social and economic ladder. Even in luxury, the pervasiveness and the evils of gender segregation appear everywhere in evidence.

Lady Mabel Grex, for example, in Trollope's *The Duke's Children*, is intelligent, witty and rich; but even she is also already bought and sold. She cannot 'love' anyone, especially the penniless Frank Tregear. Because her father has gambled away her family fortune and left her with no money of her own, she must wait for the 'right' man, that is, someone with the increasingly rare combination of wealth and title. Her own desires are unimportant. Like Lady Laura, she self-destructs, caught between a crippling system and a blank future for which she has had no preparation except to wait and expect money.

> She had begun her world with so fatal a mistake! When she was quite young, when she was little more than a child but still not a child, she had given all her love to a man [Frank Tregear] whom she soon found that it would be impossible she should ever marry. He had offered to face the world with her.... But ... the grinding need for money, the absolute necessity of luxurious living, had been pressed upon her from her childhood.... Then this boy [Palliser's son, Lord Silverbridge] had come in her way! With him all her ambition might have been satisfied.... The cup had come within the reach of her fingers, but she had not grasped it.... She had dallied with her fortune.
>
> (Trollope, 1983: 431–2, ch. XLII)

Her self-destructive mix of intelligence, honour, and carelessness of personal interest are painfully pursued to the awful last scene where she realizes that she has thrown away both her best chances: the one because he had no money, and the other because he had only money (ibid.: 89, 148, 186, 228, 280, 581).

Meanwhile, the men in the case, even the penniless ones, have no such problems. Frank Tregear transfers his affections from Mabel Grex to the wealthier Mary Palliser, just as Lord Silverbridge moves on fairly easily after being rejected by Mabel Grex to the American heiress, Isabel Boncassen. Men think of themselves, and their interests. Women do not. The men forget and move on; the women do not. His-story and herstory remain separated; he occupies public time, the time of history and project, while she stays stuck and motionless. This pattern repeats itself often in Trollope. After Laura Kennedy rejects him, Phineas Finn transfers his affection to Violet Effingham so easily that the narrator fears Finn will prove callow; but Lady Laura, meanwhile, having married the wrong man for money, remains obsessively and hopelessly attached to Phineas to the end. The segregation of His and Her space extends far, far beyond architectural considerations. When Plantagenet Palliser, the democrat who has become the Duke of Omnium, learns that his daughter, Mary Palliser, wants to wed someone he disapproves of mainly for class reasons, he consults what he takes to be his interests, not hers, and proves himself to be a despot not only by withholding his consent, but by keeping her, his own daughter, a prisoner for more than a year.

All this gendered segregation of the social world into public and private domains has a crucial temporal inflection. There is not only His and Her space, but His and Her time. Humanist time, historical time, the public time of history and project, becomes His time. It is the professional's time, common time, universal time, the time of public affairs, and wars, and heroics; it is the common denominator over millennia between us and our simian ancestors. This public time has the status of a universal, or at least of a categorical imperative. It is the time of Newton, the time of Kant, the time of history, the neutral time of emergent form, the time that encourages mobility. It includes and recovers absolutely everything; nothing escapes; nothing exists outside it. If something is not 'in' this time, it does not exist.

This is a gender problem because so much of women's experience is precisely *not* 'in' this public, common time; and because of that, so much of women's experience, so far as collective, public discourse goes, does not exist. Victorian novels satirize much of what is called middle-class 'women's work' – the drawing and dancing, the little music and less French, and above all the embroidery. This is what Adam Smith calls 'unproductive labour' – something that, therefore, has nothing to do with the affairs of a public world. Her time, her-story, differs in kind from His time and his-story. Her time conforms to local and private conditions; it is not neutral; it is flexible, defined by others, their needs, their schedules, their ambitions. These issues are perhaps first raised by Mary Wollstone-craft in her *Vindication of the Rights of Women*, and are codified by John Stuart Mill almost a century later. Even today, more than a century after Mill, little has changed; nothing has invalidated their analyses, even though the world has become exhausted by history and its projects.

Time, for example, heals nothing for Lady Mabel Grex, once she has lost her chance to marry. Like other women in Trollope (Lady Laura, Lily Dale), Lady Mabel knows that her carefully-observed rules have betrayed her. Lady Mabel can assert herself only by keeping clarity about what has happened to her. In this passage she confesses to Lord Silverbridge:

'A man has but one centre, and that is himself. A woman has two. Though the second may never be seen by her, may live in the arms of another, may do all for that other that man can do for woman, – still, still, though he be half the globe asunder from her, still he is to her the half of her existence. If she really love, there is, I fancy, no end of it.... To the end of time I shall love Frank Tregear.... A jackal is born a jackal.... So is a woman born – a woman. They are clinging, parasite things, which cannot but adhere; though they destroy themselves by adhering. Do not suppose that I take a pride in it. I would give one of my eyes to be able to disregard him.'

'Time will do it' [says optimistic Silverbridge].

'Yes; time, – that brings wrinkles and rouge-pots and rheumatism. Though I have so hated those men as to be unable to endure them, still I want some man's house, and his name, – some man's bread and wine, – some man's jewels and titles and woods and parks and gardens, – if I can get them. Time can help a man in his sorrow. If he begins at forty to make speeches, or to win races, or to breed oxen, he can yet live a prosperous life. Time is but a poor consoler for a young woman who has to be married.'

(ibid.: 581–2)

This passionate speech is Mabel's last: last in the sense that one can hear in it what Trollope is so good at conveying, the sound of a living voice. Always interested in the way tonality conveys the condition of character, Trollope catches the extent of Lady Mabel's losses in the numb, desperate, and defeated speech she makes, in her last appearance in *The Duke's Children*, when she says goodbye to Frank Tregear, now happily engaged to someone else (ibid.: ch. LXXVII, entitled 'Mabel, Goodbye'). It is as if she has died. What voice she has left comes from somewhere else, perhaps from the grammar of things that produced her ghastly choices in the first place. 'Two centres' means two systems incompatible and, as the thousands of female ghosts testify, unmediateable. It is a feudal and hierarchical distinction entirely at odds with the project of modernity.

The liberal, social and political experiments of mid-century give new importance to difference in the construction of a social entity humanly unified and sustained. The more such a polity cares for and respects differences, the more complex, and flexible, and powerful that polity will be. This is Mill's political argument in *On Liberty*, and this is the basis of historical form; in fact, George Eliot argues, 'every difference is form' (Eliot, 1963: 433). The very specialization of identity that seems to fragment the social order of things is the very basis for the inclusiveness of this essentially humanist standard. Whatever can be perceived at all, it is included; if it cannot be perceived, by definition it does not exist. Therein lies the rub for individual women: the being perceived at all. The question is not whether or not women fit into a master narrative; they do that well enough as domestic angels and economic ciphers. The question is whether or not women are excluded from the agreements – from the 'language game' or founding discourse (Lyotard, 1984: 63–4) – that constitutes the world in the first place by constructing the very medium 'in' which it, and its narratives, unfold.

While the discourse of universal inclusiveness operates mythically, in practice that discourse functions for one group at the expense of another: its agreements and consensus are, in other words, precisely Lyotard's 'terrorist apparatus'. Neutral, historical, public time that nevertheless does not include half the population, is a sham, a legend of a men's club, a clan mythology. The universal inclusiveness, which the narrative form asserts by definition, proves to have an especially terrible power of repression: to deny while appearing to include.

The number of dead women in Victorian fiction, especially dead mothers, implies that, for a female to function in the world at all, is for her to function as a sacrifice. The characteristics that make Eliot's Maggie or Hardy's Tess human and interesting are the very characteristics that make them misfits in their social order of things, and candidates for extinction. The weak ones become parasites, the strong ones either have the equivalent of nervous breakdowns, hanging on as ghosts of their former selves, or they die. Women's situation is the classic 'Catch-22': it is not possible for them to live outside social time because there is nothing outside it beyond a narrow domestic ledge; but inside it her function is to die. A lifetime of training in dependency wins out over Maggie Tulliver's valiant but 'fatally weak' efforts at independence (Ermarth, 1974a), and in the end she is drowned by her 'need to be loved'.

This problem appears elsewhere than English narrative. Women are everywhere ritual sacrifices of societies that offer them no space but privacy, no time but odd times, and no profession but 'love'. Tolstoy's Anna Karenina finds her future blank and without options when the love affair fails that had substituted for her failed marriage; when she reaches the end of the railway platform from which she falls under the train she only confirms in physical death what she has already experienced as an individual in her so-called 'life'. Flaubert's Emma Bovary, her imagination trained by romances and boredom, pursues to the point of dissolution her ever more desperate search for 'love', and in the process Flaubert even dissolves momentarily the very single-point perspective system that has sustained the narrative of *Emma Bovary* (Ermarth, 1982). The problem of women and time belongs to European culture at large.

The particular problems for English women, anatomized continuously by social novels, are summarised drastically in Thomas Hardy's late novel, *Tess of the D'Urbervilles: A Pure Woman* (1891). This narrative offers a particularly extended instance of how an individual woman can be literally excluded from the medium of time – in this case literally from the 'language game' that constitutes the world 'in' time. Its very title robs the heroine of her name and replaces it with a pretentious substitute. At an early age Tess is encouraged, or shall we say procured, by her mother for a relationship with Alec D'Urberville, the 'gentleman' who rapes her, and whose child, 'Sorrow', she bears and buries in one of the many aborted Victorian motherhoods.

When she meets Angel Clare he seems the gentle opposite of the Alec D'Urberville who was prone to translate all emotion into an intent of mastery. But Tess discovers there's very little to choose between a bad man and a good one, so far as a woman is concerned. The bad signs are there when Angel puts her on the familiar mythic pedestal:

> She was no longer the milkmaid, but a visionary essence of woman – a whole sex condensed into one typical form. He called her Artemis, Demeter, and other fanciful names half teasingly, which she did not like because she did not understand them.
> 'Call me Tess', she would say askance; and he did.
>
> (Hardy, 1978c: 187)

He lumps her with a generic entity, much as did those who considered the condition of 'women' and 'The Woman Question', rather than the condition of individuals participating in society. After her long, weary effort to resist Alec and to support herself against his unkindness and even persecution, Tess rests with relief on Angel's affection. But his affection is the more destructive when the call comes for him to treat her as an individual and his partner. Much later, when she says that she had thought he loved her for her *self*, he clearly has no idea what this means (ibid.: 298).

As their marriage approaches, Tess tries to tell him her 'history', partly from a sense of honour and partly from a wish to provide an antidote to his mythologizing of her identity. 'My history', says Tess; 'I want you to know it – you must let me tell you – you will not like me so well'. But Angel trifles with her seriousness and hinders her, and her courage fails her. 'Her instinct for self-preservation was stronger than her candour' (ibid.: 252–3). This is what sexism means: the exclusion from history, with all the desperate denial of material reality and actual experience that entails. This is how the discourse of consensus, the all-inclusive grammar of single-point perspective, can act as 'a terrorist apparatus'. It governs who can speak, and who keep silent; it governs who is 'in' history, and who is not. She tries to communicate *her* story by letter before their marriage but, with a disregard of rational process common in Hardy's universe, the letter goes astray.

Finally, on their wedding night, after Angel has confessed his past indiscretions, Tess is encouraged to tell him the burdensome secret of her rape and her dead child. How a woman is managed by the mythological other self maintained by men like Alec and Angel alike, Angel indicates in his response:

'You were one person, now you are another'. . . . He paused . . . then suddenly broke into horrible laughter – as unnatural and ghastly as a laugh in hell.

'Don't – don't! It kills me quite, that!' she shrieked. 'O have mercy upon me – have mercy! . . . I thought, Angel, that you loved me – me my very self' . . .

'I repeat, the woman I have been loving is not you.'

'But who?'

'Another woman in your shape.'

She perceived in his words the realization of her own apprehensive foreboding in former times. He looked upon her as a species of impostor; a guilty woman in the guise of an innocent one. Terror was upon her white face as she saw it; her cheek was flaccid, and her mouth had almost the aspect of a round little hole. The horrible sense of his view of her so deadened her that she staggered.

(ibid.: 298–9)

History is literally 'his'-story; it does not include hers. Hardy brings home in this narrative the embedded, flesh-and-blood enactments of social discourse: its materiality. 'His view' literally has 'deadened' hers. When she tries to contribute her voice to history, she is defeated by a generic 'woman'; telling her actual, individual 'history' is fatal. Her bawdry mother was right; to survive with even a good man, she must suppress *her* story. This is not just a matter of interpretation, it is a matter of whether or not she can *be* there. 'His view of her so deadened her that she staggered'. This man, the best in Hardy's horizon, switches from one generic woman to another, from the pure to the impure one, without stopping at the individual woman. The sense that he will neither see nor hear her is like a kind of death. The only place she has ever had in the middle-class social ceremony, is destroyed after only twenty-four hours. The Other Woman destroys it but, in this case, the 'other woman' is an impossible ideal in her husband's head. There is no competing with such a rival. She is the precursor of the pornographic advertising images of the twentieth century: a replacement in the mind of this conventional man for any possible real woman.

Hardy, like George Eliot with Hetty Sorrel's story, even suppresses – as beyond the communal capacity for perception – Tess's own account of her history. Tess's story, as she tells it to Angel, is dropped into the gap between books of the text. Book 4 ends as she begins to tell her story to Angel, and when Book 5 begins, she has finished it. Readers have seen the events she recounts, but Hardy deliberately eclipses her own account of her story ('herstory'). It is simply lost somewhere in the gaps of the historical narrative that purports to include her and that makes her its main subject.

Hardy makes Tess bear responsibility for her own fate to the extent that she makes self-destructive choices at crucial moments, especially choices that call on her courage to act in spite of her experience of men. She underestimates Angel's father's generosity, having a 'feminine loss of courage at the last and critical moment', and being deflected by 'omens' from seeking the help he would probably have given (ibid.: 378). But what help could she expect to find, isolated as she is in her view of the world? In such isolation, what courage is possible but a sort of generic resistance to a generic threat? Her experience bears out Baudrillard's claim that 'there are only ever stakes, defiance, that is to say something which does not proceed via a "social relation" ' (Baudrillard, 1983: 68–9).

Such resistance may be what is called for in the humanist history. And Hardy's novel does suggest indirectly that the association among women for which Charlotte Perkins Gilman praised the nineteenth century might be Tess's salvation. Certainly her happiest moments, though ephemeral, are those where she shares activity with other women: the 'votive sisterhood' of the May dance at the beginning, and the friends at the dairy whose solidarity is not undermined even by their common interest in Angel Clare.

The grammar of perspective that underlies the social order in historical novels, as in representative government, is a collaboration of all possible viewpoints that literally constructs an objective world. For this woman, the power of objectivity is obtained not with her consent but in spite of it, and even at the cost of her life. Tess's best collaborators are women, and their society is ephemeral. She is wanted by Alec mainly as something to subdue: an occasion to exert the violence that, as Mill says, the law allows to every clodhopper regardless of his class or wealth. She is wanted by Angel mainly as something to hang his fantasies on, in another, subtler form of violence. Even after he learns to see things from her point of view, and thus to give her the answering response that constitutes her actual self as part of the world, Angel disbelieves the crucial piece of information she gives him that might have saved her from capture and the gallows. Tess's history dies with her. No one in her society knows her story, or if hearing it believes it, so no one learns from it. Even Hardy's narrative sequence obliterates Tess's account of herself. Like Hester, her time is a not-history: fated by its suppression to be endlessly repeated.

There cannot be two vanishing points in humanist time; any truly alternate story destroys the neutrality of that temporal medium and thus of the entire humanist project it implies and carries. Women like Tess and Mabel Grex, however, and quite regardless of class origin, must live with two vanishing points. For them, there is no common medium 'in' which representation in art and politics and social order can exist. To be represented at all is necessarily to be recovered in the historical system of explanation, which is to say in a common world and a common time. Tess, like multitudes of her sisters then and still, can appear 'in' this putatively egalitarian system only as a sacrifice. The neutral media of time and space make possible mutual reference across even the widest of gaps. True alterity simply cannot exist in this system. True alterity emerges with the modernist perception, fostered by a new description of nature, that time is no longer neutral but instead an inflection of events. The nineteenth century historical and social novel has other agendas, but they are tested to the limit by dilemmas of difference that are evident most notoriously in the so-called Woman Question. The really appalling twist in *Tess of the D'Urbervilles* is that Hardy subjects the reader to Tess's experience, and thus to the experience of becoming invisible, cut off, cut out. Raped, ostracized, and betrayed first by her mother and then by her husband, Tess finally is executed by a society that permits and even encourages the abuse of women but offers no support for their efforts to fight back. She is there, but not there: sacrificed to 'the law'. When the black flag finally announces her execution, it announces as well the death of a particular social possibility.

An historical narrative is a fantasy realized: a fantasy of universal inclusion. The best writers, it could be said, are the ones who include most; the worst those who simplify the construction of social and private life with various mythological or typological inventions, like the woman who thrives on self-sacrifice, the all-accomplished 'polking polyglot' heroine (Eliot, 1963: 305), the handsome eligible heir. But the condition and fate of women belies these fantasies of form. The segregation of women works its way through to the very conditions that found the common social order of things in the first place. History, the realism of narrative forms, asserts as its most fundamental principle that all perspectives are incorporated into its common system and its common media, neutral space and time. A second vanishing point, even one slightly different from the first, destroys the system implicitly, and with it all its claims to rationality and inclusiveness. The dualistic habit insures the extinction of those values offered by historical forms. The putatively common temporal horizon, and with it the humanist project, exists only by 'terrorist' means; too many constituencies are left outside the pale. Clearly domesticity is a refuge only for those free to operate on both sides of that liminal threshold. But in 'the home' how many crimes are committed (Trodd, 1989) in the name of order and progress?

The historical method often conflicts with its message when that message includes irreducible, oppositional gender difference at the basis of almost every transaction. There is no finessing the choice. Either difference remains oppositional or it resolves into a more pluralist accommodation of variety. Mid-nineteenth-century England, it appears, was not ready fully to take the step to pluralism. Urban society disappears entirely in Hardy, where we go back to the village and to irreducible timeless concerns far afield from the mediation between constituencies that gives interest to so many nineteenth-century social narratives.

BIBLIOGRAPHY

NINETEENTH-CENTURY SOURCES

Alford, Henry (1869) 'The Two Religions: The Religion of the Bible and the Religion of the Church', *Contemporary Review*, 10 (March), 321–43.

Amiel, Henri Federic (1885) *Intimate Journal* (Journal in time,1881), Tr. Mrs. Humphrey Ward

Andrews, Charles Wesley (1856) *Religious Novels: An Argument Against Their Use*, New York: Anson D. F. Randolph.

Anon. (1851) 'The First Half of the Nineteenth Century', *Fraser's Magazine*, 43 (January), 1–15.

Anon. (1855) 'The Non-existence of Women', *North British Review*, 23, 536–62.

Bagehot, Walter (1928) *The English Constitution* [1867], London: Oxford University Press.

Barry, (Canon) William (1887) *The New Antigone: A Romance*, 3 vols, London and New York: Macmillan.

Bodichon, Barbara (1859) *Woman and Work* [1856], New York: C. S. Francis.

Bray, Charles (1838) *An Inquiry into the Origins of Christianity.*

Brontë, Anne (1979) *The Tenant of Wildfell Hall* [1848], Harmondsworth: Penguin.

—— (1988) *Agnes Grey* [1847], Harmondsworth: Penguin.

Brontë, Charlotte (1966) *Jane Eyre* [1847], Harmondsworth: Penguin.

—— (1972) *Villette* [1853], New York: Harper.

—— (1985) *Shirley* [1849], London: Zodiac.

—— (1987) *The Professor* [1857, posth.], Oxford: Clarendon Press.

Brontë, Emily (1965) *Wuthering Heights* [1847], Harmondsworth: Penguin.

Bulwer-Lytton, Edward (n.d.) *Eugene Aram, a Novel*, (3rd edn, later than 1847 [1831]), Chicago and New York: Rand, McNally.

Carlyle, Thomas (1829) 'Signs of the Times', *Edinburgh Review*, XLIX (June), 439–59.

—— (1970) *Sartor Resartus, or, The Tailor Retailored* [1833], New York: Holt Rinehart Winston.

Chambers, Robert (1844), *Vestiges of the Natural History of Creation*, London: John Churchill

Cobbe, Frances (1864) 'The Nineteenth Century', *Fraser's Magazine*, 69 (April), 481–94.

Cumming, (Revd) John (1886) 'The Age We Live In' [1847–48], in *Twelve Lectures Delivered before the Young Men's Christian Association in Exeter Hall*, London: James Nisbet & Co., vol. 3, pp. 337–68.

Darwin, Charles (1968) *The Origin of Species by Means of Natural Selection, or the Preservation of Favoured Races in the Struggle for Life* [1859], Harmondsworth: Penguin.

—— (1979) *Descent of Man, and Selection in Relation to Sex* [1871], Princeton: Princeton University Press.

Davies, J. Llewelyn (1873) 'Mr. Matthew Arnold's New Religion of the Bible', *Contemporary Review*, 21 (May), 842–66.

Dickens, Charles (1892) *The Mystery of Edwin Drood* [1870], Boston: Estes & Lauriat.

—— (1922) *The Life and Adventures of Martin Chuzzlewit* [1843], Boston: Houghton Mifflin Riverside.

—— (1939) *Nicholas Nickleby* [1838–9], London and Glasgow: Collins.

—— (1942) *A Tale of Two Cities* [1859], New York: Dodd, Mead.

—— (1956) *Bleak House* [1852–3], Boston: Houghton Mifflin Riverside.

—— (1958) *David Copperfield* [1849–50], Boston: Houghton Mifflin Riverside.

—— (1966) *Hard Times* [1854], New York: W. W. Norton.

—— (1967) *Little Dorrit* [1855–7], Harmondsworth: Penguin.

—— (1970) *Dombey and Son* [1846–8], Harmondsworth: Penguin.

—— (1971) *Our Mutual Friend* [1864–65], Harmondsworth: Penguin.

—— (1972) *Great Expectations* [1860–61], New York and London: Holt Rinehart Winston.

—— (1972a) *The Old Curiosity Shop* [1840–1], Harmondsworth: Penguin.

—— (n.d.) *The Posthumous Papers of the Pickwick Club* [1836–37], New York: The Modern Library.

Disraeli, Benjamin (1950) *Sybil: or, The Two Nations* [1845], London: Longmans, Green & Co.

Drysdale, George (1983) *Elements of Social Science* [1860], cited in Elizabeth K. Helsinger *et al.* (eds), *The Woman Question: Social Issues, 1837–1883*, New York: Garland., II, pp. 67–9.

Eliot, George (pseudonym of Marian Evans) (1855) 'Evangelical Teaching: Dr. Cumming', *Westminster Review*, LXIV (October), 436–62. Also in *Essays of George Eliot*, ed. Thomas Pinney.

—— (1856) 'The Antigone and Its Moral', *Leader*, 7 (March), 306. Also in *Essays of George Eliot*, ed. Thomas Pinney.

—— (1944) *Silas Marner, The Weaver of Raveloe* [1861], Harmondsworth: Penguin.

—— (1956) *Middlemarch, a Study of Provincial Life* [1871–72], Boston: Houghton Mifflin Riverside.

—— (1961) *The Mill on the Floss* [1860], Boston: Houghton Mifflin Riverside.

—— (1963) *Essays of George Eliot*, ed. Thomas Pinney, New York, Columbia University Press.

—— (1967) *Daniel Deronda* [1876], Harmondsworth: Penguin.

—— (1968) *Adam Bede* [1859], Boston: Houghton Mifflin Riverside.

—— (1972) *Felix Holt, the Radical* [1866], Harmondsworth: Penguin.

—— (1973) *Scenes of Clerical Life* [1858], Harmondsworth: Penguin. Also

BIBLIOGRAPHY

published in 1910 in *Scenes of Clerical life, Silas and Other Stories*, Foleshill Edition, Boston: Little Brown.

—— (1980) *Romola* [1862–3], Harmondsworth: Penguin.

—— See also Marian (Mary Ann) Evans as translator under Feuerbach and Spinoza.

Feuerbach, Ludwig (1957) *The Essence of Christianity*, trans. Mary Ann Evans (George Eliot) [1854] (*Das Wesen des Christenthums* [1841]), New York: Harper.

Froude, James Anthony (1904) *The Nemesis of Faith* [1849], London and New York: The Walter Scott Publishing Co.

Gaskell, Elizabeth (1952) *Cranford* [1853], London and Glasgow: Collins.

—— (1969) *Wives and Daughters, An Everyday Story* [1864–66, unfinished], Harmondsworth: Penguin.

—— (1973) *North and South* [1854–55], New York: Oxford University Press.

—— (1981) *Ruth* [1853], New York: Oxford University Press.

—— (1982) *Sylvia's Lovers* [1863], New York: Oxford University Press.

—— (1987) *Mary Barton, A Tale of Manchester Life* [1848], New York: Oxford University Press.

Gilman, Charlotte Perkins (1966) *Women and Economics: A Study of the Economic Relation Between Men and Women as a Factor in Social Evolution* [1898], New York: Harper & Row.

—— (1973) *The Yellow Wallpaper* (1892), Old Westbury, NY: The Feminist Press.

Gissing, George (1911) *The Odd Women* [1893], London: Sidgwick & Jackson.

—— (1982) *In The Year of Jubilee* [1894], New York: Dover; London: Constable.

—— (1993a) *The New Grub Street* [1891], New York: Oxford University Press.

—— (1993b) *Born in Exile* [1892], London: Dent.

Gleig, G. R. (1866) 'The Political Crisis', *Blackwood's Magazine*, 99 (June), 773–96.

Grand, Sarah (1992) *The Heavenly Twins* [1894], Ann Arbor: University of Michigan Press.

Greenwood, Frederick (1885) 'What Has Become of the Middle Classes?', *Blackwood's Magazine*, 138 (August), 175–80.

Hale-White, William (n.d.) *The Autobiography of Mark Rutherford. Edited by his Friend, Reuben Shapcott* [1881], 2nd edn, New York: Cassell.

Hardy, Thomas (1962) *The Mayor of Casterbridge* [1886], Boston: Houghton Mifflin Riverside.

—— (1978a) *Far From the Madding Crowd* [1874], Harmondsworth: Penguin.

—— (1978b) *Jude the Obscure* [1895], New York: Norton.

—— (1978c) *Tess of the D'Urbervilles* [1891], Harmondsworth: Penguin.

—— (1978d) *The Return of the Native* [1878], Harmondsworth: Penguin.

Harrison, Fredrick (1875), 'Religion and Conservative Aspects of Positivism, Parts I & II', *Contemporary Review*, 26 and 27 (Nov. and Dec.), 992–1012 and 140–59.

Hennell, Charles (1840) *The Philosophy of Necessity; or, the Law of Consequences as Applicable to Mental, Moral, and Social Science.*

Holland, Henry (1862) 'The Progress and Spirit of Physical Science', in *Essays on Scientific and Other Subjects*, London: Longman, Green, Longman, Roberts & Green. Originally in *Edinburgh Review*, 108 (July, 1858), 71–104.

Hood, E. P. (1987) *The Age and Its Architects* [1850], quoted in Barbara Dennis and David Skilton (eds), *Reform and Intellectual Debate in Victorian England*, London: Croom Helm.

Horne, Richard (1844) *A New Spirit of the Age*, 2 vols, London: Smith, Elder.

229

BIBLIOGRAPHY

Hutton, Richard Holt (1888) *Essays on Some of the Modern Guides to English Thought in Matters of Faith*, London: Macmillan.

—— (1894) *Contemporary Thought and Thinkers*, 2 vols, London: Macmillan.

James, Henry (1868) 'Modern Woman', *Nation*, 7, 332–4, cited in Elizabeth K.Helsinger *et al.* (eds) (1983), *The Woman Question: Social Issues, 1837–1883*, New York: Garland, I, pp. 120–3.

—— (1954) *What Maisie Knew* [1897], New York: Doubleday Anchor.

—— (1956a) *The Bostonians* [1886], New York: Random House.

—— (1956b) *The Portrait of a Lady* [1881], Boston: Houghton Mifflin Riverside.

Jewsbury, Geraldine (1853) *History of An Adopted Child*, New York: Harpers.

Kingsley, Charles (1983) *Alton Locke, Tailor and Poet* [1850], Oxford: Oxford University Press.

—— (1984) *The Water Babies, A Fairy Tale for a Land Baby* [1863], Harmondsworth: Puffin.

Kipling, Rudyard (1987a) *Jungle Book* [1894], Oxford: Oxford University Press.

—— (1987b) *Second Jungle Book* [1895], Oxford: Oxford University Press.

Lyell, Charles (1830–3) *Principles of Geology*, London: J. Murray Macaulay, Thomas (1830) 'Southey's Colloquies on Scotland', *Edinburgh Rev.* L (January), 528–65.

Mallock, W. H. (1898) *Aristocracy and Evolution: A Study of the Rights, the Origin, and the Social Functions of the Wealthier Classes*, London: Adam and Charles Black.

Mariotti, L. (pseudonym of Antonio Gallenga) (1841) 'The Age We Live In', *Fraser's Magazine*, 24 (July), 1–15.

Maurice, F. D. (1862) 'The New Morality: Worship of Majorities', *Macmillan's Magazine*, 5 (April), 504–6.

Mayhew, Henry (1968) *London Labour and the London Poor* [1861], 4 vols, New York: Dover Publications.

Meredith, George (1895) *The Amazing Marriage* [1895], 2 vols, New York: Charles Scribner's.

—— (1910) *Lord Ormont and His Aminta* [1894], London: Constable.

—— (1914) *Beauchamp's Career* [1875–76], London: Constable.

—— (1922) *Evan Harrington* [1896], New York: Charles Scribner's.

—— (1956) *An Essay on Comedy* [1877], Garden City: Doubleday Anchor.

—— (1968) *The Egoist* [1879], Harmondsworth: Penguin.

—— (1973) *Diana of the Crossways* [1885], New York: Norton.

—— (1984) *The Ordeal of Richard Feverel* [1859], Oxford and New York: Oxford University Press.

Mill, John Stuart (1831) 'The Spirit of the Age' (six weekly instalments in the *Examiner*, January 9, 23; February 6; March 13; April 3; May 15, 29).

—— (1924) *Autobiography* [1873], New York: Columbia University Press.

—— (1975) *Three Essays: 'On Liberty' [1859], 'Representative Government' [1861], 'The Subjection of Women'* [1869], New York and London: Oxford University Press.

Moore, George (1893) *Modern Painting*, London: W. Scott.

—— (1991) *Esther Waters* [1894], London: J. M. Dent.

Newman, John Henry (Cardinal) (1855) *Loss and Gain: or, The Story of a Convert* [1848], 2nd edn, Boston: Patrick Donahoe.

—— (1914) *Callista: A Tale of the Third Century* [1856], London: Longmans, Green & Co.

—— (1956) *Apologia Pro Vita Sua* [1864], Boston: Houghton Mifflin Riverside.

BIBLIOGRAPHY

Oliphant, Margaret (1984) *Hester* [1883], London: Virago.

—— (1987) *The Perpetual Curate* [18–], London: Virago.

Patterson, R. H. (1864) 'The Crisis of Parties', *Blackwood's Magazine*, 95 (June), 767–75.

Realism and Tradition in Art 1848–1900: Sources and Documents (1966), ed. Linda Nochlin, Englewood Cliffs, NJ: Prentice Hall.

Robinson, David (1830) *Blackwoods Magazine*, 28 (December), 900–20.

Shorthouse, J. Henry (1924) *John Inglesant: A Romance* [1881], London: Macmillan.

Smith, Adam (1986) *The Essential Adam Smith*, ed. Robert Heilbroner with Laurence J. Malone, New York: Norton.

Southey, Robert (1829) 'On The State and Prospects of the Country', *Quarterly Review*, XXXIX (April), 475–520.

Spinoza, Baruch (Benedict de) (1981) *Ethics*, trans. Mary Ann Evans (George Eliot) [1854–56], ed. Thos Deegan, Salzburg: Institute für Anglistik und Amerikanistik (Saltzburg Studies in English Literature, No. 102).

Stevenson, Robert Louis (1985) *Dr. Jekyll and Mr. Hyde* [1886], Harmondsworth: Penguin.

—— (1989a) *Kidnapped* [1886], Edinburgh: Cannongate.

—— (1989b) *Catriona, A Sequel to Kidnapped* [1893], Edinburgh: Cannongate.

Stowall, Hugh (1886) 'The Age We Live In: Its Tendencies and Its Exigencies' [1847–48], in *Twelve Lectures Delivered Before the Young Men's Christian Association in Exeter Hall*, 6, 43–74.

Tennyson, Alfred (Lord) (1958) *Poems of Tennyson*, ed. Jerome Buckley, Boston: Houghton Mifflin Riverside.

Thackeray, William Makepeace (1871) *The Memoirs of Barry Lyndon, Esq. Written by Himself; with The History of Samuel Titmarsh and the Great Hoggarty Diamond*, Philadelphia: J. B. Lippincott and Co.

—— (1871b) *The History of Pendennis: His Fortunes and Misfortunes, His Friends and His Greatest Enemy* [1848–50], 2 vols, Philadelphia: J. B. Lippincott & Co.

—— (1872) *The Paris Sketchbooks of Mr. M. A. Titmarsh* and *The Memoirs of Mr. Charles J. Yellowplush, Sometime Footman in Many Genteel Families*, Philadelphia: J. B. Lippincott and Co.

—— (1900) *The Virginians: A Tale of the Last Century* [1857–59], Special Bibliographical Collected Edition, vols 18–19, New York and London: Holt Rinehart Winston.

—— (1962) *The History of Henry Esmond, Esq.* [1852], New York and London: Holt Rinehart Winston.

—— (1963) *Vanity Fair: A Novel Without A Hero* [1847–48], Boston: Houghton Mifflin Riverside.

Thompson, William (1970) *Appeal of One Half of the Human Race, Women, Against the Pretensions of the Other Half, Men, To Restrain Them in Political and Thence Civil and Domestic Slavery; in Reply to Mr. Mill's Celebrated 'Article on Government'* [1825], London: Source Book Press; New York: Burt Franklin.

Trollope, Anthony (1950) *The Warden* [1855], New York: Random House.

—— (1967) *The Last Chronicle of Barset* [1867], Harmondsworth: Penguin.

—— (1969) *The Eustace Diamonds* [1873], Harmondsworth, Penguin.

—— (1972) *Phineas Finn* [1869], Harmondsworth: Penguin.

—— (1972a) *Can You Forgive Her?* [1864], Harmondsworth, Penguin

—— (1982) *Barchester Towers* [1857], Harmondsworth: Penguin.

—— (1982a) *The Way We Live Now* [1874–75], New York: Oxford University Press.

—— (1983) *The Duke's Children* [1879–80], New York: Oxford University Press.

—— (1983a) *Phineas Redux* [1873–74], New York: Oxford University Press.

—— (1983b) *The Prime Minister* [1876], New York: Oxford University Press.

—— (1984) *Framley Parsonage* [1861], Harmondsworth: Penguin.

—— (1991) *The Small House at Allington* [1864], Harmondsworth: Penguin.

—— (1992) *The Three Clerks* [1858], London: Omnium Publishers for the Trollope Society.

—— (1993) *An Autobiography* [1883], Harmondsworth: Penguin.

Ward, Mary Augusta (Mrs Humphrey Ward) (1911) *Robert Elsmere* [1888], vols I–II of *The Writings of Mrs Humphrey Ward*, Boston and New York: Houghton Mifflin.

Wells, H. G. (1993) *The Time Machine* [1895], London: Dent.

Westcott, Brooke F. (1868) 'Aspects of Positivism in Relation to Christianity', *Contemporary Review*, 8 (July), 371–86.

Whewell, William (1990) *Lectures on the History of Moral Philosophy in England, and Additional Lectures* [1852 and 1862], Bristol: Thoemmes.

White, William Hale (n.d.) *The Autobiography of Mark Rutherford*, 2nd edn, New York: Cassell.

Wiseman, Nicholas (Cardinal) (1885) *Fabiola; or, The Church of the Catacombs* [1854], New York: D. and J. Sadlier & Co.

TWENTIETH-CENTURY SOURCES

Alborn, Timothy L. (1995) 'The Moral of the Failed Bank: Professional Plots in the Victorian Money Market', *Victorian Studies*, 38, 2 (Winter), 199–226.

Alter, Robert (1975) *Partial Magic: The Novel as Self-Conscious Genre*, Berkeley: University of California Press.

Altick, Richard D. (1957) *The English Common Reader: A Social History of the Novel*, New York: Oxford University Press.

Ardis, Ann (1990) *New Women, New Novels: Feminism and Early Modernism*, New Brunswick: Rutgers University Press.

Armstrong, Nancy (1987) *Desire and Domestic Fiction: A Political History of the Novel*, New York: Oxford University Press.

Baker, Joseph Ellis (1932) *The Novel and the Oxford Movement*, Princeton: Princeton University Press.

Banks, J. A. and Banks, Olive (1954) *Prosperity and Parenthood*, London: Routledge.

Bann, Stephen (1990) *The Inventions of History: Essays on the Representation of the Past*, Manchester: Manchester University Press.

Barreca, Regina (ed.) (1990) *Sex and Death in Victorian Literature*, Bloomington: Indiana University Press.

Barrett, Dorothea (1989) *Vocation and Desire: George Eliot's Heroines*, London: Routledge.

Barthes, Roland (1972) 'The World as Object', in *Critical Essays*, trans. Richard Howard, Evanston: Northwestern University Press.

Baudrillard, Jean (1983) *In The Shadow of the Silent Majorities . . . Or, the End of the Social, and Other Essays*, New York: Semiotext(e).

Beer, Gillian (1970) *Meredith: A Change of Masks*, London: The Athlone Press.

BIBLIOGRAPHY

—— (1983) *Darwin's Plots: Evolutionary Narrative in Darwin, George Eliot and Nineteenth-Century Fiction*, London: Routledge.

—— (1989) *Arguing With the Past: Essays in Narrative from Woolf to Sidney*, London and New York: Routledge.

—— (1996) 'Helmholtz, Tyndall, Gerard Manley Hopkins: Leaps of the Prepared Imagination', in *Open Fields: Science in Cultural Encounter*, Oxford: Clarendon Press, pp. 242–72.

—— (1996a) 'Speaking for the Others: Relativism and Authority in Victorian Anthropological Literature', in *Open Fields: Science in Cultural Encounter*, Oxford: Clarendon Press, pp. 71–94.

Benians, E. A. (1925) 'Adam Smith's Project of an Empire', *Cambridge Historical Journal*, I, 3, 249–83.

Berg, Maxine (1980) *The Machinery Question and the Making of Political Economy, 1815–1848*, Cambridge: Cambridge University Press.

Berlin, Isaiah (1939) *Karl Marx: His Life and Environment*, London: Thornton Butterworth.

—— (1959) 'J. S. Mill and the Ends of Life', Cohen Memorial Lecture, The Council of Christians and Jews.

Best, Geoffrey (1971) *Mid-Victorian Britain, 1851–1875*, London: Weidenfeld & Nicolson.

Blake, Andrew (1989) *Reading Victorian Fiction: Cultural Context and Ideological Content*, London: Macmillan.

Boumelha, Penny (1985) *Thomas Hardy and Women: Sexual Ideology and Novel Form*, Madison: University of Wisconsin Press.

Bowler, Peter J. (1989) *The Invention of Progress: The Victorians and the Past*, Oxford: Basil Blackwell.

Breton, André (1972) *Manifestos of Surrealism* [1924, 1929], trans. Richard Seaver and Helen Lane, Ann Arbor: University of Michigan Press.

Briggs, Asa (1983) *A Social History of England*, Harmondsworth: Penguin.

Brown, Ford K. (1961) *Fathers of the Victorians: The Age of Wilberforce*, Cambridge: Cambridge University Press.

Buckley, Jerome Hamilton (1951) *The Victorian Temper: A Study in Literary Culture*, New York: Random House.

Burke, Peter (1970) *The Idea of Perfect History*, Carbondale: University of Illinois Press.

Burn, W. L. (1964) *The Age of Equipoise: A Study of the Mid-Victorian Generation*, New York: W. W. Norton & Co.

Butler, Lance St John (ed.) (1989) *Alternative Hardy*, New York: St. Martin's Press.

Butterfield, Herbert (1963) *The Whig Interpretation of History*, London: G. Bell and Sons.

—— (1969) *Man on His Past: The Study of the History of Historical Scholarship*, Cambridge: Cambridge University Press.

Calvert, Peter (1982) *The Concept of Class. An Historical Introduction*, London: Hutchinson.

—— (1993) *An Introduction to Comparative Politics*, Hemel Hempstead: Harvester.

Campbell, Karlyn Kohrs (1989) *Man Cannot Speak for Her*, vol.1: *A Critical Study of Early Feminist Rhetoric*, New York and London: Praeger.

Camus, Albert (1956) *The Rebel: An Essay on Man in Revolt* (*L'homme révolté* [1951]), trans. Anthony Bower, New York: Random House.

BIBLIOGRAPHY

Chairomonte, Nicolas (1966) *The Paradox of History: Stendhal, Tolstoy, Pasternak and Others*, Princeton: Christian Gauss Lectures.

Chapman, Raymond (1986) *The Sense of the Past in Victorian Literature*, New York: St. Martin's Press.

Cobban, Alfred (1966) 'The Idea of Empire', in *Ideas and Beliefs of the Victorians* [1949], New York: Dutton.

Colley, Linda (1986) 'Whose Nation? Class and National Consciousness in Britain, 1750–1830', *Past and Present*, 113 (November), pp. 97–117.

Conrad, Joseph (1921) *Victory* [1915], New York: Doubleday Anchor.

—— (1947) *The Portable Conrad*, New York: Viking.

—— (1953) *The Secret Agent* [1907], New York: Doubleday Anchor.

—— (1958) *Lord Jim* [1900], Boston: Houghton Mifflin.

—— (1959) *The Shadow-Line, Typhoon, and The Secret Sharer* [1917, 1902, 1912], New York: Doubleday Anchor.

—— (1960) *Nostromo* [1904], New York: Doubleday Anchor.

—— (1973) *Heart of Darkness* [1902], Harmondsworth: Penguin.

Cosslett, Tess (1982) *The Scientific Movement in Victorian Literature*, Brighton: Harvester.

—— (1988) *Woman to Woman: Female Friendship in Victorian Fiction*, Brighton: Harvester.

Cott, Nancy (1977) *Bonds of Womanhood: Woman's Sphere in New England, 1780–1835*, New Haven: Yale University Press.

Cottom, Daniel (1987) *Social Figures: George Eliot, Social History, and Literary Representation*, Minneapolis: University of Minnesota Press.

Crouzet, Francois (ed.) (1972) *Capital Formation in the Industrial Revolution*, London: Methuen.

Crowther, J. G. (1935) *British Scientists of the Nineteenth Century*, London: Kegan, Paul, Trench, Trubner & Co.

Culler, Jonathan (1975) *Structural Poetics*, Ithaca: Cornell University Press.

Cunningham, Gail (1978) *The New Woman and the Victorian Novel*, London: Macmillan.

Cunningham, Valentine (1975) *Everywhere Spoken Against: Dissent in the Victorian Novel*, Oxford: Clarendon Press.

Dale, Peter Allan (1977) *The Victorian Critic and the Idea of History*, Cambridge, Mass. and London: Harvard University Press.

Davidoff, Leonore and Hall, Catherine (1987) *Family Fortunes: Men and Women of the English Middle Classes 1780–1850*, London: Hutchinson.

Delphy, Christine (1984) *Close to Home: A Materialist Analysis of Women's Oppression*, trans. Diana Leonard, Amherst: University of Massachusetts Press.

Dennis, Barabara and Skilton, David (eds) (1987) *Reform and Intellectual Debate in Victorian England*, London: Croom Helm.

Derrida, Jacques (1978) *Writing and Difference* [1967], trans. Alan Bass, Chicago: University of Chicago Press.

Dickson, P. G. M. (1967) *The Financial Revolution in England: A Study in the Development of Public Credit, 1688–1756*, London: Macmillan.

Duras, Marguerite (1985) *The Lover* (*L'amant* [1984]), trans. Barbara Bray, New York: Random House.

Eisenman, Stephen (ed.) (1994) *Nineteenth-Century Art: A Critical History*, London: Thames & Hudson.

234

BIBLIOGRAPHY

Elliott-Binns, L. E. (1964) *Religion in the Victorian Era*, London: Lutterworth Press.

Ermarth, Elizabeth Deeds (1974a) 'Maggie Tulliver's Long Suicide', *Studies in English Literature*, 14, 4 (Autumn), 587–601.

—— (1974b) 'Incarnations: George Eliot's Conception of "Undeviating Law" ', *Nineteenth-Century Fiction* 29, 3 (December), 273–86. Reprinted 1996 in *George Eliot: Critical Assessments*, vol 4, ed. Stuart Hutchinson, E. Sussex: Helm and New York: Routledge.

—— (1982) 'Fictional Consensus and Female Casualties', in *Representation and Women* (English Institute Essays for 1981), eds Carolyn Heilbrun and Margaret Higgonnet, Baltimore: The Johns Hopkins University Press, pp. 1–18.

—— (1983) *Realism and Consensus in the English Novel*, Princeton: Princeton University Press.

—— (1986) ' "Th'Observed of All Observers": Shakespeare's Audience and George Eliot's Narrator', Stratford-upon-Avon Studies volume on *Nineteenth Century English Novel*, ed. Jeremy Hawthorn, London: Edward Arnold, pp. 127–40.

—— (1989) 'The Solitude of Women and Social Time', in *Taking our Time: Feminist Perspectives on Temporality*, ed. Frieda Forman with Caoran Jowton, Oxford and New York: Pergamon Press, Athene Series, pp. 37–46.

—— (1992) *Sequel to History: Postmodernism and the Crisis of Representational Time*, Princeton: Princeton University Press.

—— (1995) *George Eliot*, New York: Macmillan [1985].

Faure, Elie (1937) *History of Art: III, Modern Art*, trans. Walter Pach, Garden City, New York: Garden City Publishing.

Fish, Stanley (1973) 'Sequence and Meaning', in *To Tell a Story: Narrative Meaning and Practice*, Los Angeles: William Andrews Clark Memorial Library.

Fisher, Philip (1981) *Making Up Society: The Novels of George Eliot*, Pittsburgh: University of Pittsburgh Press.

Flint, Kate (1986) *Dickens*, Brighton: Harvester.

Foucault, Michel (1970) *The Order of Things: An Archaeology of the Human Sciences* (*Les mots et les choses* [1966]), New York: Random House.

—— (1971) *The Archaeology of Knowledge and the Discourse on Language* (*L'Archaeology du Savoir* [1969] and *L'ordre du discours* [1971]), trans. A. M. Sheridan Smith, London: Tavistock.

—— (1977) *Discipline and Punish: The Birth of the Prison*, trans. Alan Sheridan, New York: Pantheon.

—— (1985) 'Final Interview', *Raritan Review*, 5: 1, 1–13.

Fulton, Richard and Cotee, C. M. (comps) (1985) 'Introduction', in *Union List of Victorian Serials* (in US and Canadian libraries).

Furbank, P. N. (1985) *Unholy Pleasure: The Idea of Class*, Oxford: Oxford University Press.

Gallagher, Catherine (1985) *The Industrial Reformation of English Fiction: Social Discourse and Narrative Form, 1832–1867*, Chicago: Chicago University Press.

Garrett, Peter (1980) *The Victorian Multiplot Novel*, New Haven: Yale Univeristy Press.

Gilman, Charlotte Perkins (1975) *The Living of Charlotte Perkins Gilman: An Autobiography* [1935], New York: Harper Colophon.

Goldknopf, David (1972) *The Life of the Novel*, Chicago: Chicago University Press.

Goode, John (1978) *George Gissing: Ideology and Fiction*, London: Vision.

235

BIBLIOGRAPHY

Grafton, Anthony and Jardine, Lisa (1986) *From Humanism to the Humanities: Education and the Liberal Arts in Fifteenth- and Sixteenth-Century Europe*, Cambridge, Mass.: Harvard University Press.

Greene, Graham (1974) *The Honorary Consul*, New York: Pocket Books.

Gregor, Ian (ed.) (1980) *Rereading the Victorian Novel: Detail into Form*, New York: Barnes & Noble.

Griest, Guinevere (1970) *Mudies Circulating Library and the Victorian Novel*, Bloomington: Indiana University Press.

Grylls, David (1986) *The Paradox of George Gissing*, London: Allen & Unwin.

Halevy, Elie (1961) *A History of the English People in the Nineteenth Century*, vol. 4: *Victorian Years, 1941–1895*, trans. E. I. Watkin, New York: Barnes & Noble.

—— (1966) *The Growth of Philosophical Radicalism*, trans. Mary Morris, Boston: The Beacon Press.

Hamer, Mary (1987) *Writing by Numbers: Trollope's Serial Fiction*, Cambridge: Cambridge University Press.

Hardy, Barbara (1971) *The Appropriate Form: An Essay on the Novel*, London: Athlone.

Harvey, David (1988) *Social Justice and the City*, Oxford: Basil Blackwell.

—— (1989) *The Condition of Postmodernity: An Inquiry into the Origins of Cultural Change*, Oxford: Basil Blackwell.

Hawthorn, Jeremy (1986) *The Nineteenth-Century British Novel*, Stratford Upon Avon Studies, second series, London: Edward Arnold.

Heilbroner, Robert (1980) *The Worldly Philosophers*, New York: Simon & Schuster.

Helsinger, Elizabeth K. *et al.* (eds) (1983) *The Woman Question: Social Issues, 1837–1883*, New York: Garland.

Hill, Christopher (1990) *A Nation of Change and Novelty: Radical Politics, Religion, and Literature in Seventeenth-Century England*, London and New York: Routledge.

Himmelfarb, Gertrude (1991) *Poverty and Compassion: The Moral Imagination of the Late Victorians*, vol. 2, New York: Knopf.

Hughes, Londa K. and Lund, Michael (1991) *The Victorian Serial*, Charlottesville: Univeristy of Virginia Press.

Hulin, Jean-Paul and Coustillas, Pierre (eds) (n.d.) *Victorian Writers and the City*, Publications of the University of Lille.

Hynes, Samuel (1990) *A War Imagined*, London: Pimlico.

Irigaray, Luce (1985) 'When the Goods Get Together' (*Des marchandes entre elles*), in *This Sex Which is Not One* (*Ce sexe qui n'en est pas un* [1977]), trans. Catherine Porter with Carolyn Burke, Ithaca: Cornell University Press.

Ivins, William, Jr (1973) *On the Rationalization of Sight: With an Examination of Three Renaissance Treatises on Perspective*, Paper no. 8, Metropolitan Museum [1938], New York: Da Capo Press.

James, Henry (1964) *The Ambassadors* [1903], New York: Norton.

—— (1966) *The Golden Bowl* [1905], Harmondsworth: Penguin.

—— (1970) *The Wings of the Dove* [1902], Columbus, Ohio: Charles E. Merrill Standard Editions.

Kappeler, Susanne (1976) *The Pornography of Representation*, Minneapolis: University of Minnesota Press.

Kiely, Robert (1972) *The Romantic Novel in England*, Cambridge, Mass.: Harvard University Press.

Kincaid, James (1977) *The Novels of Anthony Trollope*, Oxford: Clarendon Press.

BIBLIOGRAPHY

Kramer, Lawrence (1990) *Music as a Cultural Practice, 1800–1900*, Berkeley: University of California Press.

Kristeva, Julia (1980) *Desire in Language: A Semiotic Approach to Literature and Art* [1969, 1977], trans. Thomas Gora, Alice Jardine and Loen S. Roudiez, New York: Columbia University Press.

La Capra, Dominick (1987) *History, Politics, and the Novel*, Cornell: Cornell University Press.

Langbaum, Robert (1957) *The Poetry of Experience: Dramatic Monologue in Modern Literary Tradition*, New York: Norton.

Lecercle, Jean-Jacques (1989) 'Violence of Style in *Tess of the D'Urbervilles*', in Lance St John Butler (ed.), *Alternative Hardy*, New York: St. Martin's Press, pp. 1–23.

Ledbetter, Steven (1993) 'Notes on the "Virtuoso Trumpet" ' (Scottish Chamber Orchestra), Telarc CD 80227.

Lee, Alan J. (1976) *The Origins of the Popular Press in England, 1855–1914*, London: Croom Helm.

Letwin, Shirley (1965) *The Pursuit of Certainty*, Cambridge: Cambridge University Press.

Levine, George (ed.) (1967) *The Emergence of Victorian Consciousness: The Spirit of the Age*, New York: Free Press.

—— (1988) *Darwin and the Novelists: Patterns of Science in Victorian Fiction*, Cambridge, Mass.: Harvard University Press.

Levy, Anita (1991) *Other Women: The Writing of Class, Race and Gender, 1832–1898*, Princeton: Princeton University Press.

Lister, Raymond (1966) *Victorian Narrative Paintings*, London: Museum Press.

Longford, Elizabeth (1964) *Queen Victoria: Born to Succeed*, New York and Evanston: Harper & Row.

Löwith, Karl (1949) *Meaning in History: The Theological Implications of the Philosophy of History*, Chicago: University of Chicago Press.

Lundahl, Mats and Wadensjö, Eskil (1984) *Unequal Treatment: A Study in the Neo-Classical Theory of Discrimination*, New York: New York University Press; London and Sydney: Croom Helm.

Lyotard, Jean-François (1984) *The Postmodern Condition: A Report on Knowledge* (*La condition postmoderne: rapport sur le savoir* [1979]), trans. Geoff Bennington and Brian Massumi, Minneapolis: University of Minnesota Press.

—— (1988) *The Differend: Phrases in Dispute* (*Le Différend* [1983]), trans. Georges Van Den Abbeele, Minneapolis: University of Minnesota Press.

MacKinnon, Catharine A. (1989) *Towards a Feminist Theory of the State*, Cambridge, Mass. and London: Harvard University Press.

Maglavera, Sultan (1994) *Time Patterns in Later Dickens*, Amsterdam: Rodophi.

Maison, Margaret (1961) *Search Your Soul, Eustace: A Survey of the Religious Novel in the Victorian Age*, London: Sheed & Ward.

Manier, Edward (1978) *The Young Darwin and His Cultural Circle: A study of influences which helped shape the language and logic of the firsts drafts of the theory of natural selection*, Dordrecht and Boston: Reidel.

Martin, Ralph G. (1969–72)*Jennie: The Life of Lady Randolph Churchill*, 2 vols, Englewood Cliffs, NJ: Prentice Hall.

Meyerhoff, Hans (1955) *Time in Literature*, Berkeley: University of California Press.

Miller, J. Hillis (1958) *Charles Dickens: The World of His Novels*, Bloomington: Indiana University Press.

Mokyr, Joel (ed.) (1985) *The Economics of the Industrial Revolution*, London: Allen & Unwin.

Mook, Delo E. and Vargish, Thomas (1987) *Inside Relativity*, Princeton: Princeton University Press.

Morris, John (1966) *Versions of the Self*, New York: Columbia University Press.

Morton, Peter (1984) *The Vital Science: Biology and the Literary Imagination*, London: Allen & Unwin.

Nalbantian, Suzanne (1983) *Seeds of Decadence in the Late Nineteenth-Century Novel: A Crisis in Values*, London: Macmillan.

Newton, Judith Lowder (1981) *Women, Power and Subversion: Social Strategies in British Fiction, 1778–1860*, Athens: University of Georgia Press.

Newton, Judith, Ryan, Mary and Walkowitz, Judith (eds) (1983) *Sex and Class in Women's History*, London: Routledge & Kegan Paul.

Nightingale, Florence (1991) *Cassandra and Other Selections from 'Suggestions for Thought'*, ed. Mary Poovey, London: Pickering & Chatto.

Nunokawa, Jeff (1994) *The Afterlife of Property: Domestic Security and the Victorian Novel*, Princeton: Princeton University Press.

Owens, Craig (1983) 'The Discourse of Others: Feminists and Postmodernism', in Hal Foster (ed.), *The Anti-Aesthetic: Essays on Postmodern Culture*, Port Townsend, Wash.: Bay Press.

Palmeggio, E. M (1993) *Crime in Victorian Fiction*, Westport, Conn. and London: Greenwood Press.

Pear, T. H. (1941–42) 'Psychological Aspects of English Social Stratification', *Bulletin of the John Rylands Library*, 26, 342–68.

Peckham, Morse (1951) 'Toward a Theory of Romanticism', *PMLA*, CXVI (March), 5–23.

—— (1961) 'Toward a Theory of Romanticism: II. Reconsiderations', *Studies in Romanticism*, I, i (Autumn), 1–8.

Pinney, Thomas (ed.) (1963) *Essays of George Eliot*, New York: Columbia University Press; London: Routledge.

Poole, Adrian (1975) *Gissing in Context*, London: Macmillan.

Poovey, Mary (1988) *Uneven Developments: The Ideological Work of Gender in Mid-Victorian England*, Chicago: University of Chicago Press.

Pressnell, L. S. (1956) *Country Banking in the Industrial Revolution*, Oxford: Clarendon Press.

Price, L. L. (1931) *A Short History of Political Economy in England from Adam Smith to Alfred Marshall*, London: Methuen.

Prigogine, Ilya and Stengers, Isabelle (1984) *Order out of Chaos: Man's New Dialogue with Nature* (*La Nouvelle Alliance* [1979]), New York: Bantam.

Proust, Marcel (1928) *Swann's Way* (*Du cote de chez Swann* [1913]), trans. C. K. Scott Moncrieff, New York: Random House.

Purvis, June (1989) *Hard Lessons: The Lives and Education of Working-class Women in Nineteenth-Centure England*, Minneapolis: University of Minnesota Press.

Pykett, Lyn (1989) *Emile Brontë*, Women Writers Series, Savage, Md: Barnes & Noble.

Quinlan, Maurice J. (1941) *Victorian Prelude: A History of English Manners 1700–1830*, New York: Columbia University Press.

BIBLIOGRAPHY

Reilly, Jim (1993) *Shadowtime: History and Representation in Hardy, Conrad and George Eliot*, London and New York: Routledge.

Robbe-Grillet, Alain (1989) *For A New Novel: Essays on Fiction* (essays from 1953–63, published as *Pour un nouveau roman* [1963]), trans. Richard Howard, Evanston: Northwestern University Press.

Robbins, Lionel (1935) *An Essay on the Nature and Significance of Economic Science*, 2nd edn, London: Macmillan.

—— (1939) *The Economic Basis of Class Conflict, and Other Essays in Political Economy*, London: Macmillan.

—— (1952, from 1939 lectures) *The Theory of Economic Policy in English Classical Political Economy*, London: Macmillan.

—— (1970) *Evolution of Modern Economic Theory*, London: Macmillan.

Rosen, Charles (1971) *The Classical Style: Haydn, Mozart, Beethoven*, New York: Viking.

—— (1995) *The Romantic Generation*, Cambridge, Mass.: Harvard University Press.

Rowbotham, Judith (1989) *Good Girls Make Good Wives: Guidance for Girls in Victorian Fiction*, Oxford: Basil Blackwell.

Rubenstein, W. D. (1993) *Capitalism, Culture, and Decline in Britain 1750–1990*, London: Routledge.

Rubin, William (ed.) (1977) *Cézanne, The Late Work* (exhibition catalogue, with contributions by Theodore Reff, Geneviève Monnier *et al.*), New York: Museum of Modern Art.

Schor, Hilary (1992) *Scheherezade in the Marketplace: Elizabeth Gaskell and the Victorian Novel*, Oxford and New York: Oxford University Press.

Schumpeter, Joseph (1954) *History of Economic Analysis*, ed. from manuscript Elizabeth Boody Schumpeter, New York: Oxford University Press.

Seaman, L. C. B. (1973) *Victorian England: Aspects of English and Imperial History 1837–1901*, London: Methuen.

Shuttleworth, Sally (1984) *George Eliot and Nineteenth-Century Science: The Make-believe of a Beginning*, Cambridge: Cambridge University Press.

Skilton, David (1972) *Anthony Trollope and his Contemporaries: A Study in the Theory and Conventions of Mid-Victorian Fiction*, London: Longman.

Smith, Peter (1984) *Public and Private Values in the Nineteenth-Century Novel*, Cambridge: Cambridge University Press.

Spacks, Patricia Meyer (1985) *Gossip*, New York: Alfred A. Knopf.

Spänberg, Sven-Johan (1971) *The Ordeal of Richard Feverel and the Traditions of Realism*, Uppsala: University of Uppsala Diss.

Spitzer, Leo (1963) *Classical and Christian Ideas of World Harmony*, Baltimore: The Johns Hopkins University Press.

Starzinger, Vincent (1991) *The Politics of the Center: The 'Juste Milieu' in Theory and Practice, France and England, 1815–1848* (originally, *Middlingness* [1965]), New Brunswick and London: Transaction Publishers.

Stern, J. P. (1973) *On Realism*, London and Boston: Routledge.

Stocking, George W., Jr (1987) *Victorian Anthropology*, New York and London: Macmillan.

Stoehr, Taylor (1985) *Words and Deeds: Essays on the Realist Imagination*, New York: AMS Press.

Stone, Donald (1980) *The Romantic Impulse in Victorian Fiction*, Cambridge, Mass.: Harvard University Press.

239

BIBLIOGRAPHY

Strachey, Lytton (1924) *Queen Victoria*, London: Chatto & Windus.

Super, R. H. (1981) *Trollope in the Post Office*, Ann Arbor: University of Michigan Press.

—— (1988) *The Chronicler of Barsetshire*, Ann Arbor: University of Michigan Press.

Sussman, Herbert L. (1968) *Victorians and the Machine: The Literary Response to Technology*, Cambridge, Mass.: Harvard University Press.

—— (1983) 'Victorian Science Fiction', *Science Fiction Studies*, 11, 324–8.

Swetz, Frank J. (1987) *Capitalism and Arithmetic: The New Math of the 15th Century, including the full text of the 'Treviso Arithemetic' of 1478*, trans. David Eugene Smith, La Salle, Ill.: Open Court Press.

Sypher, Wylie (1962) *The Loss of the Self in Modern Literature and Art*, New York: Random House.

Tayler, Irene (1990) *Holy Ghosts: The Male Muses of Emily and Charlotte Brontë*, New York: Columbia University Press.

Thompson, E. P. (1967) 'Time, Work-discipline, and Industrial Capitalism', *Past and Present*, 38, 56–97.

—— (1974) 'Patrician Society, Plebian Culture', *Journal of Social History*, 7, 382–405.

Tillotson, Kathleen (1954) *Novels of the Eighteen-Forties*, Oxford: Oxford University Press.

Trodd, Anthea (1989) *Domestic Crime and the Victorian Novel*, London: Macmillan.

Vargish, Thomas (1971) 'Revenge in *Wuthering Heights*', *Studies in the Novel*, III, i (Spring), 7–17.

—— (1985) *The Providential Aesthetic in Victorian Fiction*, Charlottesville: University of Virginia Press.

—— and Delo Mook (forthcoming) *Inside Modernism: Relativity Theory, Cubism, Narrative*

Watson, George (1973) *The English Ideology: Studies in the Language of Victorian Politics*, London: Allen Lane.

Webb, Robert K. (1955) *British Working Class Readers, 1790–1848: Literacy and Social Tension*, London: Allen & Unwin.

—— (1967) *English History, 1815–1914*, Publication no. 64, The American Historical Association, Baltimore: Waverley Press.

Whitehead, Alfred North (1938) *Modes of Thought*, New York: Macmillan.

Williams, Carolyn (1983) 'Natural Selection and Narrative Form in *The Egoist*', *Victorian Studies*, 7, 1 (Autumn), 53–79.

Williams, Ioan (1975) *The Realist Novel in England*, Pittsburgh: Pittsburgh University Press.

Williams, Raymond (1961) *The Long Revolution*, New York: Columbia University Press; London: Chatto & Windus.

—— (1970) *The English Novel from Dickens to Lawrence*, New York: Oxford University Press.

—— (1973) *The Country and the City*, New York: Oxford University Press.

Williamson, Carolyn (1983) 'Natural Selection and Narrative Form in *The Egoist*', *Victorian Studies*, 27, 1 (Autumn), 53–79.

—— (1988) *Transfigured World: Walter Pater's Aesthetic Historicism*, Ithaca: Cornell University Press.

Wilt, Judith (1975) *Meredith's Readable People*, Princeton: Princeton University Press.

—— (1980) *Ghosts of the Gothic: Austen, Eliot and Lawrence*, Princeton: Princeton University Press.

Wilton, Andrew (1980) *Turner and the Sublime* (exhibition catalogue), Chicago: University of Chicago Press.

Wrigley, E. A. (1988) *Continuity, Chance and Change: The Character of the Industrial Revolution in England*, Cambridge and New York: Cambridge University Press.

Young, G. M. (1964) *Victorian England, Portrait of an Age* [1953], New York: Oxford University Press.

Zizek, Slavoj (1989) *The Sublime Object of Ideology*, London and New York: Verso.

—— (1991) *Looking Awry: An Introduction to Jacques Lacan through Popular Culture*, Cambridge, Mass.: MIT Press.

INDEX

INDEX

INDEX

Made in the USA
Lexington, KY
29 June 2014